Young Chef's Nutrition Guide and Cookbook

by
Carolyn E. Moore, Ph.D., R.D.,
Mimi H. Kerr, and Robert J. Shulman, M.D.

New York • London • Toronto • Sydney

Dedication

To my loving husband, James Robinson Kerr, and our young chefs Caroline Davitte Kerr and Isabel Blake Kerr for their enthusiasm in the testing and tasting of many recipes.

To Michael Stephen Khourie who inspired this guide to healthful eating and Matthew Smith Khourie for his support throughout the project.

To my wife, Marta Fiorotto, Ph.D., and my family for their love and support.

© Copyright 1990 by Barron's Educational Series, Inc.
All rights reserved.
No part of this book may be reproduced in any form, by photostat, microfilm, xerography, or any other means, or incorporated into any information retrieval system, electronic or mechanical, without the written permission of the copyright owner.

All inquiries should be addressed to:
Barron's Educational Series, Inc.
250 Wireless Blvd.
Hauppauge, New York 11788

International Standard Book No. 0-8120-5789-9
Library of Congress Catalog Card No. 89-18218

Library of Congress Cataloging-in-Publication Data
Moore, Carolyn E.
    The Young Chef's Nutrition Guide and Cookbook / by Carolyn E. Moore, Mimi H. Kerr, Robert J. Shulman.
      p. cm.
     ISBN 0-8120-5789-9
    1. Cookery. 2. Children—Nutrition. I. Kerr, Mimi H.
II. Shulman, Robert J. III. Title.
TX714.M6667 1990
641.5′123—dc20
     89-18218
     CIP

PRINTED IN USA
012 8800 987654321

Contents

GOOD FOOD

Diet and Disease	2
A Good Diet and Good Health	6
Diets for Problems and Problem Diets	18
Designing Your Own Diet	20
The Foods You Buy	22
Welcome to the Kitchen	34

THE RECIPES

Beverages	41
Breads	50
Snacks	69
Sandwiches	103
Soups	114
Entrees	122
Vegetables	184
Pasta	206
Rice	212
Salads	218
Fruits	229
Cakes	246
Cookies	256
Frozen Desserts	273

INDEX   282

Acknowledgments

We would like to thank the children attending the Le Panier Cooking School, Houston, Texas, who helped test the more than 150 recipes in our book. Their participation made the project both fun and worthwhile. We are also grateful to Christine Lanzisera for her editorial review of the manuscript, and appreciate the assistance of Barbara S. Callender, Annie Elliott, and Cary Lauritzen in typing the cookbook.

Good Food

Good food does more than just taste good. It's good for you too. It helps you grow, gives you energy to do the things you enjoy, makes you healthy, and keeps you healthy.

Just about any food is good as long as it is part of a balanced diet. It's the balance that is important. Too much of some foods is just as bad as too little.

In this book we would like to show you what we mean by a healthful diet, what kinds of food you need and when—because how much you need to eat changes as you grow older—and how you can choose a good diet for yourself. There are over 150 recipes here that you can make as part of a healthful diet. Each recipe includes information about the nutritional value of the final dish so you can see where it fits into your own diet plan.

Diet and Disease

It used to be that you got sick from what you *didn't* eat. That's still true in much of the world, where people are suffering from malnutrition or even dying of starvation. But in the United States today, people are more apt to be suffering from illnesses that are caused by eating too much of the wrong things.

You may have friends or relatives who are on special diets because they have problems with their weight, with high blood pressure, or with high blood cholesterol. Those friends and relatives may have trouble staying on their diets and do a lot of complaining because they can't eat the things they used to eat. Sometimes their doctors have put them on very restricted diets, trying to make up for years of bad eating habits. And any kind of bad habit is hard to break.

The best way to avoid problems like these is to develop good eating habits when you are young. You don't have to give up anything you like. You just need to make sure that your diet is balanced, and that you aren't leaving out any of the nutrients you need.

Cholesterol and Fat

Cholesterol is a type of fat that accumulates in the blood and builds up deposits called plaque on the walls of the blood vessels that carry the blood through the body. Everyone has cholesterol, but people who eat excessive amounts of fat in their diet may have high levels of cholesterol in their blood. People with high cholesterol levels are more likely to suffer from heart disease and high blood pressure.

Actually, there are two kinds of cholesterol. Cholesterol attaches to proteins in the blood called lipoproteins. Low-density lipoproteins (LDL) carry cholesterol that builds up the plaque, so LDL-cholesterol is considered "bad" cholesterol. High-density lipoproteins (HDL), on the other hand, carry cholesterol to the liver, where the body can get rid of it, and so they are the "good" cholesterol.

DIET AND DISEASE

Probably the most unhealthy fats we eat are the saturated fats. Most of these are animal fats, from red meat (beef, lamb, pork) or whole-milk dairy products (milk, butter, cream, cheese, ice cream). These are the fats that can raise your cholesterol level. One of the major diet problems in the United States today is that people eat far more meat than is necessary for the amount of protein they need, so they end up eating more saturated fat than is good for them.

The recipes in this cookbook use ingredients that are low in saturated fats: nonfat and low-fat milk products, low-fat milk cheeses, lean cuts of meat, and margarine instead of butter. Using these ingredients, you get the protein and calcium you need without getting too much saturated fat.

Other kinds of fats—polyunsaturated and monounsaturated fats—may actually help to lower the level of blood cholesterol when they are substituted for saturated fats. Polyunsaturated fats are found in corn, cottonseed, sesame, soybean, and safflower oil and in many fish. Good sources of monounsaturated fats are olive oil, peanut butter, peanut oil, avocados, some nuts, and canola oil.

For the most part, the recipes in this cookbook use polyunsaturated margarine or safflower oil instead of butter. Other vegetable oils can be substituted.

Another major source of cholesterol is egg yolks. Our recipes frequently use egg whites and egg substitutes to keep the cholesterol content low.

Salt

Salt (sodium is the scientific term) helps your body retain water. This keeps you from drying out. But some people seem to be sensitive to salt, and their bodies retain too much water. This can lead to high blood pressure, and increases the risk of heart attack, stroke, or kidney disease.

The chief source of sodium in your diet is the salt that you sprinkle on your food at the table or while you are cooking it. However, processed foods—foods that you buy already prepared like canned soups or frozen dinners—almost all have some kind of salt added to them, and sometimes the salt content is very high. You can cut way down on the amount of salt you eat just by cooking your own food instead of relying on canned or frozen foods, and by using herbs and spices for flavoring.

Caffeine

Caffeine is a stimulant. That means it makes your heart beat faster and makes your body operate a little more quickly. Many people find that coffee, a major source of caffeine for adults, tends to make them nervous and keeps them awake—whether they want to stay awake or not.

Children and teenagers may not drink much coffee, but that doesn't mean they avoid caffeine. Many soft drinks also contain caffeine, and so does chocolate. We recommend that you not drink more than one 12-ounce serving of a caffeine-containing drink each day.

Diet and Health

Health problems that have been linked to diet include heart disease, high blood pressure, some kinds of cancer, and obesity (being too fat). People who eat a balanced diet, one that avoids too much fat and salt and includes all the necessary nutrients and fiber, are more likely to live long and healthy lives.

TEN RECOMMENDATIONS FOR A HEALTHY DIET

1. Eat enough calories to keep yourself growing at a normal rate and to remain at a healthy weight.
2. Each day, no more than thirty percent of your total calories should come from fat.

3. Only ten percent of your total calories should come from saturated fat.

4. Ten percent of your total calories should come from polyunsaturated fat and ten percent from monounsaturated fat.

5. You should not eat more than 300 milligrams of cholesterol each day.

6. Eat plenty of starches (complex carbohydrates).

7. Avoid foods with table sugar (sucrose), and don't satisfy your taste for sweets with artificial sweeteners.

8. Eat foods containing dietary fiber each day.

9. Use table salt sparingly and avoid foods high in salt.

10. Limit your intake of caffeine.

A Good Diet and Good Health

To start with, a diet isn't something that makes you lose weight, although it can accomplish that. Your diet is simply the foods you eat.

Foods are generally divided into six basic groups: dairy products, vegetables, fruits, breads and other grains, meat, and fat. You need to eat foods from all these groups—everyone does. But there is no single food from any of the groups that you have to eat. There are plenty of other foods in each group.

Together, these food groups provide all the nutrients your body needs. These nutrients in turn fall into several groups that affect your body and your health in different ways.

Calories

You have probably heard people who are trying to lose weight talk about counting their calories or say, "Oh, I can't eat that. Too many calories." You may have assumed that calories are something that makes you fat. That's not exactly true.

Calories are a measurement of energy, energy your body needs to grow, to walk, to breathe—to do anything at all. Everyone needs calories. But not everyone needs the same number of calories. How many calories you need depends on how big you are, how much you are growing, and what you do during the day. If your diet doesn't provide enough calories, you will get thin, you won't grow properly, you may get tired and cranky, and you may catch colds and other illnesses more easily. If your diet provides too many calories, your body will store them by turning them into fat.

Children and teenagers grow in spurts, and while you are in a growth spurt you need more calories than usual. Babies, for example, grow very quickly. The average newborn baby weighs about seven and a half pounds, and the average one-year-old weighs twenty pounds. That's nearly triple in size. Imagine how big you would be if you tripled in size by next year. It's no wonder that babies seem to want to eat all the time.

After the first year of life, you grow more slowly, gaining about five pounds a year, until you hit your next growth spurt. For girls, this usually comes when they are about nine years old, and lasts about three years. For boys, the growth spurt generally starts when they are about eleven years old, and it lasts four to six years. Of course, these are only averages. For lots of people the growth spurt starts or ends earlier or later. When you hit your growth spurt, your body will need more calories, so your appetite will probably grow too. Children who do not get enough calories over several months will not grow at expected rates.

The chart below will give you an idea of how many calories you need. It is based on average weight and height for different ages. If you are big or small for your age, your calorie needs will be bigger or smaller. How many calories you need also depends on what you do. If you spend all your spare time running with the track team, you will need more calories than someone whose hobby is making model ships.

RECOMMENDED CALORIE INTAKE OF CHILDREN BASED ON AVERAGE WEIGHT AND HEIGHT

	Age	Weight (lb)	Height (in)	*Average Calorie Needs*
Children	1–3	29	35	1,300
	4–6	44	44	1,800
	7–10	62	52	2,000
Boys	11–14	99	62	2,500
	15–18	145	69	3,000
Girls	11–14	101	62	2,200
	15–18	120	64	2,200

Adapted from The National Academy of Sciences-National Research Council, Recommended Dietary Allowances. *Tenth Edition, Washington, DC: National Academy of Sciences, 1989.*

A GOOD DIET AND GOOD HEALTH

However, the right number of calories is not enough to guarantee a good diet. All foods provide you with calories. When you design your diet, you need to make sure that the foods you choose give you all the other nutrients you need as well as the appropriate number of calories.

Protein

Protein is the basic material that is needed for growth. Your body can't store protein, so you need it in your diet every day, and you need even more than usual during growth spurts. Generally speaking, you should be getting about twenty percent of your calories from protein, which has 120 calories per ounce (4 calories per gram).

Protein is made up of a group of materials called amino acids. There are several essential amino acids that your body needs, and there are several ways you can get them.

Meat, fish, eggs, and dairy products like milk and cheese supply "high-quality" protein. That means they have all the essential amino acids in the right proportion. Unfortunately, many of these animal sources also have a lot of fat and cholesterol. However, fish, chicken, turkey, and low-fat milk and cheese provide high-quality protein without too much fat.

You can also get proteins from different vegetables, like beans, but no one vegetable has all the essential amino acids. You have to eat these in combinations to get the protein you need. Many traditional dishes provide the right combinations, like peanut butter and bread, rice and beans, or corn and beans.

Getting enough protein can be a problem for people on vegetarian (non-meat) diets, especially for those people who do not eat either dairy products or eggs. Planning a vegetarian diet is complicated, because you must also make sure you get enough of the nutrients that are scarce in vegetables, like iron,

A GOOD DIET AND GOOD HEALTH

calcium, riboflavin, zinc, vitamin B12 and vitamin D. If you are a vegetarian, you may need vitamin and mineral supplements. Since vegetables are so low in calories, you also have to make a special effort to get enough calories to allow you to grow properly.

Fat

Like the amino acids of protein, certain fats are essential for your body. Fat is a good, concentrated source of energy, with 270 calories per ounce (9 calories per gram)—more than twice the energy in carbohydrates or protein—and provides vitamins A, D, E, and K. You don't need too much of it, however, and because you don't usually sit down to eat plain fat, you may not realize how much of it you eat.

All the meat you eat has fat in it. All milk and cheese has fat, some more than others. Butter, which is made from cream, has the most fat, while skimmed milk has had the fat removed—skimmed off. These are all animal fats.

Then there are vegetable fats, like corn oil, olive oil, and margarine. There is fat in chocolate, but not very much fat in cocoa powder.

There is likely to be at least some fat in anything you eat other than fresh fruits and some vegetables, and vegetables are often cooked or served with fat. Since not more than thirty percent of your calories should come from fat, this is a part of your diet that needs special attention.

Carbohydrates

These are the starches and sugars that provide most of our energy. The starches are foods like bread, cereal, and potatoes that are called "complex carbohydrates," as opposed to the simple sugars like table sugar (sucrose) or honey. Carbohydrates have 120 calories per ounce (4 calories per gram). Ideally, ten to fifteen percent of your total calories

A GOOD DIET AND GOOD HEALTH

should come from simple sugars, and forty percent should come from complex carbohydrates.

Getting people to eat enough sugar is not a problem. Even newborn babies like sugar water better than plain water. The problem is that many sweet foods can fill you up with carbohydrates without giving you all the other nutrients you need.

Complex carbohydrates, on the other hand, are an important part of any diet. Breads and cereals, especially those made with whole grain flours, provide a wide range of vitamins, minerals, fiber, and even protein. Starchy vegetables like potatoes, corn, beans, and peas are an important source of the B vitamins. Potatoes have vitamin C, and beans are a good source of protein and iron.

Vitamins

There are two groups of vitamins: water-soluble (the B vitamins and vitamin C) and fat-soluble vitamins (A, D, E, and K). Your body can't store the water-soluble vitamins, so you need to eat these every day. Fat-soluble vitamins can be stored in your body.

Diseases caused by a lack of vitamins—diseases like scurvy and pellagra—were a serious problem in the past, when a wide variety of fresh fruits and vegetables were hard to get. Today, such diseases are uncommon in the United States because many foods that people eat regularly are rich in vitamins: B vitamins in whole grain and enriched cereals and breads; vitamins A and D in fortified milk; vitamin C in citrus fruits; vitamin E in vegetable oils; and folic acid (one of the B vitamins) in green leafy vegetables.

Sometimes young people don't get enough of vitamins A and C. Vitamin A is particularly important for healthy skin and for night and color vision. Vitamin C, also called ascorbic acid,

A GOOD DIET AND GOOD HEALTH

helps keep your body in good condition. A good source of vitamin A is carrots, and a good source of vitamin C is citrus fruits like oranges, so recipes in this cookbook that are especially rich in these vitamins are identified by a carrot or an orange.

Minerals

Your body also needs a wide variety of minerals to keep itself in good working order, most of them in very small quantities. Two of the most important ones as you are growing are calcium and iron.

Almost all the calcium in your body—about 99 percent of it—is in your bones, and as you are growing, you need extra calcium to make sure your bones grow properly. Milk and dairy products are the richest sources of calcium, so recipes with plenty of calcium are identified by a milk bottle in the cookbook. Vitamin D helps your body absorb calcium. That is why milk has vitamin D added to it. If you don't like milk or if you are allergic to milk, you may need to take calcium supplements.

Iron is an important part of your red blood cells, which carry oxygen in your body. Without enough of it, you will be weak and anemic. It is particularly important during your growth spurts, and that is when your body's need for iron is at its highest. Lean cuts of meat, poultry, fish, and enriched cereals are all good sources of iron. However, the iron in red meat is absorbed most easily by your body. Recipes in the cookbook that are rich in iron are identified with a piece of lean meat. Your need for iron is greatest during your teen years, and iron deficiency is probably the most common nutritional deficiency in young people.

Fiber

When we are talking about food, fiber doesn't mean threads or bits of cloth. Dietary fiber is the parts of foods made from

A GOOD DIET AND GOOD HEALTH

plants that your body doesn't digest. That may sound as if fiber is something you don't need, but it is actually very important to keep your digestive system working properly, getting rid of whatever your body doesn't absorb in normal bowel movements.

Fresh fruit (with the skin), vegetables, and baked goods and cereals made with whole grain flours are particularly good sources of fiber.

How Much Is Enough?

The Food and Nutrition Board of the National Academy of Sciences—National Research Council has developed recommended dietary allowances (RDA) for twenty nutrients including calories. These are based on the amount of these nutrients required each day to maintain good nutrition in most healthy people.

FOOD AND NUTRITION BOARD, NATIONAL ACADEMY OF SCIENCES—NATIONAL RESEARCH COUNCIL RECOMMENDED DIETARY ALLOWANCES,[a] Revised 1989

Designed for the maintenance of good nutrition of practically all healthy people in the United States

Category	Age (Years)	Weight[b]		Height[b]		Protein	Fat-Soluble Vitamins			
		(kg)	(lb)	(cm)	(in)	(g)	Vitamin A (μg RE)[c]	Vitamin D (μg)[d]	Vitamin E (mg α-TE)[e]	Vitamin K (μg)
Children	1-3	13	29	90	35	16	400	10	6	15
	4-6	20	44	112	44	24	500	10	7	20
	7-10	28	62	132	52	28	700	10	7	30
Males	11-14	45	99	157	62	45	1,000	10	10	45
	15-18	66	145	176	69	59	1,000	10	10	65
Females	11-14	46	101	157	62	46	800	10	8	45
	15-18	55	120	163	64	44	800	10	8	55

[a] The allowances, expressed as average daily intakes over time, are intended to provide for individual variations among most normal persons as they live in the United States under usual environmental stresses. Diets should be based on a variety of common foods in order to provide other nutrients for which human requirements have been less well defined. The median weights and heights of those under 19 years of age were taken from Hamil, P.V.V., T.A. Drizd, C.L. Johnson

A GOOD DIET AND GOOD HEALTH

The chart on pages 12 and 13 summarizes the RDA for children and teenagers based on their ages.

In general, you can get all these nutrients by eating a variety of foods without taking vitamin or mineral supplements. Such supplements can actually cause problems. In an effort to make sure they are getting all the vitamins and minerals they need, some people go overboard and take such high doses that they make themselves sick. Although your body will simply get rid of excess amounts of many vitamins, others—particularly the fat-soluble vitamins A, D, E, and K—are stored in the body where they can reach levels that are too high for good health. Signs of excess doses of vitamin A, for example, include dry skin, bone pain, headaches, liver damage, and failure to gain weight. The tables beginning on page 14 will give you more information about the major vitamins and minerals.

Water-Soluble Vitamins							Minerals						
Vitamin C (mg)	Thiamin (mg)	Riboflavin (mg)	Niacin (mg NE)	Vitamin B_6 (mg)	Folate (µg)	Vitamin B_{12} (µg)	Calcium (mg)	Phosphorus (mg)	Magnesium (mg)	Iron (mg)	Zinc (mg)	Iodine (µg)	Selenium (µg)
40	0.7	0.8	9	1.0	50	0.7	800	800	80	10	10	70	20
45	0.9	1.1	12	1.1	75	1.0	800	800	120	10	10	90	20
45	1.0	1.2	13	1.4	100	1.4	800	800	170	10	10	120	30
50	1.3	1.5	17	1.7	150	2.0	1,200	1,200	270	12	15	150	40
60	1.5	1.8	20	2.0	200	2.0	1,200	1,200	400	12	15	150	50
50	1.1	1.3	15	1.4	150	2.0	1,200	1,200	280	15	12	150	45
60	1.1	1.3	15	1.5	180	2.0	1,200	1,200	300	15	12	150	50

et al. 1979. Physical growth: National Center for Health Statistics Percentiles. Am. J. Clin. Nutr. 32: 607–629. The use of these figures does not imply that the height-to-weight ratios are ideal.

^{c}Retinol equivalents. 1 retinol equivalent = 1 µg retinol or 6 µg β-carotene. One RE = 3.35 international unit (IU). Vitamin A content of food in this book is reported in IU.

A GOOD DIET AND GOOD HEALTH

FUNCTION, SOURCES, AND NUTRITIONAL RISKS OF THE MAJOR VITAMINS

Vitamin	Functions	Good Sources	Nutritional Risks	
			Inadequate Intake	Excessive Intake
A	Night and color vision; healthy skin; growth and repair of tissue; proper bone development	Liver; yellow fruits and vegetables; egg yolk; butter; dark green, leafy vegetables; fish and liver oils	Night blindness; rough, dry skin; retarded growth; dry eyes	Headaches; joint and bone pain; loss of hair, dry skin; fatigue; abnormal growth; liver damage
D	Calcium absorption from the intestine; bone mineralization; proper tooth formation	Fortified milk products; fish-liver oil; butter; egg yolks	Rickets (abnormal bone growth) in children; osteomalacia (porous bone) in adults; muscular weakness	Calcium deposits in tissues; nausea, vomiting, loss of appetite; elevated blood cholesterol
E	Antioxidant (prevents breakdown of fats and oils by oxygen); muscle formation; maintenance of red blood cell membranes	Vegetable oils, margarine; whole grain cereals; wheat germ; soy beans, sprouts; nuts	Breakdown of red blood cells; nerve damage	Headache; blurred vision; skin rash
K	Blood clotting	Green leafy vegetables; cabbage, cauliflower; soybeans	Impaired blood clotting	Unknown
B_1 (Thiamin)	Metabolism of carbohydrates for energy; growth and repair of tissue—especially nerves, heart, and muscle	Whole grain cereals and breads; yeast; wheat germ; liver, pork products; legumes	Beri beri: muscle weakness, confusion, enlargement of the heart, loss of appetite	Unknown
B_2 (Riboflavin)	Metabolism of carbohydrate, protein, and fat for energy; growth and repair of tissue	Liver; dairy products; eggs; whole grain cereals and breads; salmon	Cracks in the skin around the lips and corners of the mouth; sensitivity to light	Unknown

FUNCTION, SOURCES, AND NUTRITIONAL RISKS OF THE MAJOR VITAMINS

Vitamin	Functions	Good Sources	Nutritional Risks	
			Inadequate Intake	Excessive Intake
B_3 (Niacin)	Metabolism of carbohydrate, protein, and fat for energy	Liver; whole grain cereals and breads; yeast; peanut butter	Pellagra: skin discoloration, confusion, swollen tongue, irritability, dermatitis, diarrhea, loss of appetite, insomnia	Flushing or itching of the skin; abnormal heartbeat; high blood sugar; ulcers
B_6 (Pyridoxine)	Metabolism of protein; absorption of fat; formation of red blood cells	Whole grain cereals and fruits; seeds and nuts	Skin changes such as dermatitis and eczema; dizziness; sores on the mouth, tongue, and lips; anemia; numbness; convulsions	Disorders of the nervous system. Dependency can develop on high doses, and deficiency symptoms can occur when intake is reduced to normal levels.
B_{12}	Metabolism of carbohydrate, protein, and fat; synthesis of genetic code (DNA and RNA); formation of red blood cells	Liver; milk; eggs	Pernicious anemia; red tongue; irritability, drowsiness, depression	Unknown
C	Synthesis of collagen (substance that holds cells together); formation of connective tissue in skins, bones, muscles; protection against destruction of vitamins A, E, thiamin, and riboflavin by oxygen	Citrus fruits; vegetables; potatoes	Scurvy: bleeding gums, abnormal blood clotting, weight loss, weakness, poor wound healing, irritability	Dependency can develop on high doses, and deficiency symptoms of scurvy may occur when intake is reduced to normal levels

A GOOD DIET AND GOOD HEALTH

FUNCTION, SOURCES, AND NUTRITIONAL RISKS OF THE MAJOR MINERALS

Mineral	Functions	Good Sources	Nutritional Risks	
			Inadequate Intake	Excessive Intake
Calcium	Growth and maintenance of bones and teeth; blood clotting; contraction of muscles	Dairy products: milk, cheese, yogurt; spinach, chard, mustard greens, broccoli; sardines	Rickets (abnormal bone growth) in children; osteoporosis (porous bones that break) in adults	Deposits of calcium in the body; decreased absorption of magnesium, zinc, and iron
Phosphorous	Growth and maintenance of bones and teeth; metabolism of carbohydrates, protein, and fat; storage and release of energy; firing of nerves	Liver; yeast; dairy products; nuts, seeds; tofu; oatmeal; eggs; soft drinks	Weakness; loss of appetite; poor formation of bones and teeth; cramps and weakness in muscles	Imbalance of the calcium to phosphorus ratio that may cause a deficiency of calcium
Sodium	Fluid balance	Table salt; cured meats; food in brine solution	Muscular weakness and cramps; low blood pressure; headaches	Fluid retention causing swelling of hands and feet; high blood pressure; heart disease
Potassium	Fluid balance; muscle contraction; nerve function; maintenance of normal heartbeat; release of energy from carbohydrates, proteins, and fats	Fruits and vegetables; whole grains; yeast; meats; dairy products; molasses	Abnormal heartbeat; muscle cramps, weakness, lethargy, abdominal pain	Abnormal heartbeat; muscular paralysis
Zinc	Formation of genetic material (DNA and RNA); component of many enzymes; normal bone formation; absorption of B vitamins	Liver; wheat germ; eggs; nuts; oysters; whole grains; some legumes; bran	Poor growth; failure to mature sexually; poor wound healing and appetite	Nausea, vomiting, fever, anemia; premature birth; skin rash

FUNCTION, SOURCES, AND NUTRITIONAL RISKS OF THE MAJOR MINERALS

Mineral	Functions	Good Sources	Nutritional Risks	
			Inadequate Intake	Excessive Intake
Iodine	Formation of thyroid hormones which help control metabolism, growth, and energy production	Iodized salt; seafood	Goiter (enlarged thyroid gland); mental retardation; protruding abdomen, swollen features in newborns when mother deficient	Potentially could cause iodine poisoning; thyroid gland disease
Iron	Synthesis of hemoglobin (protein in the blood that carries oxygen); part of several enzymes	Liver, red meat; yeast; dark green, leafy vegetables; egg yolk; apricots, prunes; molasses; enriched and whole-grain cereals	Anemia; weakness	Heart, liver, and pancreas disease
Copper	Formation of hemoglobin; part of several enzymes	Oysters; nuts, seeds; cocoa powder; oatmeal; liver; milk	Abnormal blood count; bone disease	Nausea, vomiting; diarrhea; headache
Fluoride	Formation of strong bones, teeth	Fluoridated water; seafood	Tooth decay; osteoporosis	Stained teeth; brittle bones

Diets for Problems and Problem Diets

The most common nutritional problem among children and teenagers is obesity (being overweight). Obesity is a problem not just because it's fashionable to be slim, but because it can lead to future health problems. Obesity can put stress on your bones, which may not be strong enough to support the extra weight. High blood pressure and high levels of blood cholesterol often come along with excess weight and are associated with heart disease later in life. Overweight children often have trouble metabolizing sugars effectively and this can lead to diabetes later on.

However, weight problems can generally be solved—and remain solved—for most people by adopting a sensible diet. People who weigh too much simply eat more calories than are being used each day for growth or other activities. Leftover calories are stored as fat. About 3,500 extra calories produce a pound of body fat. This means that 3,500 fewer calories should get rid of a pound of body fat. Cutting 500 calories a day out of your diet will generally lead to a safe and sensible weight loss of a pound a week and will not leave you so hungry that you can't think about anything but food. At the same time, try to get more exercise. This will not only help you lose weight but will be good for your general health. (People who are severely overweight or who have medical problems that are being aggravated by overweight should have their diet supervised by a doctor.)

If you are trying to lose weight, here are a few suggestions.
1. Keep a record of everything you eat so you can keep track of your calories.
2. Don't eat while you are doing something else. This will keep you from eating when you are not actually hungry.
3. Sit down while eating.
4. Don't eat too fast. Give your body a chance to notice that it has had enough to eat.
5. Eat meals and snacks only in those parts of your home intended for eating.

DIETS FOR PROBLEMS AND PROBLEM DIETS

Fad Diets

Many young people are preoccupied about their weight—some wanting to lose weight and others wanting to "bulk up" to make the wrestling team or the football team. They often try various fad diets, which can be dangerous.

Almost any diet will work in the short run, but fad diets are hard to stay on for a long time and are nutritionally unbalanced.

Low carbohydrate diets The authors of these diets promise quick weight loss if you don't eat starches and sugars. What they don't tell you is that the pounds lost result from water loss and that the weight is regained rapidly when you start to eat carbohydrates again. Such diets can cause dehydration, diarrhea, low sodium levels, low blood pressure and dizziness, and they do not include enough vitamins and minerals to maintain a healthy body.

High protein diets Because high protein diets are usually also low carbohydrate diets, the same problems and risks are present. High protein diets can also cause the body to lose calcium and bone. Athletes often try high protein diets to promote muscle growth and strength, but there is little scientific evidence to show that this will work. Your body can only use so much protein at a time. Any excess is just extra calories.

High fat diets Since fat is digested slowly, you feel full for a longer period of time on these diets. The bad news is that they are high in saturated fats and cholesterol. Like other fad diets, high fat diets can lead to dehydration and other problems associated with loss of body water.

Protein-sparing modified fast diets These diets, in which protein powders are added to water or only a small amount of meat is allowed, are one step away from starvation. These were designed for extremely overweight adults who need to lose 100 pounds or more and who are under strict medical supervision. Children and teenagers do not belong on these diets *ever* without the close supervision of a doctor.

Designing Your Own Diet

Most of us lead busy lives. Hardly any family gets to sit down and eat three meals a day together. Breakfast is usually a rush, with everyone in a hurry to get to work or to school. From the day they start school until the day they retire, most people only eat lunch at home on weekends and on vacations. If your family is like most, the only time you eat together is dinner, and even that depends on who's doing what that evening. And you probably have snacks during the day, when you get home from school, while you are doing your homework or watching television.

That means you are already making a lot of decisions about your diet. Your parents may not have time to make sure you eat your breakfast. They may send you off to school with a good nutritious lunch, but they aren't there to see what you eat and what you throw away or swap. When you eat out in a restaurant, they probably let you choose what you want to order. And they may have no idea of what you eat as a snack when they aren't around. Since you are already making all these decisions for yourself, maybe you should pay some attention to what you are doing.

First, figure out how well you're doing already. Keep track of everything you eat for a week. That's everything you actually eat. It does not include the cereal you dump into the garbage or the meat you feed to the dog.

Next divide the foods you ate into the basic food groups—dairy products, fruits, vegetables, breads and other grains, meats, and fat. (Examples of foods in the different groups can be found in the chart beginning on page 25. You may want to ask your parents to help you with this.) Many of the foods will belong in more than one category. For example, a bowl of cereal with milk has both a grain, the cereal, and a dairy product, the milk. Make a separate category for anything that doesn't seem to fit into any of the categories, like a spoonful of sugar or a can of soda.

On pages 29–31, there are charts that show you how many

DESIGNING YOUR OWN DIET

servings a day you need from each food group and how big a serving is, depending on your age. Compare your list with the one in the book. If they are pretty much the same, you and your family are eating good, healthful meals. If there is a big difference between what you should be eating and what you actually are eating, it's time for a change. You need to design a diet that is better for you. But it has to be a diet that you will enjoy eating. Don't start by looking at what you ate last week and decide that you can never eat French fries again. Especially if French fries are one of your absolutely favorite foods.

Start from the other end. Make a list of all the foods you like in each of the basic food groups. You can use the list starting on page 25 as a starting point. You'd better get plenty of paper, because this will be a long list. Even if you think there are lots of foods you don't like, there are probably even more that you do like.

Now start planning your diet. Get your family involved in this too. It will help your parents to plan meals if they know you will eat certain things. As you get more skilled in the kitchen, you can even prepare some meals or snacks yourself. Remember to be realistic in your planning. Don't say you will have a nice hot bowl of oatmeal for breakfast every day when you know you never get out of bed until ten minutes before the school bus comes. However, you really should eat a good breakfast, so try to plan something you can get ready the night before. If you are really in a rush, maybe you can take something to eat on the school bus. An apple is better than nothing. And don't say you will stop having a snack when you get home from school if, like most kids, you come home from school absolutely starving. Plenty of nutritious foods make great snacks. This might even be a good time for that bowl of oatmeal. No law says you can only eat oatmeal in the morning.

You will soon discover that it is possible to eat a good, well balanced diet that's full of foods you really like.

The Foods You Buy

You have the most control over foods that you or your parents cook from scratch at home. Then you know exactly what ingredients are going in, and if you use the recipes in this cookbook, you will know exactly what the nutritional value of the dish is. But realistically, you aren't going to eat all your meals at home, and even when you do eat at home, you will buy some of the food already prepared, at least to some extent. You will buy bread at the supermarket, make spaghetti using canned tomatoes, bring home a pizza for supper.

HOW TO READ A LABEL

NUTRITION INFORMATION. You will see nutrition information on food labels expressed as a percent of the USRDA for protein, five vitamins (riboflavin, thiamin, niacin, vitamin A and vitamin C) and two minerals (calcium and iron).

SERVING SIZE tells the specific portion on which nutrition information is based. If the food is consumed several times a day, you might find nutrition information for multiple servings.

SERVINGS PER CONTAINER tell how many people you can expect to serve. It also helps you calculate cost per serving. To do so, divide the cost per container by the number of servings. For example:

$$\frac{\$2}{4 \text{ svg per container}} = 50 \text{ cents}$$

Here you find the number of CALORIES and grams of PROTEIN, FAT, and CARBOHYDRATE in one serving.

If the product is normally combined with other food, such as cereal with milk, nutrition information may show you the percent of the USRDA provided by the food alone and also by the combination.

SODIUM. A new regulation requires sodium labeling. You'll find sodium expressed as milligrams per serving and also as milligrams per 100 grams of the food. FDA definitions to sodium labeling are:

Very Low Sodium—35 mg or less per serving.

Low Sodium—140 mg or less per serving.

THE FOODS YOU BUY

At the store

You can find out a lot about the nutritional value—or lack of value—in the foods you buy at the market by reading the labels. Many prepared foods have nutrition information on the label, including how much of your daily requirements a serving provides, how big a serving is, and what ingredients went into it (see below).

Reduced Sodium—Processed to reduce normal level by 75 percent.

You may also find OPTIONAL INFORMATION on 12 other vitamins and minerals, cholesterol, types of fats, and carbohydrates. These may be provided voluntarily by the manufacturer.

INGREDIENTS are listed in order of amounts present in food. They are listed by weight, not by volume. Food additives are listed but specific kinds of spices, flavors, and colors do not have to be named. The FDA has set standards of identity (or "recipes") for over 360 common food products such as bread, ketchup, mayonnaise, and ice cream. Individual ingredients do not have to be listed for products having a standard of identity.

Name and place of business of either manufacturer, packer, or distributor must be on the label. Comments and questions about the product may be sent to this address.

Adapted from Safeway's Nutrition Awareness Program Booklet

THE FOODS YOU BUY

People frequently worry about the additives in prepared foods. These are chemicals, either artificial or natural, that the manufacturer adds to the food while it is being prepared or packaged. You may get the impression that additives mean bad food, as opposed to fresh, natural foods. But some additives, like BHT, BHA, and calcium propionate, preserve food and keep it from spoiling. Others, like the vitamin D added to milk, make foods more, not less, nutritious. Still others, like food colorings, make foods look more attractive. Nonetheless, some of the additives are of doubtful value, and some can cause health problems for some people. If you eat a wide variety of foods, especially fresh foods or foods made without processed ingredients, you are unlikely to get too much of any one additive.

At a fast food restaurant

Most children and teenagers love fast foods—burgers, fries, milkshakes, fried chicken, tacos, hot dogs, pizza—and the restaurants serving these foods fit well into the lives of busy families. You don't have to plan ahead or get dressed up to eat in fast-food restaurants. You know what you are getting, and the prices are fairly reasonable. Nutritionally speaking, fast foods may not be perfect, but they aren't all "junk food." Typical fast-food meals are high in calories for the nutrition they provide, high in saturated fats, salt, and sugar, and low in fiber and vitamins. But most fast-food restaurants offer choices, and if you put them together properly, you will end up with fairly well-balanced meals.

To help you choose your fast-food meals, we have provided nutritional charts (starting on page 32) based on information from the corporate headquarters of each restaurant. The number of calories, and the amount of protein, carbohydrate, total fat, saturated fat, cholesterol, and sodium of different foods are listed. The best choices are checked.

GUIDE TO GOOD FOOD

	Recommended	*Not Recommended*
MILK AND MILK PRODUCTS	**Milk** Buttermilk (skim or low-fat) Chocolate milk (1-2%) Low-fat or skim milk (fluid, evaporated, or powdered) **Cheese** Low-fat cheese (less than 15% fat) Low-fat (1-2% fat) cottage cheese Mozzarella, part skim milk Ricotta, part skim milk Skim milk cheese **Yogurt** Nonfat, plain Low-fat, fruited, flavored, or frozen **Miscellaneous** Ice milk	**Milk** Buttermilk (from whole) Chocolate milk (from whole) Evaporated (from whole) Whole **Cheeses** Blue cheese Cheddar Cream Creamed cottage cheese Mozzarella, whole milk Parmesan Ricotta, whole milk Swiss **Yogurt** Whole, plain or fruited **Miscellaneous** Butter Half and half Ice cream Cream (light, sour, and whipping)
MEAT OR MEAT ALTER- NATIVES	**Beef (Choice or Good)** Chuck Flank steak Ground (lean, 10% fat) Round, bottom or top Rump, all cuts **Lamb** Leg Rib, chop or roast **Luncheon Meat** Thin sliced lean meat Turkey franks, Turkey ham, Turkey pastrami **Fish and Shellfish** Any fresh or frozen fish or seafood Tuna, canned in water	**Beef (Prime)** Brisket Canned Corned Ground (15%-20% fat) Roast, rib Sausage **Lamb** Breast Ground Mutton **Luncheon Meat** Bologna Bratwurst Frankfurters, beef and pork Salami **Organ Meat (high in cholesterol)** Liver Sweetbreads

GOOD FOOD GUIDE

GUIDE TO GOOD FOOD

	Recommended	Not Recommended
	Pork Canadian bacon Leg, whole rump Ham, center or rump Loin, rib or chop Ribs, center or shank	**Pork** Country-style ham Deviled ham Loin, back ribs Pork, ground Sausage Spare ribs
	Veal Cutlets Leg Loin Rib Shank Shoulder	**Veal** Breast
	Poultry Chicken Cornish hen Turkey	**Poultry** Duck, domestic
	Meat Alternatives Peas or beans, dried Egg white or egg substitute	**Egg (high in cholesterol)** Egg yolk
BREADS, CEREALS, AND OTHER GRAINS	**Breads** French or Italian Pita Pumpernickel Raisin Rye Whole wheat White Bagel, small Bun, hamburger, hot dog Cornbread English muffin Muffin Pancake Roll, plain Tortilla, corn or wheat Waffle	**Breads** Biscuit Butter roll Cheesebread Croissants Doughnut Egg bread Sweet roll
	Cereal Barley, cooked Bulgar, cooked Bran flakes Cold cereal Hot cereal Grits, cooked Corn meal, dry	**Cereal** Cereals, presweetened Cereals, with coconut

GUIDE TO GOOD FOOD

Recommended	Not Recommended
Pasta	**Pasta**
Macaroni	Noodles, egg
Noodles	Noodles, chow mein
Lasagna	
Spaghetti	
Crackers	**Crackers**
Arrowroot	Cheese puffs
Bread sticks	Corn chips
Graham	Potato chips
Matzo	Tortilla chips
Pretzels, no salt	Other commercial crackers
Pretzel sticks, no salt	
Rye wafers	
Saltines, low sodium	
Soda	
Wheat	
Starchy Vegetables	**Starchy Vegetables**
Corn	Beans seasoned with bacon
Dried beans, peas, and lentils	or ham hocks
Hominy	Creamed corn
Peas	Fried rice
Potato	Potatoes, French fried
Pumpkin	
Rice (white/brown)	
Sweet potato	
Winter squash	
Miscellaneous	**Miscellaneous**
Bread crumbs	Pies
Corn starch	Popcorn, buttered and salted
Popcorn, air-popped	

FRUITS AND JUICES	All other fresh	Fruit pie filling
		Fruit roll ups
		Fruit in sugar syrup, light
		Fruit in sugar syrup, heavy
		Fruit whips
		Sweetened juices

VEGETABLES	All other	**Fried Vegetables**
		Vegetables with Sauces
		Vegetables in butter sauce
		Vegetables in cream sauce
		Vegetables in cheese sauce

GUIDE TO GOOD FOOD

	Recommended	*Not Recommended*
FAT	Avocado Margarine Nuts Olives	Butter Bacon, bacon fat Chocolate Coconut Cream Lard Hydrogenated vegetable oils
	Oil Canola Corn Cottonseed Olive Peanut Safflower Sesame Soybean Sunflower Walnut	**Oil** Coconut Palm

	Salad Dressing
	Caesar
	French
	French, low-calorie
	Italian
	Italian, low-calorie
	Mayonnaise
	Mayonnaise, light
	Thousand Island
	Thousand Island, low-calorie
	Vinegar and oil
		Salad Dressing
		Blue cheese
		Creamy
		Green goddess
		Salad dressings
		  with sour cream
		  or cheese
		Tartar sauce

**MISCEL-
LANEOUS**
	Angel food cake
	Cakes and cookies
	  made with
	  recommended
	  ingredients
	Fruit ice
	Gelatin, sweetened
	Frozen yogurt
	Ice milk
	Sherbet
		Cake (with icing)
		Cupcakes (with icing)
		Ice cream
		Pies, fruit
		Sugar
		Honey
		Jams
		Jellies

FOOD GROUP GUIDE

BASIC FOOD GROUP GUIDE FOR PRESCHOOL CHILDREN, AGES 4 TO 6 YEARS

Food Group	Recommended Number of Servings	Serving Size
Milk and Dairy Products	3 to 4	
Low-fat (2%) milk		¾ cup
Low-fat cheese		½ to ¾ ounces
Low-fat yogurt, cottage cheese		½ cup
Powdered skim milk		2 tablespoons
Fruits	2 or more	
Fruits	1 or more citrus (source of vitamin C)	
Juice		½ cup
Raw		½ to 1 small
Canned		¼ to ½ cup
Vegetables	2 or more	
Yellow or green*	1 or more (source of vitamin A)	¼ cup
Others		¼ cup
Breads, Cereals, and Starchy Vegetables	3 or more	
Whole-grain or enriched white bread		1 slice
Rolls, muffins, bagels, etc.		½
Ready-to-eat, unsweetened cereal		¾ cup
Cooked cereal, pasta, potato, or rice		¼ to ½ cup
Crackers		2 or 3
Meat and Meat Alternatives	4 to 6	
Lean meat, fish, poultry		1 ounce
Egg or egg substitute		1 small
Legumes (dried peas, beans)		¼ cup
Peanut butter		2 tablespoons
Fat	5 or more	
Margarine (vitamin A fortified)		1 teaspoon
Salad dressing, mayonnaise		2 teaspoons
Vegetable oil		1 teaspoon
Miscellaneous		
Desserts	In moderation	
Cake, pie		1 small slice
Cookies		1 medium
Ice cream, ice milk, sherbet, pudding		½ cup
Sugar, honey, jams, jellies	In moderation	1 tablespoon

*Good sources of vitamin A: vegetables, such as broccoli, carrots, spinach, and squash; also fruits such as cantaloupe and apricots.

FOOD GROUP GUIDE

BASIC FOOD GROUP GUIDE FOR SCHOOL CHILDREN, AGES 7 TO 10 YEARS

Food Group	Recommended Number of Servings	Serving Size
Milk and Dairy Products	4	
Low-fat (2%) milk		1 cup
Low-fat cheese		1 ounce
Low-fat yogurt		1 cup
Low-fat cottage cheese		¾ cup
Powdered skim milk		3 to 4 tablespoons
Fruits	2 or more	
Fruits	1 or more citrus (source of vitamin C)	
Juice		½ cup
Raw		1 small
Canned		½ cup
Vegetables	2 or more	
Yellow or green*	1 or more (source of vitamin A)	¼ cup
Other		¼ cup
Breads, Cereals, and Starchy Vegetables	4 or more	
Whole-grain or enriched white bread		
Rolls, muffins, bagels, etc.		1 slice
Ready-to-eat, unsweetened dry cereal		1
Cooked cereal, pasta, potato, or rice		1 cup ½ cup
Crackers		3 or 4
Meat and Meat Alternatives	5 to 7	
Lean meat, fish, or poultry		1 ounce
Egg or egg substitute		1 medium
Legumes (dried peas, beans)		½ cup
Peanut butter		3 tablespoons
Fat	7 or more	
Margarine (vitamin A fortified)		1 teaspoon
Salad dressing, mayonnaise		2 teaspoons
Vegetable oil		1 teaspoon
Miscellaneous		
Desserts	In moderation	
Cake, pie		1 small slice
Cookies		2 medium
Ice cream, ice milk, sherbet, pudding		½ cup
Sugar, honey, jams, jellies	In moderation	1 tablespoon

*Good sources of vitamin A: vegetables, such as broccoli, carrots, spinach, and squash; also fruits such as cantaloupe and apricots.

FOOD GROUP GUIDE

BASIC FOOD GROUP GUIDE FOR TEENAGERS, AGES 11 TO 17 YEARS

Food Group	Recommended Number of Servings	Serving Size
Milk and Dairy Products	4	
Low-fat (2%) milk		1 cup
Low-fat cheese		1½ ounces
Low-fat yogurt, cottage cheese		1 cup
Powdered skim milk		4 tablespoons
Fruits	2 or more	
Fruits	1 or more citrus	
Juices	(source of vitamin C)	1 cup
Raw		1 medium
Canned		1 cup
Vegetables	2 or more	
Yellow or green*	1 or more (source of vitamin A)	½ cup
Other		½ cup
Breads, Cereals, and Starchy Vegetables	4 or more	
Whole-grain or enriched white bread		1 slice
Rolls, muffins, bagels, etc.		1 large
Ready-to-eat, unsweetened dry cereal		1 to 1½ cup
Cooked cereal, pasta, potato, or rice		1 cup
Crackers		4 to 6
Meat and Meat Alternatives	6 to 8	
Lean meat, fish, or poultry		1 ounce
Egg or egg substitute		1 large
Legumes (dried peas, beans)		1 cup
Peanut butter		4 tablespoons
Fat	9 or more	
Margarine (vitamin A fortified)		2 teaspoons
Salad dressing, mayonnaise		4 teaspoons
Vegetable oil		2 teaspoons
Miscellaneous		
Desserts	In moderation	
Cake, pie		1 medium slice
Cookies		2 or 3 medium
Ice cream, ice milk, sherbet, pudding		¾ cup
Sugar, honey, jams, jellies	In moderation	1 tablespoon

*Good source of vitamin A: vegetables, such as broccoli, carrots, spinach, and squash; also fruits such as cantaloupe and apricots.

FAST FOOD GUIDE

Restaurant	Calories	Protein (Grams)	Carbohydrates (Grams)	Fat (Grams)	Saturated Fat (Grams)	Cholesterol (Milligrams)	Sodium (Milligrams)
Burger King							
Apple Pie	305	3	44	12	4	4	412
Breakfast Bagel Sandwich	387	17	46	14	5	268	780
✓ Cheeseburger	317	17	30	15	7	48	651
✓ Chicken Tenders	204	20	10	10	2	47	636
French Fries, Regular	227	3	24	13	7	14	160
French Toast Sticks	499	9	49	29	5	74	498
✓ Hamburger	275	15	29	12	5	37	509
Scrambled Egg Plate	468	15	33	30	NA	370	808
Specialty Chicken Sandwich	688	26	56	40	8	82	1423
Vanilla Shake	321	9	49	10	NA	NA	205
Whopper	628	27	46	36	12	90	880
✓ Whopper, Jr.	322	15	30	17	6	41	486
Dairy Queen							
Chicken Breast Fillet	608	27	46	34	NA	78	725
Chicken Nuggets	276	16	23	18	NA	39	505
Dipped Cone, Regular	340	6	42	16	NA	60	100
Fish Fillet	430	20	45	18	NA	40	674
Float	410	5	82	7	NA	20	85
Hot Dog	280	11	21	16	NA	45	830
Malt, Regular	760	14	134	18	NA	50	260
"Mr. Misty," Regular	250	0	63	0	NA	10	10
Shake, Regular	710	14	120	19	NA	50	260
✓ Single Hamburger	360	21	33	16	NA	45	630
✓ Soft Ice Cream	140	3	22	4	NA	10	45
Sundae, Regular	310	5	56	8	NA	70	120
Domino's							
✓ Cheese Pizza	376	22	56	10	5.5	19	483
Deluxe Pizza	498	27	59	20	9.3	40	954
Pepperoni Pizza	460	24	56	18	8.4	28	825
Veggi Pizza	498	31	60	19	10.2	36	1035
Jack in the Box							
Apple Turnover	401	4	45	24	10.8	15	350
✓ Beef Fajita Pita	333	24	27	14	5.9	45	635
Breakfast Jack®	307	18	30	13	5.2	203	871
✓ Cheeseburger	315	15	33	14	5.7	41	746
Chef Salad	295	32	3	18	9.4	107	812
✓ Chicken Fajita Pita®	292	24	29	8	2.9	34	703
✓ Hamburger	267	13	28	11	4.1	26	556
Jumbo Jack©	584	26	42	34	11.0	73	733
✓ Regular Taco	191	8	16	11	5.2	21	406
Super Taco	288	12	21	17	8.0	37	765
Taco Salad	503	34	28	31	13.4	92	1600
Kentucky Fried Chicken							
Biscuit	232	4	27	11	2.9	1	539
✓ Cole Slaw	119	1	13	7	1.0	4	197
✓ Corn on the Cob	176	5	32	3	1	1	21
Extra Crispy							
Breast	354	27	14	21	5	93	842
Drumstick	173	13	6	11	3	65	346
Kentucky Fries	244	3	31	12	3	2	139
Kentucky Nuggets, 6 pieces	276	17	13	17	4	71	840
✓ Mashed Potatoes and Gravy	71	2	12	2	0.5	1	342

*NA = Not Available

FAST FOOD GUIDE

Restaurant	Calories	Protein (Grams)	Carbohydrates (Grams)	Fat (Grams)	Saturated Fat (Grams)	Cholesterol (Milligrams)	Sodium (Milligrams)
Original Recipe							
Breast	283	28	9	15	4	93	672
✓ Drumstick	146	13	4	9	2	67	275
Long John Silver							
Battered Fish, 1 piece	150	12	9	8	1.8	30	510
✓ Chicken Plank, 1 piece	110	8	6	6	1.4	15	320
Children's Meal							
1 fish, fries, and 1 hushpuppy	440	16	49	20	4.9	30	590
2 planks, fries, and 1 hushpuppy	510	20	52	24	5.9	30	730
✓ Clam Chowder	140	11	10	6	1.8	20	590
✓ Coleslaw	140	1	20	6	1.0	15	260
✓ Corn on the Cob	270	6	38	14	2.6	5	95
Crispy Fish Sandwich	600	29	60	28	6.3	30	1220
✓ Garden Salad	140	8	9	8	NA	5	330
✓ Homestyle Fish, 1 piece	125	7	9	7	1.6	20	200
Ocean Chef Salad	250	24	19	9	0.7	80	1340
McDonald's							
Apple Pie	260	2	30	15	6	5	240
Big Mac	560	25	43	32	10	103	950
✓ Cheeseburger	310	15	31	14	5	53	750
Chicken Nuggets	290	19	14	16	4	65	520
Egg McMuffin	290	18	28	11	4	226	740
English Muffin with Butter	170	5	27	5	2	9	270
Fish-O-Filet	440	14	38	26	5	50	1030
French Fries, Regular	220	3	26	12	5	9	110
✓ Hamburger	260	12	31	10	4	37	500
McDonald Cookies	290	4	47	9	2	0	300
Scrambled Eggs	140	12	1	10	3	399	290
✓ Garden Salad	110	7	6	7	3	83	160
Vanilla Shake	350	10	56	10	5	41	170
Taco Bell							
Beef Burrito	397	23	38	17	7.4	57	926
Bean Burrito	356	13	54	10	2.9	9	888
Burrito Supreme	407	18	45	18	7.7	33	796
✓ Chicken Fajita	225	14	20	10	3.7	44	619
Encharito	382	20	31	20	9.3	54	1243
✓ Pintos and Cheese	190	9	19	9	3.6	16	642
Soft Taco	228	12	18	12	5.4	32	516
✓ Steak Fajita	234	15	19	11	4.8	14	485
✓ Taco	183	10	11	11	4.6	32	276
Taco Salad	941	36	63	61	19.0	80	1662
✓ Tostada	243	9	27	11	4.1	16	596
Wendy's							
✓ Chef Salad	180	15	10	9	NA	120	140
Chicken Breast Filet Sandwich	430	26	41	19	NA	60	705
Chili	230	21	16	9	NA	50	960
French Fries	310	4	38	15	NA	15	105
Frosty	400	8	59	14	NA	50	220
✓ Garden Salad	102	7	9	5	NA	0	110
✓ Kid's Hamburger	260	13	30	9	NA	30	510
✓ Plain Potato	250	6	52	2	NA	trace	60
Wendy's Big Classic	580	24	47	34	NA	80	1015

Welcome to the Kitchen

The kitchen is the best place to be when it comes to good food. The cooking is fun and so is the eating. You can make snacks, meals, special holiday treats for yourself and for your whole family.

If you haven't done much cooking before, you should have an adult with you who can show you how to use kitchen equipment and guide you through the various techniques cooks use. We will describe some of these techniques, but reading about something isn't always enough. For example, it is much easier to fold in beaten egg whites when someone shows you how than it is when you have only read about it.

Never cook by yourself until your parents have agreed that you are ready. You don't want a mistake in your recipe, and you don't want to hurt yourself. Stoves, broilers, knives, mixers, grinders—many pieces of kitchen equipment can be very dangerous if you don't use them properly. Learning how to use them takes practice.

When you have chosen a recipe, read it through. Make sure you have all the ingredients you need and all the equipment.

Take out everything you will need, and measure your ingredients. Have everything ready before you start preparing the recipe.

Remember to clean up. The cook is responsible for making sure the kitchen is clean at the end of the cooking session. Return ingredients that are left over to their proper places. Wash, dry, and put away dishes, pots, pans, and utensils. When you are finished, sweep the floor and wipe the counter. Make your kitchen shine!

SAFETY FIRST

1. Dress safely. Roll up long sleeves and pull your hair back so nothing gets into the food that doesn't belong there. And wear an apron so that the food doesn't get where it doesn't belong.

WELCOME TO THE KITCHEN

2. Wash your hands whenever they get messy so things you are trying to hold don't slip through your fingers.
3. Keep your fingers away from the sharp edge of a knife. Pick knives up by the handle, not by the blade. Always cut food on a cutting board, not while holding food in your hand.
4. Make sure electric appliances are turned off before you plug them in.
5. Never put your fingers or a utensil into the bowl of a blender, mixer, or food processor while it is on. NEVER!
6. Use pot holders or hot pads when you pick up pots from the stove or put things in or take things out of the oven.
7. Don't let the handles of pots stick out over the side of the stove where someone could bump into them.
8. Turn the oven or stove burner off as soon as you have finished with it.

KITCHEN KNOW HOW

How to Measure

Dry ingredients Mound ingredients into the correct size dry measuring cup. Level with the flat edge of a table knife or spatula.

Liquid ingredients Place a liquid measuring cup on a level surface. Bend down so the cup is at eye level. Carefully fill the cup with liquid to the correct measurement.

Small quantities For liquid ingredients, choose the correct measuring spoon and fill it just to the top. Hold the spoon over an empty bowl or cup while you measure to catch accidental spills or overflow. For dry ingredients, mound the ingredients in the correct measuring spoon and level with the flat edge of a spatula or table knife.

Brown sugar Firmly pack brown sugar into the correct dry measuring cup so that when it is turned out, it will keep its shape.

Margarine A quarter of a pound of margarine (one stick) equals half a cup, and the wrapper on a ¼ pound stick is marked with measurements for 8 tablespoons. Place wrapped margarine on a cutting board and cut through the paper with a small, sharp knife at the correct mark. For melted margarine, measure before melting or, if already melted, use measuring spoons.

How to Grate

Mouli or rotary grater Use the grater with the smallest holes for hard cheeses like Parmesan. For cheddar and mozzarella, fit the grater with the wheel with the largest holes. Cut the cheese into 1 to 1½-inch cubes using a chef's knife on a cutting board. Put the cheese cubes in the grater next to the blade and put the clamp down. Hold the grater over a bowl and turn the handle clockwise to grate the cheese into the bowl. (When grating semisoft cheese like mozzarella, put the cheese cubes in the freezer for fifteen minutes. Firmer cheese is easier to grate.)

Upright or four-sided grater Use this type of grater with care because it is sharp and can cut your knuckles and fingers. It can be used for cheese, onions, carrots, zucchini, and citrus rinds. When grating vegetables or mozzarella or cheddar cheese, use the side with the largest holes. For Parmesan, use the smallest holes. Place a sheet of wax paper under the grater to catch the grated food. Move the food over the grater side from the top down. For citrus rinds, place the grater on its side with the smallest holes facing up. Place a piece of parchment paper over the holes. Move the fruit across the parchment-covered grater. The rind will grate onto the parchment. Remove the paper from the grater and slide the edge of a rubber spatula over it to collect the rind.

How to Chop, Slice, Dice, and Peel

Chef's knife Always work on a cutting board. When chopping, hold the knife parallel to you with the handle in your writing hand and your other hand on the dull top of the blade. Lift the handle up and down, rocking the blade on the pointed end to chop the ingredients.

For onions, place the onion on a cutting board and cut in half from root to shoot. Place the onion flat side down, slice off the top, and pull the papery skin down over the root end. Hold the onion down at the root end with one hand. Slice the onion lengthwise about six times, but not through the root (it holds the onion together), and then cut across the slices to make small pieces.

For potatoes, cut the potatoes in half lengthwise, place the flat side down, and cut into the desired size and shape.

For garlic, flatten the clove with a dough scraper or chef's knife by pressing the flat side down firmly on the clove until the skin pops. The skin should slip off easily. Chop the garlic with the chef's knife, rocking the blade on the pointed end, until it is finely chopped.

Small or medium-size knife Hold the handle with your writing hand and place the food parallel to you on a cutting board. Hold the large end of the food item with your other hand, keeping your hand away from the blade. Cut across the food, bringing the handle back toward you.

Mezzaluna Place the food on a cutting board. Hold each handle of the mezzaluna and rock the blade back and forth over the food. When the chopped pieces spread, scrape them back to the center of the board and continue chopping. Use the mezzaluna to chop fresh herbs as well as vegetables.

WELCOME TO THE KITCHEN

Serrated knife Place round foods on the cutting board and cut them in half using a sawing motion. Put the flat side down and cut the food into the desired shapes and sizes. Use a serrated knife for tomatoes, citrus fruit, and breads.

Bread Place the bread parallel to you on a cutting board. Cut it crosswise into slices using a sawing motion.

Peeling Cup the handle of a u-shaped peeler with the blade extended across the top in the palm of your writing hand, grasping it between your thumb and index finger. Hold the food to be peeled against a cutting board with your other hand. Push the sharp swivel blade of the peeler across the food away from your hand.

How to Crack, Separate, and Beat an Egg

Cracking an egg Hold the egg in one hand. Gently but firmly tap the middle of the egg against the rim of a bowl, making an even, crosswise break. Hold the egg cracked side down over the bowl. Using your thumbs, pull the edges of the shell apart letting the egg drop gently into the bowl.

Separating the yolk from the white Egg whites will not beat foamy or stiff if even a trace of yolk mixes in with the white. Use three clean, dry bowls. Crack eggs one at a time into the first bowl. Cup clean, dry fingers under the yolk and lift it out carefully. Transfer the yolk to the second bowl. Transfer the white to the third bowl, which will be just for whites. Repeat for as many eggs as your recipe needs. If the yolk breaks into the white, put the egg into a fourth bowl or jar and save it for another use.

Beating egg whites Use an electric mixer or a whisk. Beat egg whites at the last minute before they are to be used, or they become deflated. Put the egg whites in a bowl large enough to hold the beaten whites. Beat them on high speed, or as quickly as you can if beating by hand. Egg whites are stiffly beaten if the tips of the peaks stand up straight when you pull up the beater, or if the bowl can be turned upside down and the whites cling to the bottom of the bowl.

Folding egg whites Fold egg whites into a mixture with a rubber spatula, working quickly and gently by lifting the mixture from the bottom of the bowl over the top. Continue until the egg whites are completely combined with the rest of the mixture.

How to Melt Margarine

Conventional method Cut margarine into tablespoon-size pieces. Put it in a small saucepan over medium heat on the stove and stir it until it is melted. Remove from heat.

Microwave method Cut margarine into tablespoon-size pieces. Place in a 2-cup microwave-safe measure and cover loosely with a paper towel or wax paper. Cook on high (100%) power for 30 seconds to 1 minute or until melted.

The Recipes

All the recipes in this book are accompanied by nutritional charts that provide information that will be particularly useful to you as you design your own diet. We have tried to minimize those elements you don't want too much of—saturated fats, cholesterol, and sodium. In the charts, these nutrients appear in italics, and the amount in each serving is specified. We have also listed those nutrients that are most often lacking in young people's diets—iron, calcium, vitamins A and C, and fiber. Good sources of these nutrients appear in bold. Finally, so that you can see how a particular recipe will fit into your overall diet, we have included the number of calories and the precise amounts of carbohydrate, protein, and fat.

The recipes are also labeled so that you can see which food group or groups they belong to:

V for Vegetables

F for Fruits and fruit juices

M for Meat, fish, poultry, and eggs

G for Grain products, like bread, pasta, and rice

D for Dairy products like milk and cheese

Finally, symbols mark those recipes that are particularly rich in certain important nutrients:

○ for vitamin C

🥕 for vitamin A

🥩 for iron

🥛 for calcium

BEVERAGES

Apple-Lime Cooler

Skill Level: Beginner   Serves 1

INGREDIENTS
¼ cup apple juice
2 tablespoons sparkling water or seltzer water
2 ice cubes
¼ lime

EQUIPMENT
glass
liquid measuring cup
measuring spoons
cutting board
serrated knife

In a serving glass, combine apple juice and sparkling water over ice. Rub lime around the glass and squeeze lime juice into apple juice mixture. Serve.

NUTRITIONAL INFORMATION

Calories per serving	34	Fiber	0.2 g
Carbohydrate	9 g	Vitamin A	2 IU
Protein	0 g	Vitamin C	5 mg
Total fat	0 g	Calcium	11 mg
Saturated fat	*0 g*	*Sodium*	*10 mg*
Cholesterol	*0 mg*	Iron	0.3 mg

BEVERAGES

Banana Smoothy

Skill level: Beginner   Serves 3

INGREDIENTS
1½ cups lowfat (2%) milk
1   medium-size ripe banana (at room temperature or frozen), broken into 3 pieces
1   tablespoon honey
½   teaspoon vanilla

EQUIPMENT
liquid measuring cup
measuring spoons
blender

Combine all ingredients in a blender and mix until smooth and frothy.

NUTRITIONAL INFORMATION	
Calories per serving 142	Fiber .... 0.3 g
Carbohydrates .... 26 g	Vitamin A .... 296 IU
Protein .... 5 g	Vitamin C .... 7 mg
Total fat .... 3 g	Calcium .... 180 mg
Saturated fat .... 1.6 g	*Sodium* .... 73 mg
Cholesterol .... 9 mg	Iron .... 0.3 mg

BEVERAGES

Fruit Frappé

Skill Level: Beginner   Serves 6

INGREDIENTS
- 2 bananas, peeled and cut into pieces
- ½ pint fresh strawberries, washed and hulled
- 1 6-ounce can orange juice concentrate
- 3 cups crushed ice

EQUIPMENT
- table knife
- cutting board
- blender
- dry measuring cups
- rubber spatula
- tall glass

1. Place bananas, strawberries, and orange juice concentrate in a blender. Cover.

2. Start the blender and slowly add ice, blending until the mixture is smooth and chunks of fruit are well mixed.

3. Serve in a tall glass.

NUTRITIONAL INFORMATION

Calories per serving..... 81	Fiber .... 0.4 g
Carbohydrate .... 20 g	Vitamin A.......... 104 IU
Protein .... 1 g	**Vitamin C .... 51 mg**
Total fat .... 0 g	Calcium........... 26 mg
Saturated fat .... 0 g	*Sodium .... 1 mg*
Cholesterol.......... 0 mg	Iron............. 0.3 mg

BEVERAGES

Lemon-Apple-Ade

Skill Level: Beginner   Serves 8

INGREDIENTS
2½ cups apple juice
3 tablespoons sugar
½ cup fresh lemon juice
10 ice cubes
fresh mint leaves

EQUIPMENT
liquid measuring cup
ice cube trays
measuring spoons
cutting board
serrated knife
juicer
blender or food processor

1. Pour apple juice into ice cube trays; freeze 2 hours or until almost firm.
2. Combine apple juice cubes, sugar, and lemon juice in container of a blender or food processor; cover and process just until slushy.
3. Add ice, cover, and process until smooth. Garnish servings with mint.

NUTRITIONAL INFORMATION	
Calories per serving 58	Fiber . . . . 0.2 g
Carbohydrate . . . . 15 g	Vitamin A . . . . 4 IU
Protein . . . . 0 g	Vitamin C . . . . 8 mg
Total fat . . . . 0 g	Calcium . . . . 6 mg
Saturated fat . . . . 0 g	Sodium . . . . 2 mg
Cholesterol . . . . 0 mg	Iron . . . . 0.3 mg

Mighty Milk Shake

Skill Level: Beginner   Serves 1

INGREDIENTS
- ½ cup low-fat vanilla frozen yogurt
- ½ cup low-fat (2%) milk
- 1 egg white
- 1 teaspoon unsweetened cocoa powder
- ¼ teaspoon vanilla

EQUIPMENT
- dry measuring cups
- liquid measuring cup
- measuring spoons
- blender

Combine all ingredients in a blender. Blend on high speed until frothy. Serve.

NUTRITIONAL INFORMATION	
Calories per serving 201	Fiber .... 0 g
Carbohydrate .... 27 g	Vitamin A .... 338 IU
Protein .... 13 g	Vitamin C .... 2 mg
Total fat .... 5 g	**Calcium .... 317 mg**
Saturated fat .... *3.1 g*	*Sodium* .... *204 mg*
Cholesterol .... *16 mg*	Iron .... 0.2 mg

BEVERAGES

Orange Juliette

Skill Level: Beginner   Serves 2

INGREDIENTS
1   cup fresh orange juice
½   cup low-fat vanilla frozen yogurt

EQUIPMENT
cutting board
serrated knife
juicer
liquid measuring cup
dry measuring cups
blender
rubber spatula
chilled glass

Put orange juice and frozen yogurt in a blender and blend until frothy, about 1 minute. Serve in a chilled glass.

NUTRITIONAL INFORMATION

Calories per serving 102
Carbohydrate . . . . 20 g
Protein . . . . 2 g
Total fat . . . . 1 g
Saturated fat . . . . 0.9 g
Cholesterol . . . . 5 mg
Fiber . . . . 0.1 g
Vitamin A . . . . 301 IU
Vitamin C . . . . 62 mg
Calcium . . . . 115 mg
Sodium . . . . 55 mg
Iron . . . . 0.3 mg

BEVERAGES

Orange Squeeze

Skill Level: Beginner   Serves 1

INGREDIENTS
2   oranges, chilled
1   strawberry
1   mint sprig

EQUIPMENT
serrated knife
cutting board
juicer
serving glass

1. Roll oranges on work surface to soften them.
2. Cut oranges in half with a serrated knife. Juice with a juicer. Pour juice into serving glass.
3. Split a strawberry in half lengthwise, leaving stem intact. Garnish glass of juice with strawberry and mint.

NOTE: For larger quantities of juice, use an electric juicer.

NUTRITIONAL INFORMATION	
Calories per serving 129	**Fiber. . . . . 1.2 g**
Carbohydrate . . . . 31 g	Vitamin A. . . . . 542 IU
Protein . . . . 2 g	**Vitamin C . . . . 148 mg**
Total fat . . . . 0 g	Calcium . . . . 106 mg
Saturated fat . . . . *0 g*	*Sodium* . . . . *1 mg*
Cholesterol. . . . . *0 mg*	Iron . . . . 0.6 mg

BEVERAGES

Strawberry Shake

Skill Level: Beginner   Serves 2

INGREDIENTS
- 1 cup low-fat (2%) milk
- ¾ cup fresh or frozen hulled strawberries
- 1 egg white
- 1 tablespoon sugar
- ¼ teaspoon vanilla

EQUIPMENT
- liquid measuring cup
- dry measuring cups
- measuring spoons
- blender
- rubber spatula
- 2 chilled glasses

1. Combine all ingredients in a blender.
2. Blend on high speed for about 2 minutes, until smooth and frothy. Serve in tall, chilled glasses.

NOTE: When strawberries are too ripe to eat, they can be frozen and used in this recipe. They should be hulled, washed, patted dry, and placed in a plastic bag for freezing. Using frozen strawberries makes this shake icy and cool.

NUTRITIONAL INFORMATION

Calories per serving 117	Fiber .... 0.3 g
Carbohydrate .... 17 g	Vitamin A. .... 265 IU
Protein .... 7 g	**Vitamin C .... 33 mg**
Total fat .... 3 g	Calcium .... 186 mg
Saturated fat .... *1.5 g*	*Sodium* .... *98 mg*
Cholesterol .... *10 mg*	Iron .... 0.3 mg

BEVERAGES

Thunderbird

Skill Level: Beginner   Serves 1

INGREDIENTS
½ cup fresh orange juice
½ cup grape juice
ice

EQUIPMENT
cutting board
serrated knife
juicer
liquid measuring cup
beverage glass
iced tea spoon

1. Combine orange juice and grape juice in a glass.
2. Add ice and stir.

NUTRITIONAL INFORMATION

Calories per serving 134	Fiber . . . . 0 g
Carbohydrate . . . . 32 g	Vitamin A . . . . 107 IU
Protein . . . . 2 g	**Vitamin C . . . . 49 mg**
Total fat . . . . 0 g	Calcium . . . . 22 mg
Saturated fat . . . . 0 g	Sodium . . . . 5 mg
Cholesterol . . . . 0 mg	Iron . . . . 0.4 mg

BREADS

Banana Bran Muffins

Skill Level: Intermediate   Yield: 12 muffins

INGREDIENTS
nonstick vegetable cooking spray
¼ cup margarine
⅓ cup brown sugar
1¼ cups mashed bananas
   (about 3)
1 egg
½ cup whole wheat pastry flour
½ cup cake flour
1 teaspoon baking soda
¼ teaspoon salt
1 cup bran cereal

EQUIPMENT
12-cup muffin tin
paper liners (optional)
large mixing bowl
dry measuring cups
electric mixer
rubber spatula
measuring spoons
hot pads
cake tester
cooling rack

1. Preheat oven to 375°F. Coat a 12-cup muffin tin with nonstick vegetable cooking spray or use paper liners.
2. In a mixing bowl, cream together margarine and brown sugar with an electric mixer on medium high until blended, about 1 minute. Add bananas and egg, then beat with the electric mixer about 1 minute. Push batter from sides of bowl with a rubber spatula.
3. Add whole wheat pastry flour, cake flour, baking soda, and salt. Beat about 1 minute on medium-high speed.
4. Add bran and beat until just combined.
5. Fill prepared muffin cups with batter, using a ⅓-cup measuring cup.
6. Bake 15 to 20 minutes until tester inserted in muffin comes out clean. Cool muffin tins on cooling racks for about 5 minutes. Turn muffins out onto cooling racks.

NUTRITIONAL INFORMATION

Calories per serving 131	Fiber. . . . . 0.7 g
Carbohydrate . . . . 22 g	Vitamin A. . . . . 343 IU
Protein . . . . 2 g	Vitamin C . . . . 4 mg
Total fat . . . . 5 g	Calcium. . . . . 15 mg
Saturated fat . . . . 0.8 g	*Sodium*. . . . . 120 mg
Cholesterol. . . . . 23 mg	Iron . . . . 1.5 mg

BREADS

Blueberry-Citrus Muffins

Skill Level: Intermediate   Yield: 12

INGREDIENTS
- nonstick vegetable cooking spray
- ¼ cup margarine, melted
- 1 egg
- 2 egg whites
- ½ cup sugar
- 1 cup low-fat lemon yogurt
- ¼ cup fresh orange juice
- 1 teaspoon grated orange rind or lemon rind
- 1 cup all-purpose flour
- 1 cup whole wheat pastry flour
- 1 teaspoon baking powder
- ½ teaspoon baking soda
- 1 1-pound bag frozen blueberries, thawed and drained, or 1 pint fresh blueberries, washed and patted dry

EQUIPMENT
- 12-cup muffin tin
- large mixing bowl
- measuring spoons
- dry measuring cups
- electric mixer
- rubber spatula
- cutting board
- serrated knife
- juicer
- liquid measuring cup
- grater
- parchment paper
- strainer
- hot pads
- cake tester
- cooling rack

1. Preheat oven to 375°F. Coat a 12-cup muffin tin with nonstick vegetable cooking spray.
2. In a large bowl, cream together margarine, egg, egg whites, and sugar with an electric mixer on medium-high speed for about 2 minutes.
3. Add yogurt, orange juice, and grated rind to egg mixture. Beat on medium speed until well combined. Push down batter from sides with a rubber spatula.
4. Add both flours, baking powder, and baking soda to batter. Beat on medium-high speed until just blended, about 30 seconds.
5. With a rubber spatula, gently fold in blueberries.
6. Using a ⅓-cup measure, fill 12 muffin cups half-full with muffin batter.

Continued on next page

BREADS

7. Bake muffins for 25 minutes, or until a tester inserted in the center of one muffin comes out clean.
8. Transfer pan to cooling rack and cool muffins in pan for 10 minutes, then turn out onto cooling rack.

NUTRITIONAL INFORMATION

Calories per serving 177	**Fiber. . . . . 0.7 g**
Carbohydrate . . . . 30 g	Vitamin A. . . . . 228 IU
Protein . . . . 5 g	Vitamin C . . . . 5 mg
Total fat . . . . 5 g	Calcium. . . . . 47 mg
Saturated fat . . . . *1.1 g*	*Sodium*. . . . . *150 mg*
Cholesterol . . . . *24 mg*	Iron . . . . 0.8 mg

BREADS

Cinnamon Bears

Skill Level: Intermediate   Serves 3

INGREDIENTS
- 2 teaspoons sugar
- ½ teaspoon cinnamon
- 3 slices whole wheat bread
- 1 tablespoon margarine
- 9 raisins

EQUIPMENT
- small bowl
- measuring spoons
- 3-inch bear-shaped cookie cutter
- baking sheet
- toaster oven (optional)
- hot pads
- spreader

 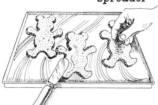 

1. Combine sugar and cinnamon in a small bowl.
2. Preheat oven to broil or use toaster oven.
3. Use a bear-shaped cookie cutter to create bears out of whole wheat bread slices. Place bears on a baking sheet.
4. Toast bears until lightly browned, about 30 seconds to 1 minute, on second rack from top of oven. Turn the bears over.
5. Spread margarine on top side of each bear and sprinkle with cinnamon sugar.
6. Broil 1 to 2 minutes until cinnamon sugar crystallizes.
7. Remove from oven. Use raisins to create eyes and mouth.

NUTRITIONAL INFORMATION

Calories per serving 121	Fiber .... 0.2 g
Carbohydrate .... 19 g	Vitamin A.......... 156 IU
Protein .... 2 g	Vitamin C .... 0 mg
Total fat .... 4 g	Calcium........... 25 mg
Saturated fat .... *0.8 g*	*Sodium* .... *62 mg*
Cholesterol.......... *0 mg*	Iron .... 0.4 mg

BREADS

Cornmeal Pancakes

Skill Level: Advanced   Serves 8

INGREDIENTS	EQUIPMENT
1 cup cornmeal	large mixing bowl
¾ cup all-purpose flour	dry measuring cups
1 tablespoon sugar	measuring spoons
1 teaspoon baking soda	mixing spoon
¼ teaspoon salt	liquid measuring cup
2 cups buttermilk	medium mixing bowl
4 tablespoons safflower oil, divided	electric mixer
	rubber spatula
2 stiffly beaten egg whites	basting brush
	nonstick griddle or skillet
	ladle
	metal spatula

1. Combine cornmeal, flour, sugar, baking soda, and salt in a large mixing bowl.

2. Add buttermilk and 3 tablespoons oil, and stir to combine.

3. Gently fold in beaten egg whites and let stand 10 minutes.

4. Lightly coat a nonstick griddle or skillet with some of remaining tablespoon safflower oil using a basting brush, and heat over medium-high until hot. Ladle ¼ cup batter into the skillet to form a round pancake. Cook until the top begins to bubble and the bottom is golden.

5. Flip pancake with a metal spatula and cook until the bottom is golden brown. Repeat with remaining batter, oiling skillet between batches.

NOTE: Serve with Strawberry Spread (page 100) for a tasty alternative to syrup.

BREADS

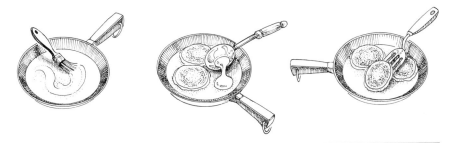

NUTRITIONAL INFORMATION

Calories per serving 212
Carbohydrate . . . . 26 g
Protein . . . . 5 g
Total fat . . . . 9 g
Saturated fat . . . . *1.1 g*
Cholesterol . . . . *2 mg*
Fiber . . . . 0.1 g
Vitamin A . . . . 97 IU
Vitamin C . . . . 1 mg
Calcium . . . . 75 mg
Sodium . . . . *195 mg*
Iron . . . . 0.8 mg

BREADS

Drop Biscuits

Skilled Level: Intermediate   Serves 12

INGREDIENTS
nonstick vegetable cooking spray
2   cups plus 1 tablespoon all-purpose flour (divided)
2   tablespoons sugar
1   tablespoon baking powder
¼   teaspoon salt
½   cup low-fat (2%) milk
½   cup buttermilk

EQUIPMENT
baking sheet
large mixing bowl
dry measuring cups
measuring spoons
mixing spoon
liquid measuring cup
hot pads
metal spatula

1. Preheat oven to 425°F. Lightly coat baking sheet with nonstick vegetable spray.
2. In a large mixing bowl, combine 2 cups flour, sugar, baking powder, and salt. Stir together.
3. Quickly stir in milk and buttermilk, stirring just until ingredients are blended. Sprinkle dough with 1 tablespoon flour and knead a few times until smooth.
4. Use a spoon to scoop about 2 tablespoons of dough, and place scoops 2 inches apart on the baking sheet.
5. Bake about 12 to 14 minutes, or until biscuits are lightly browned.
6. Remove with metal spatula and serve hot.

NUTRITIONAL INFORMATION

Calories per serving 89	Fiber . . . . 0.1 g
Carbohydrate . . . . 18 g	Vitamin A . . . . 42 IU
Protein . . . . 3 g	Vitamin C . . . . 0 mg
Total fat . . . . 1 g	Calcium . . . . 33 mg
Saturated fat . . . . 0.3 g	*Sodium* . . . . 164 mg
Cholesterol . . . . 2 mg	Iron . . . . 0.6 mg

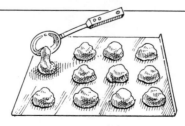

BREADS

Frenchy Toast

Skill Level: Intermediate   Serves 5

INGREDIENTS
1   egg
3   egg whites
2   tablespoons low-fat (2%) milk
¾   teaspoon vanilla
¼   teaspoon cinnamon
2   teaspoons margarine, divided
5   slices whole wheat bread
4   teaspoons powdered sugar

EQUIPMENT
shallow bowl
whisk
measuring spoons
nonstick skillet
metal spatula
hot pad

1. Combine egg and egg whites in a shallow bowl and beat with a small whisk until frothy.
2. Add milk, vanilla, and cinnamon. Whisk to combine.
3. Heat 1 teaspoon margarine in a nonstick skillet over medium-high heat.
4. Dip a slice of bread into the egg mixture, coating both sides evenly.
5. Put the bread slice in the skillet and cook on each side for 2 minutes or until browned. Dip the remaining bread slices in the egg mixture and cook them one at a time, adding remaining margarine after 2 slices have been cooked.
6. Sprinkle Frenchy Toast with powdered sugar. Serve hot.

NUTRITIONAL INFORMATION

Calories per serving 116	**Fiber**. . . . . **1.1 g**
Carbohydrate . . . . 15 g	Vitamin A. . . . . 127 IU
Protein . . . . 6 g	Vitamin C . . . . 0 mg
Total fat . . . . 4 g	Calcium. . . . . 33 mg
Saturated fat . . . . *0.6 g*	*Sodium*. . . . . *156 mg*
Cholesterol . . . . *55 mg*	Iron . . . . 0.9 mg

BREADS

Garlic Bread

Skill Level: Intermediate   Serves 6
Conventional and Oven Method   Microwave and Oven Method

INGREDIENTS
1   small loaf French bread
¼   cup margarine
2   garlic cloves, slightly crushed

EQUIPMENT
serrated knife or bread knife
cutting board
small saucepan or microwave-safe 1-cup measure
dry measuring cups
dough scraper
paper towels (optional)
hot pads
pastry brush
foil

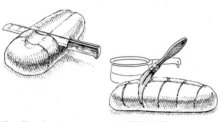

1. Preheat oven to 350°F.
2. Cut bread with a serrated knife or bread knife into 6 even sections, but only cut almost to the base of the loaf each time.
3. Put margarine and garlic in a small saucepan and melt over low heat, or place margarine and garlic in a microwave-safe 1-cup measure, cover with a paper towel, and cook at high (100%) power for 1 minute.
4. Use a pastry brush to apply the garlic-flavored margarine to each side of the bread slices.
5. Wrap foil around the bread loaf. Heat in the oven for 8 to 10 minutes.

NUTRITIONAL INFORMATION

Calories per serving 142
Carbohydrate . . . . 14 g
Protein . . . . 2 g
Total fat . . . . 8 g
Saturated fat . . . . *1.7 g*
Cholesterol . . . . *0 mg*
Fiber . . . . 0 g
Vitamin A . . . . 312 IU
Vitamin C . . . . 0 mg
Calcium . . . . 14 mg
Sodium . . . . *234 mg*
Iron . . . . 0.6 mg

BREADS

Good Morning Coffee Cake

Skill Level: Intermediate   Serves 15

INGREDIENTS
nonstick vegetable cooking spray
1   cup whole wheat flour
1¼ cups all-purpose flour
2   teaspoons cinnamon
¼   teaspoon ginger
½   cup brown sugar
½   cup granulated sugar
½   cup safflower oil
¼   cup apple juice
½   cup chopped pecans
1   teaspoon baking soda
1   teaspoon baking powder
1   egg, beaten
1   cup buttermilk

EQUIPMENT
13×9×2-inch baking pan
large mixing bowl
dry measuring cups
measuring spoons
liquid measuring cup
mixing spoon
small mixing bowl
electric mixer
rubber spatula
hot pads
cake tester

1. Coat a 13×9×2-inch baking pan with nonstick vegetable cooking spray. Preheat oven to 350°F.

2. In a large mixing bowl, stir together whole wheat and all-purpose flour, cinnamon, ginger, brown sugar, granulated sugar, safflower oil, and apple juice. Place ¾ cup of the batter in a small mixing bowl.

3. Add pecans to the batter in the small mixing bowl to make the topping. Stir well and set aside.

4. To the remaining batter, add baking soda, baking powder, egg, and buttermilk. Combine all ingredients with an electric mixer on high for 1 to 2 minutes. Push batter from sides with a rubber spatula.

Continued on next page

BREADS

5. Pour batter into prepared baking pan. Sprinkle the topping mixture evenly over the surface of the coffee cake. Bake for 40 to 45 minutes, or until a tester inserted in the middle comes out clean.

NUTRITIONAL INFORMATION	
Calories per serving 217	Fiber . . . . 0.3 g
Carbohydrate . . . . 28 g	Vitamin A . . . . 27 IU
Protein . . . . 3 g	Vitamin C . . . . 0 mg
Total fat. . . . . 11 g	Calcium . . . . 35 mg
Saturated fat . . . . *1.1 g*	*Sodium.* . . . . *108 mg*
Cholesterol . . . . *19 mg*	Iron . . . . 1.0 mg

BREADS

Parmesan Bread Sticks

Skill Level: Intermediate   Yield: 24   1 serving = 3 sticks

INGREDIENTS
4   whole wheat hot dog buns
3   tablespoons olive oil
¼   cup grated Parmesan cheese

EQUIPMENT
serrated knife
cutting board
measuring spoons
pastry or basting brush
baking sheet
grater
hot pads

1. Preheat oven to 250°F.
2. Split each hot dog bun in half lengthwise using a serrated knife, then cut each half into 3 long strips.
3. Brush each bread stick with olive oil and place on a baking sheet. Sprinkle with Parmesan cheese.
4. Bake for 1 hour until bread sticks are crisp and golden.

NOTE: Leftovers can be stored in zip-close plastic bags.

NUTRITIONAL INFORMATION

Calories per serving 122   Fiber .... 0.1 g
Carbohydrate .... 13 g   Vitamin A .... 18 IU
Protein .... 3 g   Vitamin C .... 0 mg
Total fat .... 6 g   Calcium .... 57 mg
Saturated fat .... 1.2 g   Sodium .... 179 mg
Cholesterol .... 2 mg   Iron .... 0.3 mg

BREADS

Powerhouse Oatmeal Muffins

Skill Level: Intermediate   Yield: 12

INGREDIENTS
- 2 cups buttermilk
- 1 cup rolled oats
- nonstick vegetable cooking spray
- 1 egg
- 2 egg whites
- ½ cup dark brown sugar
- 1⅔ cups whole wheat flour
- 2 tablespoons toasted wheat germ
- 1 teaspoon baking powder
- ¼ teaspoon salt
- 2 tablespoons safflower oil

EQUIPMENT
- mixing bowl
- liquid measuring cup
- dry measuring cups
- 12-cup muffin tin
- large mixing bowl
- whisk
- spoon
- measuring spoons
- hot pads
- cake tester
- cooling rack

1. Put buttermilk and oats into a mixing bowl and stir them together. Cover and chill overnight. (If you forget to do this the night before, you can combine buttermilk and oats at baking time.)
2. Coat a 12-cup muffin tin with nonstick vegetable cooking spray. Preheat oven to 400°F.
3. In a large mixing bowl, whisk together the egg, egg whites, and brown sugar until the mixture is smooth. Add the buttermilk mixture and stir until ingredients are well combined.
4. Stir flour, wheat germ, baking powder, salt, and oil into oatmeal mixture.
5. Using a ⅓-cup measure, fill each muffin cup ⅓ full with batter.

BREADS

6. Bake for 15 to 20 minutes, or until cake tester comes out clean.
7. Turn muffins out onto cooling racks.

NOTE: For a delicious treat, serve with Strawberry Spread (page 100).

NUTRITIONAL INFORMATION

Calories per serving 161	**Fiber............. 0.5 g**
Carbohydrate .... 27 g	Vitamin A .... 35 IU
Protein .... 6 g	Vitamin C .... 0 mg
Total fat .... 4 g	Calcium........... 69 mg
Saturated fat........ 0.6 g	*Sodium........... 105 mg*
Cholesterol......... 24 mg	Iron .... 1.3 mg

BREADS

Tiny Tart Shells

Skill Level: Intermediate   Yield: 20   1 serving = 2 tart shells

INGREDIENTS
1 cup all-purpose flour
½ cup part-skim ricotta cheese
¼ cup margarine

EQUIPMENT
mixing bowl
dry measuring cups
mixing spoon
2 12-cup nonstick miniature muffin tins
hot pads
cooling racks

1. Preheat oven to 425°F.
2. In a mixing bowl, combine flour, ricotta, and margarine. Knead together with your fingers until well blended.
3. Form 20 balls from dough. Press dough balls into miniature cups. Gently press your thumb into the center of each one to create a hollow space.
4. Bake for 12 to 15 minutes until lightly browned.
5. Cool muffin tins on cooling racks.
6. Remove tart shells.

NOTE: For a tea-time treat, fill tart shells with "Always A Favorite Chicken Salad" (page 149). Tart shell dough can also be pressed into an 8-inch pie plate for a pie crust.

NUTRITIONAL INFORMATION

Calories per serving 46
Carbohydrate . . . . 4 g
Protein . . . . 1 g
Total fat . . . . 3 g
Saturated fat . . . . *0.7 g*
Cholesterol . . . . *2 mg*
Fiber . . . . 0 g
Vitamin A . . . . 120 IU
Vitamin C . . . . 0 mg
Calcium . . . . 18 mg
Sodium . . . . *9 mg*
Iron . . . . 0.1 mg

BREADS

Valentine Scones

Skill Level: Intermediate   Yield: 15   1 serving = 1 scone

INGREDIENTS
nonstick vegetable cooking spray
1½ cups plus 2 tablespoons all-purpose flour, divided
¾ cup whole wheat pastry flour
¼ cup sugar
1¼ teaspoons baking powder
¼ teaspoon salt
½ cup chilled margarine
1 egg, lightly beaten
¼ cup milk
1 egg white, lightly beaten
1 tablespoon colored sugar

EQUIPMENT
baking sheet
mixing bowl
sifter
dry measuring cups
measuring spoons
cutting board
small knife
2 small bowls
2 forks
liquid measuring cup
plastic wrap (optional)
2½-inch heart-shaped cookie cutter
pastry brush
hot pads
cooling rack
metal spatula

1. Preheat oven to 375°F. Coat a baking sheet with nonstick vegetable cooking spray.
2. In a mixing bowl, sift together 1½ cups all-purpose flour, whole wheat flour, sugar, baking powder, and salt.
3. Cut margarine into 8 pieces. Use your fingertips to blend margarine into dry ingredients until the mixture resembles coarse cornmeal.
4. Stir egg and milk into mixture, then gently knead a few times until dough is moist and holds together.
5. Wrap dough in plastic wrap and chill, or immediately pat dough into a ½-inch-thick circle with your palms on a work surface sprinkled with 2 tablespoons flour.
6. Cut dough into hearts with a cookie cutter, starting at the edge of the circle and going toward the center. Gently knead scraps together, flatten the dough into a circle, and cut remaining hearts. Place heart scones on the prepared baking sheet as you cut them.

Continued on next page

BREADS

7. Brush top of each scone with egg white. Sprinkle each with colored sugar.

8. Bake 15 to 20 minutes until bottoms are lightly browned. Remove pan from oven and place on a cooling rack. Remove warm scones with a metal spatula.

9. Serve warm.

NOTE: For a Valentine's Tea Party, serve scones with molded, heart-shaped Strawberry Spread (page 100).

NUTRITIONAL INFORMATION

Calories per serving 144	Fiber . . . . 0.2 g
Carbohydrate . . . . 18 g	Vitamin A. . . . . 276 IU
Protein . . . . 3 g	Vitamin C . . . . 0 mg
Total fat . . . . 7 g	Calcium. . . . . 15 mg
Saturated fat . . . . *1.4 g*	*Sodium*. . . . . *148 mg*
Cholesterol . . . . *18 mg*	Iron . . . . 0.4 mg

BREADS

Whole Wheat Crepes

Skill Level: Advanced   Serves 8   Yield: 16–18 crepes
         1 serving = 2 crepes

INGREDIENTS
½ cup whole wheat flour
½ cup all-purpose flour
1½ cups low-fat (2%) milk
1 egg
⅛ teaspoon salt
5 teaspoons safflower oil, divided

EQUIPMENT
mixing bowl
dry measuring cups
liquid measuring cup
measuring spoons
electric mixer
rubber spatula
nonstick 6-inch skillet
basting brush
ladle or ¼-cup measure
paper towels
small metal spatula
wax paper

1. In a mixing bowl, combine flours, milk, egg, salt, and 3 teaspoons oil. Beat with an electric mixer on high speed about 1 minute until blended.
2. Brush a nonstick skillet with a small amount of the remaining oil and heat over high heat. Remove pan from heat. Using ladle, put about 2 tablespoons of batter in the skillet, immediately tipping and shaking it to spread the batter over the bottom evenly. Return the skillet to the stove and heat at medium high until the crepe is browned, about 30 seconds.
3. Turn the skillet upside down over paper towels and remove crepe using a small metal spatula. Repeat to make 16 to 18 crepes, adding a small amount of oil to the skillet occasionally with the basting brush.
4. For breakfast or dessert, spread each warm crepe with 2 teaspoons all-fruit jam, fold in quarters, and sprinkle with powdered sugar.

Continued on next page

BREADS

For a main dish, spread each crepe with 2 tablespoons of grated low-fat mozzarella cheese, roll up into a cylinder, put in a baking dish, and bake at 350° for about 8 minutes until cheese melts.

NOTE: Crepes can be prepared ahead of time. Stack cooled crepes between sheets of wax paper, wrap stack in foil, and refrigerate until ready to use. Nutrient analysis does not include fillings.

NUTRITIONAL INFORMATION

Calories per serving 112	Fiber .... 0.2 g
Carbohydrate .... 13 g	Vitamin A. .... 126 IU
Protein .... 4 g	Vitamin C .... 1 mg
Total fat .... 5 g	Calcium .... 74 mg
Saturated fat .... 1.1 g	*Sodium* .... 70 mg
Cholesterol .... 38 mg	Iron .... 0.5 mg

SNACKS

Apple Leather

Skill Level: Intermediate   Serves 4

INGREDIENTS
nonstick vegetable cooking spray
1½ cups unsweetened applesauce

EQUIPMENT
15×10×1-inch baking sheet
rubber spatula
dry measuring cups
hot pads
scissors

1. Preheat oven to 400°F. Coat baking sheet with nonstick vegetable cooking spray.
2. Using a rubber spatula, spread applesauce evenly over the baking sheet.
3. Place baking sheet in oven. Lower heat to 200°F. Bake for approximately 3 hours until the apple leather can be peeled from the baking sheet.
4. Cut apple leather into 4×4-inch pieces with scissors. Serve. Store leftovers in plastic wrap.

NUTRITIONAL INFORMATION

Calories per serving	40	**Fiber**	**0.5 g**
Carbohydrate	10 g	Vitamin A	26 IU
Protein	0 g	Vitamin C	1 mg
Total fat	0 g	Calcium	3 mg
Saturated fat	*0 g*	*Sodium*	*2 mg*
Cholesterol	*0 mg*	Iron	0.1 mg

SNACKS

Bean Dip

Skill Level: Advanced   Serves about 8   1 serving = ½ cup
Microwave and Conventional Methods

Microwave Method

INGREDIENTS
- 4 cups pinto beans, boiled until tender
- ½ teaspoon ground cumin
- 1 4-ounce can chopped green chilies
- 2 tablespoons margarine
- ½ cup chopped onion
- 1 garlic clove, minced
- 1½ teaspoons fresh lime juice

EQUIPMENT
- dry measuring cups
- colander
- food processor or blender
- measuring spoons
- rubber spatula
- 2-quart microwave-safe bowl
- cutting board
- chef's knife
- dough scraper
- hot pads
- wooden spoon
- serrated knife
- plastic wrap
- juicer

1. Drain beans in a colander. Transfer beans to food processor or blender and puree until smooth, about 2 minutes.
2. Add cumin and green chilies; puree until well combined. Set aside.
3. In a 2-quart microwave-safe bowl, combine margarine, onion, and garlic. Microwave on high (100%) power 3 minutes. Stir with a wooden spoon.
4. Remove beans from the food processor or blender container, scraping the sides with a rubber spatula, and add to onion mixture. Stir to combine.
5. Cover bowl with plastic wrap and microwave on medium-high (70%) power for 5 minutes or until hot.
6. Stir lime juice into bean mixture. Serve.

SNACKS

Conventional Method

EQUIPMENT
dry measuring cups
colander
food processor or blender
measuring spoons
rubber spatula
large nonstick skillet
cutting board
chef's knife
dough scraper
hot pads
wooden spoon
serrated knife
juicer

Follow Steps 1 and 2 from the microwave method.

3. In a large nonstick skillet, sauté onion and garlic in margarine over medium heat for 5 minutes or until they are limp. Stir with a wooden spoon.

4. Remove beans from food processor or blender container, scraping sides with a rubber spatula, and add to onion mixture. Stir to combine.

5. Cook over medium heat for about 10 minutes or until mixture is hot. Stir occasionally.

6. Stir lime juice into bean mixture. Serve.

NOTE: Serve with Corn Tortilla Chips (page 81). Chips are not included in nutritional analysis.

NUTRITIONAL INFORMATION

Calories per serving 151	**Fiber** . . . . **3.5 g**
Carbohydrate . . . . 24 g	Vitamin A . . . . 122 IU
Protein . . . . 7 g	Vitamin C . . . . 2 mg
Total fat . . . . 3 g	Calcium . . . . 45 mg
Saturated fat . . . . 0.5 g	Sodium . . . . 203 mg
Cholesterol . . . . 0 mg	**Iron** . . . . **2.3 mg**

SNACKS

Breakfast Sundae

Skill Level: Beginner   Serves 1

INGREDIENTS
1   ripe banana
⅓   cup low-fat strawberry
    custard-style yogurt
2   tablespoons bran cereal

EQUIPMENT
cutting board
table knife
dry measuring cups
measuring spoons

1. Peel banana and cut into ⅓-inch slices. Place in a serving bowl.
2. Add yogurt and sprinkle with bran cereal. Serve immediately.

NUTRITIONAL INFORMATION

Calories per serving 195
Carbohydrate .... 44 g
Protein .... 5 g
Total fat .... 1 g
Saturated fat........ 0.7 g
Cholesterol.......... 3 mg
Fiber............. 0.8 g
Vitamin A......... 344 IU
Vitamin C .... 13 mg
Calcium .... 113 mg
Sodium .... 86 mg
Iron............. 0.8 mg

Cheese Pimento Spread In Celery Boats

Skill Level: Beginner   Serves 8

INGREDIENTS
- ½ cup (2 ounces) grated low-fat mozzarella cheese
- ½ cup (2 ounces) grated cheddar cheese
- ¼ cup chopped green, red, or yellow pepper (or a combination)
- 2 tablespoons light mayonnaise
- 4 stalks celery

EQUIPMENT
- mixing bowl
- grater
- dry measuring cups
- cutting board
- small, sharp knife
- measuring spoons
- spoon
- dish cloth or paper towels

1. Combine the mozzarella and cheddar cheeses with chopped pepper in a mixing bowl.
2. Stir in mayonnaise until cheese spread is well combined.
3. Wash celery stalks well and dry. Cut off 1 inch from both ends of each stalk. Remove any tough strings on outside of celery stalk. Slice stalks into uniform pieces about 2 inches long.
4. Spoon 1 tablespoon cheese mixture into the hollow portion of the celery.

NUTRITIONAL INFORMATION

Calories per serving	66	Fiber	0.2 g
Carbohydrate	1 g	Vitamin A	227 IU
Protein	3 g	Vitamin C	6 mg
Total fat	5 g	Calcium	99 mg
Saturated fat	2.6 g	Sodium	118 mg
Cholesterol	13 mg	Iron	0.2 mg

SNACKS

Cheesy Popcorn

Skill Level: Advanced   Serves 8

INGREDIENTS
½ cup popping corn
3 tablespoons safflower oil
¼ cup margarine, melted
½ cup grated Parmesan cheese
¼ teaspoon salt

EQUIPMENT
dry measuring cups
measuring spoons
large covered saucepan or
  popcorn popper
hot pads
extra large mixing bowl
grater
2 mixing spoons

1. To prepare 4 quarts of popped corn, place corn and oil into a pan with a tight-fitting lid or into a popcorn popper.
2. Cover and heat. Leave pan lid slightly ajar to allow steam to escape. If using a popcorn popper, follow manufacturer's instructions.
3. When popping slows, remove pan from heat or unplug popper.
4. Place popcorn in an extra-large bowl and gradually pour margarine over it.
5. Gradually add Parmesan cheese and salt. Toss until popcorn is evenly coated and serve.

NUTRITIONAL INFORMATION

Calories per serving 165
Carbohydrate . . . . 9 g
Protein . . . . 4 g
Total fat . . . . 13 g
Saturated fat . . . . 2.5 g
Cholesterol . . . . 4 mg
Fiber . . . . 0.3 g
Vitamin A . . . . 269 IU
Vitamin C . . . . 0 mg
Calcium . . . . 74 mg
Sodium . . . . 227 mg
Iron . . . . 0.5 mg

SNACKS

Chip-Dipping Salsa

Skill Level: Intermediate   Yield: 1 quart   Serves 12

INGREDIENTS
- 2   28-ounce cans tomatoes, drained
- ½   cup chopped yellow onion
- 1   garlic clove, chopped
- ½   cup cilantro leaves
- 2½   teaspoons wine vinegar
- ¾   teaspoon salt
- ¼   teaspoon sugar

EQUIPMENT
- colander
- cutting board
- chef's knife
- dry measuring cups
- dough scraper
- measuring spoons
- food processor or blender

1. Combine all ingredients in a food processor or blender for about 1½ to 2 minutes, depending on whether a smooth or chunky sauce is desired.
2. Serve immediately or chill in a covered container.

NOTE: Serve Salsa with Corn Tortilla Chips (page 81). Tortilla chips are not included in the nutritional analysis.

NUTRITIONAL INFORMATION	
Calories per serving..... 28	**Fiber**............. **0.5 g**
Carbohydrate .... 6 g	**Vitamin A**....... **1024 IU**
Protein .... 1 g	Vitamin C .... 20 mg
Total fat .... 0 g	Calcium........... 10 mg
Saturated fat .... 0 g	*Sodium*........... 281 mg
Cholesterol......... 0 mg	Iron.............. 0.6 mg

SNACKS

Christmas Spinach Dip

Skill Level: Intermediate   Yield: 3 cups   Serves 24

INGREDIENTS
- 2 10-ounce packages frozen chopped spinach, thawed
- ¾ cup low-fat cottage cheese
- ½ cup light mayonnaise
- ¼ cup grated Parmesan cheese
- 3 tablespoons finely chopped onion
- 3 tablespoons chopped parsley
- 4 teaspoons fresh lemon juice
- ½ teaspoon finely chopped garlic
- ½ teaspoon salt
- ¼ teaspoon pepper
- pinch of cayenne pepper
- pinch of dried thyme

EQUIPMENT
- food processor or blender
- measuring spoons
- cutting board
- dough scraper
- chef's knife
- mezzaluna (optional)
- grater
- dry measuring cups
- serrated knife
- juicer
- rubber spatula
- storage container

1. Squeeze liquid from spinach.
2. Combine all ingredients in a food processor or blender and blend until combined. Transfer to storage container and chill until serving time.

NOTE: Serve during the Christmas season or any time with crackers. For a holiday party, serve dip in a bread round by slicing the top from a whole round of bread with bread knife. Scoop out the center of the bread with your hands. Tie a festive ½-inch-wide ribbon around the center width of the bread loaf. Fill the hollowed center with spinach dip.

NUTRITIONAL INFORMATION

Calories per serving..... 33	Fiber .... 0.2 g
Carbohydrate .... 1 g	**Vitamin A** .... **1985 IU**
Protein .... 2 g	Vitamin C .... 8 mg
Total fat .... 2 g	Calcium .... 41 mg
Saturated fat .... *0.2 g*	*Sodium* .... *114 mg*
Cholesterol .... *1 mg*	Iron .... 0.6 mg

SNACKS

Christmas Vegetable Tree

Skill Level: Intermediate   Serves 8

INGREDIENTS
- 5 carrots, peeled
- 1 red pepper
- 1 head green leaf lettuce
- 2 cups broccoli, cut into small florets
- 2 cups cauliflower, cut into small florets
- 1 cup cherry tomatoes

EQUIPMENT
- peeler
- cutting board
- toothpicks
- mixing bowl
- small, sharp knife
- scissors
- 18-inch styrofoam cone
- dry measuring cups

1. Using a peeler, cut peeled carrot into long strips by running the peeler along the side of the carrot. Repeat several times. When you have cut to the middle of the carrot, turn the carrot over and cut strips from the other side. Roll each carrot strip into a curl, then secure it with a toothpick. Chill curls in ice water.

2. Place red pepper on its side and use a small, sharp knife to make a cut about 1 inch around the stem, being careful not to cut through the stem. Grasp under the rim with your fingers and turn to loosen. Pull the stem away from the pepper to remove the core. Remove the white ribs from the pepper. Using scissors, cut the pepper into festive shapes.

3. Loosely cover a styrofoam cone with lettuce leaves, using toothpicks to secure them.

4. Insert additional toothpicks into the cone. Decorate the tree by spearing broccoli and cauliflower florets, cherry tomatoes, and red pepper onto toothpicks. Place carrot curls on the tree with the toothpicks that hold them together.

Continued on next page

SNACKS

NOTE: Serve the Christmas Vegetable Tree with extra vegetables and a dip (pages 76, 102). Nutritional analysis does not include extra vegetables or dip.

NUTRITIONAL INFORMATION			
Calories per serving	52	**Fiber**	**2 g**
Carbohydrate	11 g	**Vitamin A**	**6267 IU**
Protein	4 g	**Vitamin C**	**107 mg**
Total fat	0 g	Calcium	89 mg
Saturated fat	*0 g*	*Sodium*	*35 mg*
Cholesterol	*0 mg*	Iron	1.4 mg

"Circles and Squares" Snack Mix

Skill Level: Intermediate Serves 18 1 serving = ½ cup
Microwave and Conventional Methods

Microwave Method

INGREDIENTS
- ¼ cup margarine, cubed
- 3 tablespoons Worcestershire sauce
- 1 tablespoon red wine vinegar
- ½ teaspoon garlic powder
- 4 cups ring-shaped oat cereal
- 4 cups square-shaped bran cereal
- ¾ cup unsalted peanuts

EQUIPMENT
- large, microwave-safe bowl
- measuring spoons
- small, sharp knife
- cutting board
- hot pads
- 2 wooden spoons
- dry measuring cups
- airtight container

1. Put margarine in a large microwave-safe bowl. Microwave on high (100%) power for about 1 minute, or until margarine is melted.
2. Add Worcestershire sauce, red wine vinegar, and garlic powder to margarine. Stir to combine.
3. Add oat and bran cereals and peanuts to the bowl, stirring well to coat evenly.
4. Microwave on high for a total of 6 minutes, stirring well every 2 minutes.
5. Cool before storing. Store in an airtight container.

Continued on next page

SNACKS

Oven Method

EQUIPMENT
small saucepan
measuring spoons
small, sharp knife
cutting board
hot pads
2 wooden spoons
13×9×2-inch baking pan
dry measuring cups
airtight container

1. Preheat oven to 325°F.
2. Melt margarine in a small saucepan over medium-low heat.
3. Remove melted margarine from heat and stir in the Worcestershire sauce, red wine vinegar, and garlic powder.
4. In a 13×9×2-inch baking pan, combine oat and bran cereals and peanuts.
5. Pour margarine mixture over cereals and stir well to coat evenly.
6. Bake for 25 minutes, or until cereal is crisp and lightly browned, stirring the mixture well every 8 minutes.
7. Cool before storing. Store in an airtight container.

NUTRITIONAL INFORMATION

Calories per serving 109	**Fiber** . . . . **0.7 g**
Carbohydrate . . . . 13 g	Vitamin A . . . . 154 IU
Protein . . . . 3 g	Vitamin C . . . . 5 mg
Total fat . . . . 6 g	Calcium . . . . 37 mg
Saturated fat . . . . *1.2 g*	*Sodium* . . . . *158 mg*
Cholesterol . . . . *0 mg*	**Iron** . . . . **2.6 mg**

SNACKS

Corn Tortilla Chips

Skill Level: Intermediate   Serves 4

INGREDIENTS
4 corn tortillas
1 tablespoon safflower oil

EQUIPMENT
cutting board
small, sharp knife or kitchen scissors
15×10×1-inch baking sheet
pastry brush
measuring spoons
hot pads

1. Preheat oven to 400°F.
2. Cut tortillas into 8 wedges on a cutting board by using a small, sharp knife, or cut them with kitchen scissors.
3. Place tortilla wedges on a baking sheet. Brush both sides of each wedge with oil.
4. Bake for 10 minutes or until wedges become crisp and lightly golden.

NOTE: Serve the Corn Tortilla Chips with Chip-Dipping Salsa (page 75), Bean Dip (page 70), or Pico de Gallo (page 93).

NUTRITIONAL INFORMATION	
Calories per serving 93	Fiber .... 0.3 g
Carbohydrate .... 14 g	Vitamin A .... 6 IU
Protein .... 2 g	Vitamin C .... 0 mg
Total fat .... 4 g	Calcium .... 60 mg
Saturated fat .... 0.3 g	Sodium .... 33 mg
Cholesterol .... 0 mg	Iron .... 0.9 mg

SNACKS

Cream Cheese Spread with Whole Wheat Crackers

Skill Level: Beginner   Serves 6

INGREDIENTS
- 4 ounces light cream cheese
- 2 tablespoons low-fat cottage cheese
- 1 tablespoon fresh lemon juice
- 2 teaspoons low-sodium soy sauce
- 18 whole wheat low-sodium crackers

EQUIPMENT
- small mixing bowl
- measuring spoons
- cutting board
- serrated knife
- juicer
- fork or electric mixer
- rubber spatula
- spreader or table knife

1. In a small mixing bowl, combine cream cheese, cottage cheese, lemon juice, and soy sauce.
2. Using a fork or an electric mixer, cream together mixture until smooth.
3. Cover and chill until serving time.
4. Spread onto crackers.

NOTE: The Cream Cheese Spread can also be served as a dip for raw vegetables or as a sauce for cooked vegetables.

NUTRITIONAL INFORMATION

Calories per serving..... 95	Fiber .... 0.3 g
Carbohydrate .... 10 g	Vitamin A......... 114 IU
Protein .... 4 g	Vitamin C .... 1 mg
Total fat .... 4 g	Calcium........... 32 mg
Saturated fat........ 0.1 g	*Sodium*........... *259 mg*
Cholesterol......... *11 mg*	Iron .... 0.3 mg

SNACKS

Creamy Oatmeal for One

Skill Level: Intermediate   Serves 1
Microwave Method

INGREDIENTS
⅓ cup rolled oats
1 tablespoon oat bran
½ cup low-fat (2%) milk
¼ cup water
¼ teaspoon vanilla
1 teaspoon margarine
1 teaspoon sugar

EQUIPMENT
dry measuring cups
measuring spoons
liquid measuring cup
microwave-safe bowl
hot pads
spoon
cereal bowl

1. Combine oats, oat bran, milk, water, and vanilla in a microwave-safe bowl.
2. Microwave on medium (50%) power for 5 minutes.
3. Stir ingredients together to combine, then add margarine and sugar to oatmeal. Transfer to cereal bowl and serve.

NOTE: All milk or all water can be substituted for milk and water combination.

NUTRITIONAL INFORMATION	
Calories per serving 228	**Fiber............. 2.2 g**
Carbohydrate .... 30 g	Vitamin A......... 406 IU
Protein............. 9 g	Vitamin C.......... 1 mg
Total fat .... 8 g	**Calcium .... 192 mg**
Saturated fat........ 2.6 g	Sodium........... 118 mg
Cholesterol......... 10 mg	Iron .... 1.3 mg

SNACKS

Fresh Fruit Kabobs

Skill Level: Beginner   Serves 8

INGREDIENTS
- ½ pound seedless grapes
- 2 cups pineapple cubes
- 1½ cups strawberries
- 2 tangerines, peeled and sectioned
- 1 cup fresh blueberries

EQUIPMENT
- dry measuring cups
- serrated knife
- cutting board
- wooden skewers

Pierce fruit onto wooden skewers, alternating types of fruit.

NOTE: Making Fresh Fruit Kabobs is a good group project.

NUTRITIONAL INFORMATION

Calories per serving..... 94	**Fiber............... 1 g**
Carbohydrate .... 24 g	Vitamin A.......... 262 IU
Protein .... 1 g	**Vitamin C .... 35 mg**
Total fat .... 0 g	Calcium........... 16 mg
Saturated fat .... *0 g*	*Sodium* .... *3 mg*
Cholesterol.......... *0 mg*	Iron.............. 0.5 mg

SNACKS

Fun Fruits with a Dip

Skill Level: Intermediate   Serves 6

INGREDIENTS
¾ cup plain low-fat yogurt
2 tablespoons powdered sugar
1 tablespoon fresh lemon juice
1 ripe nectarine
1 cup strawberries
1 apple
½ pineapple, peeled and cored

EQUIPMENT
small mixing bowl
dry measuring cups
measuring spoons
small whisk or a serving spoon
cutting board
serrated knife
juicer
paper towels or dish cloth
small, sharp knife
serving dish
apple corer and slicer
small serving bowl

1. To prepare fruit dip, put yogurt, powdered sugar, and lemon juice in a small mixing bowl. Blend the ingredients with a small whisk or serving spoon until the mixture is smooth. Chill the dip until serving time.

2. Wash and dry the nectarine, then cut it in half and remove the pit. Place the halves flat side down on a cutting board and cut each lengthwise into four slices. Place the slices on a serving dish.

3. Wash strawberries and pat them dry. Place strawberries on the serving dish with the nectarine slices.

4. Wash and dry the apple, then core and slice it using an apple corer and slicer. Add apple slices to the serving dish.

Continued on next page

SNACKS

5. Place the pineapple flat side down on the cutting board. Cut into four lengthwise slices, cut each slice into thirds, and add them to the serving dish.

6. Transfer dip to a serving bowl and place on serving dish with fruit.

NUTRITIONAL INFORMATION

Calories per serving..... 86	**Fiber............. 0.7 g**
Carbohydrate .... 19 g	Vitamin A......... 217 IU
Protein .... 2 g	Vitamin C .... 26 mg
Total fat .... 1 g	Calcium........... 62 mg
Saturated fat........ *0.3 g*	*Sodium* .... *21 mg*
Cholesterol.......... *2 mg*	Iron............. 0.4 mg

SNACKS

Ghost Treats

Skill level: Beginner   Serves 1

INGREDIENTS
1   rice cake
1   tablespoon light cream cheese
3   raisins

EQUIPMENT
measuring spoons
table knife or spreader

1. With hands, break off edges of the rice cake to create a ghostly shape.
2. Spread rice cake with cream cheese.
3. Use raisins for the ghost's eyes and mouth. Serve.

NUTRITIONAL INFORMATION

Calories per serving	82	Fiber	0 g
Carbohydrate	11 g	Vitamin A	161 IU
Protein	2 g	Vitamin C	0 mg
Total fat	4 g	Calcium	12 mg
Saturated fat	2.1 g	Sodium	67 mg
Cholesterol	11 mg	Iron	0 mg

SNACKS

Honey Bear Granola

Skill Level: Intermediate Serves 12

INGREDIENTS
nonstick vegetable cooking spray
½ cup apple juice
⅓ cup honey
3 cups rolled oats
⅓ cup toasted wheat germ
⅓ cup slivered almonds
⅓ cup chopped pecans
1 teaspoon cinnamon
⅓ cup raisins

EQUIPMENT
15×10×1-inch baking pan
small bowl
dry measuring cups
liquid measuring cup
spoon or small rubber spatula
measuring spoons
hot pads
metal spatula

1. Preheat oven to 350°F. Coat a 15×10×1-inch baking pan with nonstick vegetable cooking spray.
2. In a small bowl, stir together apple juice and honey until well combined.
3. Pour oats, wheat germ, almonds, and pecans onto prepared baking sheet. Combine these ingredients with your hands. Add cinnamon and toss to coat.
4. Pour apple juice-honey mixture on granola mixture, stirring with a large spoon or tossing with your hands to coat evenly.
5. Bake for 30 minutes, stirring well every 10 minutes with a metal spatula.
6. Remove from oven. Stir in raisins. Cool. Store in airtight container.

NOTE: Eat Honey Bear Granola alone as a snack or use as a topping for sliced fruit, cereal, low-fat yogurt, or frozen yogurt.

NUTRITIONAL INFORMATION

Calories per serving 134	Fiber .... 0.3 g
Carbohydrate .... 20 g	Vitamin A .... 4 IU
Protein .... 3 g	Vitamin C .... 0 mg
Total fat .... 5 g	Calcium .... 19 mg
Saturated fat .... 0.6 g	*Sodium* .... 1 mg
Cholesterol .... 0 mg	*Iron* .... 0.8 mg

SNACKS

Oatmeal Cups

Skill Level: Intermediate   Serves 12   1 serving = 2 cups

INGREDIENTS
nonstick vegetable cooking spray
2   cups rolled oats
1   cup whole-wheat flour
¼   teaspoon cinnamon
¼   teaspoon salt
½   cup "lite" maple syrup
½   cup safflower oil
½   cup all-fruit strawberry jam

EQUIPMENT
2 12-cup miniature muffin tins
blender or food processor
dry measuring cups
measuring spoons
liquid measuring cup
hot pads
2 spoons
2 cooling racks

1. Preheat oven to 350°F. Coat 2 miniature muffin tins (24 cups) with nonstick vegetable cooking spray.
2. In a blender or food processor, combine oats, flour, cinnamon, and salt. Process until the mixture is coarse.
3. Add syrup and oil to mixture and process until sticky dough forms, about 30 seconds to 1 minute.
4. Form mixture into 1-inch balls, then press the balls into miniature cups. Gently press your thumb into the center of each ball to create a hollow space for jam. (Do not add jam at this point.)
5. Bake oatmeal cups for 10 minutes. Carefully remove the muffin tins from the oven and place them on a heatproof surface.
6. Using 2 spoons, one to scoop jam and the other to push jam into oatmeal cup, fill each cup.
7. Bake an additional 10 minutes until jam is heated through.
8. Cool on cooling racks. Serve at room temperature.

NUTRITIONAL INFORMATION

Calories per serving 235	Fiber............. 0.5 g
Carbohydrate .... 34 g	Vitamin A .... 0 IU
Protein .... 3 g	Vitamin C .... 0 mg
Total fat............ 10 g	Calcium .... 27 mg
Saturated fat .... 0.8 g	*Sodium* .... 48 mg
Cholesterol.......... 0 mg	Iron............. 1.2 mg

SNACKS

Orange Spread

Skill Level: Intermediate   Serves 8

INGREDIENTS
1   orange
1   8-ounce package light cream cheese
1   tablespoon honey

EQUIPMENT
peeler
food processor or blender
measuring spoons
rubber spatula

1. Use a peeler to cut 3 strips of rind from the orange. Finely chop the peel in the food processor or blender.

2. Add the cream cheese and honey to the peel, then blend the ingredients together until light and fluffy, about 1 minute.

NOTE: For a tasty breakfast change, serve Orange Spread on whole wheat English muffins, pumpkin bread, or mini bagels.

NUTRITIONAL INFORMATION

Calories per serving..... 90	Fiber............... 0 g
Carbohydrate .... 3 g	Vitamin A.......... 355 IU
Protein .... 5 g	Vitamin C.......... 9 mg
Total fat .... 7 g	Calcium........... 28 mg
Saturated fat........ *4.2 g*	*Sodium*........... *113 mg*
Cholesterol......... *22 mg*	*Iron*.............. *0.1 mg*

SNACKS

Peanut Butter Points

Skill Level: Intermediate   Serves 10
Microwave and Conventional Methods

Oven/Microwave Method

INGREDIENTS
- 10 slices extra-thin whole wheat bread
- ½ cup smooth natural peanut butter
- 3 tablespoons safflower oil
- 1 tablespoon honey
- ½ cup toasted wheat germ
- 4 teaspoons sesame seeds

EQUIPMENT
- bread knife or serrated knife
- cutting board
- baking sheet
- hot pads
- dry measuring cups
- measuring spoons
- microwave-safe bowl
- wooden spoon
- shallow bowl
- wax paper
- pastry or basting brush

1. Preheat oven to 250°F.
2. Cut crust from bread using a bread knife or serrated knife, then cut each slice diagonally, twice, to form 4 triangles.
3. Place bread on a baking sheet. Bake for 15 minutes or until crisp and lightly browned.
4. Combine peanut butter, safflower oil, and honey in a microwave-safe bowl. Microwave on medium-high (70%) power for 2 minutes, stirring well after 1 minute.
5. Combine wheat germ and sesame seeds in a shallow bowl.
6. Place a sheet of wax paper on work surface.
7. Brush each triangle with peanut butter mixture, then coat with wheat germ and sesame seeds. Place the triangles on wax paper.
8. Let the triangles stand about 1 hour or until dry. Store in an airtight container.

Continued on next page

SNACKS

Oven/Conventional Method

EQUIPMENT

Same as above, but substitute a small saucepan for the microwave-safe bowl.

Follow all the steps as above but substitute the following for Step 4:

4. Combine peanut butter, safflower oil, and honey in a small saucepan. Stir ingredients together over low heat for 2 to 3 minutes until mixture is smooth and well blended.

NUTRITIONAL INFORMATION

Calories per serving 260	Fiber . . . . 0.3 g
Carbohydrate . . . . 32 g	Vitamin A . . . . 0 IU
Protein . . . . 7 g	Vitamin C . . . . 0 mg
Total fat. . . . . 11 g	Calcium. . . . . 36 mg
Saturated fat . . . . *1.7 g*	*Sodium*. . . . . *211 mg*
Cholesterol. . . . . *0 mg*	Iron . . . . 1.4 mg

SNACKS

Pico De Gallo

Skill Level: Intermediate   Serves 6

INGREDIENTS
3   cups diced fresh tomato
1   cup diced onion
¼   cup fresh lime juice
3   tablespoons chopped cilantro
½   teaspoon salt

EQUIPMENT
cutting board
serrated knife
chef's knife
dry measuring cups
mixing bowl
spoon
juicer
liquid measuring cup
mezzaluna (optional)
measuring spoons

Stir tomato and onion together in a mixing bowl. Add lime juice, cilantro and salt. Stir to combine. Cover and refrigerate until serving time.

NOTE: Pico de Gallo is a great dipping sauce for Corn Tortilla Chips (page 81), or serve with grilled fish, chicken, or pinto beans. For spicy Pico de Gallo, add diced fresh jalapeños.

NUTRITIONAL INFORMATION	
Calories per serving..... 33	**Fiber**............. 0.7 g
Carbohydrate .... 8 g	**Vitamin A** .... 834 IU
Protein .... 1 g	Vitamin C .... 28 mg
Total fat .... 0 g	Calcium........... 21 mg
Saturated fat .... *0 g*	*Sodium*........... *183 mg*
Cholesterol.......... *0 mg*	Iron .... 0.6 mg

SNACKS

Pizza Snack

Skill Level: Intermediate   Serves 1

INGREDIENTS
1   whole wheat pita bread round
1   ¾-ounce slice lean ham
2   tablespoons spaghetti sauce
1   ounce grated low-fat mozzarella cheese

EQUIPMENT
kitchen scissors
cutting board
baking sheet
hot pads
metal spatula
measuring spoons
grater
cooling rack

1. Preheat oven to 400°F.
2. Using kitchen scissors, cut a circle out of the top layer of a pita bread round, leaving about a ¾-inch rim.
3. Place pita round upside-down on a baking sheet and toast in the oven until lightly browned; keep oven on.
4. Cut ham into thin strips with kitchen scissors.
5. Using a metal spatula, turn pita round over, and cover with spaghetti sauce. Top with ham strips and mozzarella cheese. Bake for 5 minutes until cheese has melted.
6. Transfer baking sheet to cooling rack. Cool pizza for a few minutes. Use kitchen scissors to cut into quarters before serving.

NUTRITIONAL INFORMATION

Calories per serving 266	Fiber . . . . 0.3 g
Carbohydrate . . . . 27 g	Vitamin A . . . . 323 IU
Protein . . . . 15 g	Vitamin C . . . . 8 mg
Total fat . . . . 10 g	Calcium . . . . 180 mg
Saturated fat . . . . 4.9 g	Sodium . . . . 694 mg
Cholesterol . . . . 38 mg	Iron . . . . 1.2 mg

SNACKS

Popcorn Olé

Skill Level: Advanced   Serves 8

INGREDIENTS
¼ cup popping corn
3½ tablespoons safflower oil, divided
1 teaspoon chili con carne seasoning
4 drops Tabasco sauce
¼ teaspoon salt

EQUIPMENT
dry measuring cups
measuring spoons
large covered saucepan or popcorn popper
hot pads
extra-large mixing bowl
small bowl
spoon
2 large mixing spoons

1. To prepare 8 cups popped corn, place corn and 1½ tablespoons oil into a pan with a tight-fitting lid or into a popcorn popper.
2. Cover and heat. Leave pan lid slightly ajar to allow steam to escape. If using a popcorn popper, follow manufacturer's instructions.
3. When popping slows, remove pan from heat or unplug popper.
4. Place popped corn in a extra-large mixing bowl.
5. Combine 2 tablespoons oil, chili con carne seasoning, Tabasco sauce, and salt in a small bowl. Mix well with a spoon.
6. Gradually add seasoned oil to popcorn, tossing with 2 large mixing spoons to coat evenly.

NUTRITIONAL INFORMATION

Calories per serving	78	Fiber	0.1 g
Carbohydrate	5 g	Vitamin A	0 IU
Protein	1 g	Vitamin C	0 mg
Total fat	6 g	Calcium	1 mg
Saturated fat	*0.5 g*	*Sodium*	*166 mg*
Cholesterol	*0 mg*	*Iron*	*0.2 mg*

SNACKS

 # Ranch Dip

Skill Level: Beginner   Serves 10

INGREDIENTS
- ½ cup plain low-fat yogurt
- ¼ cup commercial low-calorie ranch-style dressing
- 2 tablespoons grated carrot

EQUIPMENT
- small bowl
- dry measuring cups
- grater
- measuring spoons
- spoon

1. In a small bowl, stir together yogurt and dressing.
2. Stir grated carrot into yogurt mixture.
3. Serve, or cover and chill.

NUTRITIONAL INFORMATION

Calories per serving	14	Fiber	0 g
Carbohydrate	1 g	Vitamin A	416 IU
Protein	1 g	Vitamin C	0 mg
Total fat	1 g	Calcium	26 mg
Saturated fat	*0.3 g*	*Sodium*	*81 mg*
Cholesterol	*1 mg*	Iron	0 mg

SNACKS

Rosh Hashanah Apples and Honey

Skill Level: Beginner   Serves 6

INGREDIENTS
2   large Granny Smith apples (or any other type of apple can be used)
1   teaspoon fresh lemon juice
2   tablespoons honey

EQUIPMENT
apple corer and slicer
cutting board
serrated knife
juicer
measuring spoons
small bowl

1. Core and slice apples with an apple corer and slicer.
2. Toss apple slices with lemon juice to prevent browning.
3. Put honey in a small bowl. Place honey bowl on a serving dish with apple slices, dip apples into honey as you eat them.

NOTE: Although apples and honey are traditionally served at the Jewish New Year, Rosh Hashanah, to express hope that the coming year will be sweet, they can be used as a snack any time.

NUTRITIONAL INFORMATION	
Calories per serving..... 73	**Fiber............. 0.5 g**
Carbohydrate .... 19 g	Vitamin A .... 37 IU
Protein .... 0 g	Vitamin C .... 4 mg
Total fat .... 0 g	Calcium............ 6 mg
Saturated fat .... 0 g	*Sodium .... 1 mg*
Cholesterol.......... 0 mg	Iron.............. 0.2 mg

SNACKS

Snap, Crackle, Pop Cheese Wafers

Skill Level: Intermediate   Yield: 4 dozen   1 serving = 1 wafer

INGREDIENTS
nonstick vegetable cooking spray
2 cups grated sharp cheddar cheese (8 ounces)
1 cup margarine, room temperature
1 cup all-purpose flour
1 cup whole wheat flour
⅛ teaspoon cayenne pepper
⅛ teaspoon salt
1 teaspoon Worcestershire sauce
2 cups Rice Krispies cereal

EQUIPMENT
2 baking sheets
large mixing bowl
dry measuring cups
grater
electric mixer
rubber spatula
measuring spoons
2 spoons
hot pads
2 cooling racks
metal spatula
airtight container

1. Preheat oven to 375°F. Coat 2 baking sheets with nonstick vegetable cooking spray.
2. In a large mixing bowl, cream cheese and margarine together with an electric mixer at medium-high speed for 2 minutes. Push batter from sides with a rubber spatula.
3. Add all-purpose and whole wheat flours, cayenne pepper, salt, and Worcestershire sauce to cheese and margarine mixture. Beat with mixer at low speed until ingredients are just combined, then increase speed to medium-high and beat for 2 minutes.
4. Gently knead Rice Krispies into dough with hands.
5. Drop dough by teaspoonfuls onto prepared baking sheets by using two spoons, one to scoop dough and the other to push it off. Flatten dough with two fingers.

6. Bake for 10 minutes or until lightly browned. Transfer baking sheets to cooling racks. Remove wafers from baking sheet with a metal spatula. Cool.
7. Store in an airtight container.

NUTRITIONAL INFORMATION

Calories per serving..... 66	Fiber................ 0 g
Carbohydrate .... 5 g	Vitamin A......... 233 IU
Protein .... 1 g	Vitamin C.......... 0 mg
Total fat .... 5 g	Calcium........... 19 mg
Saturated fat .... 2 g	Sodium .... 32 mg
Cholesterol.......... 2 mg	Iron .... 0.3 mg

SNACKS

Strawberry Spread

Skill Level: Beginner   Yield: 1 cup
1 serving = 1 generous tablespoon

INGREDIENTS
½ cup margarine
½ cup strawberry all-fruit jam
½ teaspoon fresh lemon juice

EQUIPMENT
food processor or blender
measuring spoons
dry measuring cups
cutting board
serrated knife
juicer
rubber spatula
covered bowl or butter molds

1. In a food processor or blender, process margarine, jam, and lemon juice for 1 to 2 minutes until evenly blended. Push spread down from sides with rubber spatula.
2. Chill strawberry spread in a covered bowl in the refrigerator, or freeze it in butter or candy molds for 30 minutes. Remove frozen spread from molds and store in plastic freezer bags. Allow to soften on a serving dish 10 minutes before use.

NOTE: Strawberry Spread is delicious on pancakes, biscuits, or bagels. You can be creative and think of other ways to serve it.

NUTRITIONAL INFORMATION

Calories per serving	104	Fiber	0.1 g
Carbohydrate	9 g	Vitamin A	312 IU
Protein	0 g	Vitamin C	0 mg
Total fat	8 g	Calcium	6 mg
Saturated fat	*1.5 g*	*Sodium*	*90 mg*
Cholesterol	*0 mg*	Iron	0.1 mg

Tuna Snacker

Skill Level: Beginner   Serves 4

INGREDIENTS
- 1 6½-ounce can tuna packed in water
- ¼ cup diced celery
- 3 tablespoons chopped chives
- ⅛ to ¼ teaspoon pepper
- 1 tablespoon olive oil
- 1 scant tablespoon fresh lemon juice
- 16 melba rounds

EQUIPMENT
- mixing bowl
- spoon
- cutting board
- small, sharp knife
- dry measuring cups
- measuring spoons
- serrated knife
- juicer

1. Stir together tuna, celery, chives, pepper, olive oil, and lemon juice in a mixing bowl.
2. Spoon tuna mixture onto melba rounds.

NUTRITIONAL INFORMATION

Calories per serving 152	Fiber . . . . 0.1 g
Carbohydrate . . . . 12 g	Vitamin A. . . . . 115 IU
Protein. . . . . 15 g	Vitamin C . . . . 4 mg
Total fat . . . . 4 g	Calcium. . . . . 13 mg
Saturated fat . . . . 0.4 g	*Sodium . . . . 40 mg*
Cholesterol . . . . 29 mg	Iron . . . . 0.8 mg

SNACKS

Yogurt Vegetable Dip

Skill Level: Beginner   Serves 8

INGREDIENTS
- ½ cup light mayonnaise
- ½ cup plain low-fat yogurt
- 1 tablespoon prepared mustard
- 1 teaspoon dried dillweed or 1 tablespoon chopped fresh dill
- 1 teaspoon low-fat (2%) milk

EQUIPMENT
- small mixing bowl
- dry measuring cups
- measuring spoons
- cutting board
- chef's knife or mezzaluna
- mixing spoon

Combine all ingredients in a small mixing bowl and stir together. Chill and serve.

NUTRITIONAL INFORMATION

Calories per serving 75	Fiber .... 0 mg
Carbohydrate .... 1 g	Vitamin A .... 30 IU
Protein .... 2 g	Vitamin C .... 0 mg
Total fat .... 7 g	Calcium .... 29 mg
Saturated fat .... 0.9 g	Sodium .... 73 mg
Cholesterol .... 1 mg	Iron .... 0.1 mg

Berry-Good Turkey Sandwiches

Skill Level: Beginner   Serves 4

INGREDIENTS
- 8 slices whole wheat bread
- 3 tablespoons margarine, softened
- 3 tablespoons jellied cranberry sauce
- 8 ounces smoked turkey breast, sliced

EQUIPMENT
- spreader
- measuring spoons
- serrated knife or bread knife
- cutting board

1. Spread one side of each slice of bread with margarine and cranberry sauce.
2. Place turkey over the cranberry sauce on 4 slices of the bread. Cover each with one of the remaining slices of bread.
3. Cut each sandwich in half and serve.

NUTRITIONAL INFORMATION

Calories per serving 334	Fiber . . . . 0.3 g
Carbohydrate . . . . 36 g	Vitamin A. . . . . 351 IU
Protein. . . . . 21 g	Vitamin C . . . . 1 mg
Total fat. . . . . 12 g	Calcium. . . . . 61 mg
Saturated fat . . . . 2.5 g	*Sodium. . . . . 403 mg*
Cholesterol . . . . 39 mg	Iron . . . . 1.6 mg

SANDWICHES

CLT's (Cheese, Lettuce, and Tomato Sandwiches)

Skill Level: Beginner   Serves 2

INGREDIENTS
- 4 slices oatmeal or whole wheat bread
- 4 teaspoons light mayonnaise
- 4 leaves Boston bibb lettuce
- 1 tomato, thinly sliced
- ⅛ teaspoon pepper
- 2 ¾-ounce slices low-fat cheddar cheese

EQUIPMENT
- measuring spoons
- spreader
- cutting board
- serrated knife or bread knife

1. Spread one side of each slice of bread with mayonnaise.
2. Place 2 lettuce leaves each on 2 slices of bread, and top with tomato. Sprinkle tomato with pepper, and cover with cheese slice and remaining bread.

NUTRITIONAL INFORMATION

Calories per serving 266	**Fiber.** .... **0.8 g**
Carbohydrate .... 33 g	**Vitamin A** .... **999 IU**
Protein. .... **11 g**	Vitamin C .... 22 mg
Total fat. .... 11 g	**Calcium** .... **200 mg**
Saturated fat .... 1.0 g	Sodium. .... 774 mg
Cholesterol .... 12 mg	Iron .... 1.4 mg

SANDWICHES

Ham and Cheese "Hot Dogs"

Skill Level: Beginner   Serves 4

INGREDIENTS
- 2 teaspoons light mayonnaise
- 4 whole wheat hot dog buns
- 1 teaspoon prepared mustard
- 4 1-ounce slices boiled lean ham
- 4 1-ounce cylinders string cheese

EQUIPMENT
- measuring spoons
- spreader or small spatula

1. Spread mayonnaise on the inside of each hot dog bun.
2. Spread mustard on one side of the 4 slices of ham.
3. Roll the ham around each cheese cylinder. Place ham and cheese inside a hot dog bun and serve.

NUTRITIONAL INFORMATION

Calories per serving 261	Fiber .... 0.1 g
Carbohydrate .... 23 g	Vitamin A .... 181 IU
Protein .... 16 g	Vitamin C .... 8 mg
Total fat .... 11 g	**Calcium .... 241 mg**
Saturated fat .... 4.7 g	*Sodium* .... 768 mg
Cholesterol .... 31 mg	Iron .... 1.2 mg

SANDWICHES

 # Lox and Mini Bagels

Skill Level: Intermediate   Serves 6

INGREDIENTS
- 6 mini bagels
- 1 tablespoon margarine, melted
- 3 ounces light cream cheese
- 3 ounces thinly sliced smoked salmon
- 1 teaspoon chopped fresh dill (optional)

EQUIPMENT
- serrated knife or bread knife
- cutting board
- measuring spoons
- pastry brush
- baking sheet
- hot pads
- cooling rack
- spreader
- chef's knife or mezzaluna

1. Preheat oven to 350°F.
2. Slice bagels in half using a serrated knife or bread knife.
3. Brush cut surfaces of bagels lightly with melted margarine using a pastry brush. Place on a baking sheet.
4. Bake bagels for 5 to 7 minutes until light golden brown.
5. Transfer baking sheet to a cooling rack. Cool bagels.
6. Spread cream cheese over bagels.
7. Top each bagel with smoked salmon. Sprinkle with dill and serve.

NUTRITIONAL INFORMATION

Calories per serving 181	Fiber .... 0 g
Carbohydrate .... 20 g	Vitamin A .... 118 IU
Protein .... **9 g**	Vitamin C .... 0 mg
Total fat .... 6 g	Calcium .... 26 mg
Saturated fat .... 1.7 g	*Sodium .... 114 mg*
Cholesterol .... 16 mg	Iron .... 1 mg

SANDWICHES

PB&S (Peanut Butter and Strawberries)

Skill Level: Beginner   Serves 4

INGREDIENTS
- 4 slices whole wheat bread
- ¼ cup natural peanut butter
- 2 tablespoons toasted wheat germ
- 8 strawberries, thinly sliced

EQUIPMENT
- heart-shape cookie cutter or serrated knife
- cutting board
- small bowl
- measuring spoons
- dry measuring cups
- spoon
- spreader
- small, sharp knife

  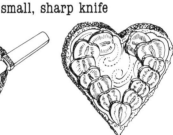

1. Cut bread slices into heart shapes with a cookie cutter or with a serrated knife on a cutting board.
2. Stir together peanut butter and wheat germ in a small bowl.
3. Spread one side of each slice of bread with peanut butter mixture.
4. Layer strawberry slices in a fan pattern, from the bottom point of the heart and up toward the rounded edges at the top. Serve.

NUTRITIONAL INFORMATION

Calories per serving 177	**Fiber.** .... 0.7 g
Carbohydrate .... 19 g	Vitamin A .... 3 IU
Protein .... 7 g	Vitamin C .... 7 mg
Total fat .... 9 g	Calcium .... 34 mg
Saturated fat .... *2.2 g*	*Sodium.* .... *229 mg*
Cholesterol. .... *0 mg*	Iron .... 1.0 mg

SANDWICHES

Pocket Sandwich with Ham and Cheese

Skill Level: Beginner   Serves 6

INGREDIENTS
- 3 tablespoons light mayonnaise
- 1 teaspoon Dijon-style mustard
- ¼ teaspoon prepared horseradish
- 8 ounces sliced lean ham
- ½ cup finely chopped celery
- 3 whole wheat pita breads
- 2 ounces (½ cup) low-fat mozzarella cheese, grated

EQUIPMENT
- mixing bowl
- measuring spoons
- spoon
- kitchen scissors
- small, sharp knife
- cutting board
- grater
- plastic wrap

1. In a mixing bowl, stir together mayonnaise, mustard and horseradish.
2. Use kitchen scissors to cut ham into ½-inch-wide strips.
3. Add ham and celery to mayonnaise mixture. Stir until well coated.
4. Using kitchen scissors, cut each pita round in half. Open bread to make a pocket.
5. Fill each pita pocket with ham and celery filling and top with grated cheese.
6. Serve or store wrapped in plastic wrap.

NUTRITIONAL INFORMATION

Calories per serving 171	Fiber............. 0.5 g
Carbohydrate .... 15 g	Vitamin A .... 96 IU
Protein............ **12 g**	Vitamin C .... 9 mg
Total fat .... 7 g	Calcium .... 101 mg
Saturated fat........ *2.0 g*	*Sodium*........... *717 mg*
Cholesterol........ *20 mg*	Iron............. 1.2 mg

SANDWICHES

Reindeer Sandwich

Skill Level: Beginner   Serves 3

INGREDIENTS
½ cup creamy natural peanut butter
2 tablespoons honey
3 slices whole wheat bread
6 raisins
3 red peanut M&Ms
6 pretzel twists, unsalted

EQUIPMENT
small bowl
spoon
dry measuring cups
measuring spoons
cutting board
serrated knife or bread knife
spreader

1. Combine peanut butter and honey in a small bowl. Stir until smooth.
2. Place bread slices on a cutting board and cut each into triangles using a serrated knife or bread knife.
3. Spread triangles with peanut butter. Create a reindeer by decorating each triangle with two raisins for eyes, a red M&M for the nose, and two pretzel twists for the antlers.

NUTRITIONAL INFORMATION			
Calories per serving	399	Fiber	0.9 g
Carbohydrate	39 g	Vitamin A	13 IU
Protein	**13 g**	Vitamin C	0 mg
Total fat	24 g	Calcium	58 mg
Saturated fat	5 g	Sodium	400 mg
Cholesterol	0 mg	Iron	1.2 mg

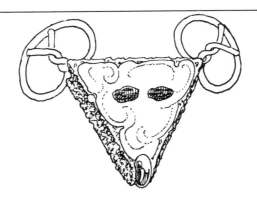

SANDWICHES

Star Egg

Skill Level: Intermediate   Serves 1

INGREDIENTS
1 slice whole wheat bread
1 egg substitute
1 teaspoon margarine

EQUIPMENT
star-shaped cookie cutter or small, sharp knife
cutting board
cup
fork
measuring spoons
nonstick skillet
hot pads
metal spatula

1. Use a star-shaped cookie cutter or a small knife to cut out the center of a slice of whole wheat bread. Only the outside portion of the bread will be used.
2. Lightly beat egg substitute in a cup with a fork.
3. Melt the margarine in a nonstick skillet over medium heat. Place the bread in the skillet and pour the egg substitute into the star. Cook until the bottom of the egg is set and the bread is lightly browned. Flip the bread and egg over using a metal spatula. Cook until the bottom of the egg is set.

NUTRITIONAL INFORMATION	
Calories per serving 140	Fiber . . . . 0.1 g
Carbohydrate . . . . 13 g	**Vitamin A . . . . 1171 IU**
Protein . . . . 8 g	Vitamin C . . . . 0 mg
Total fat . . . . 6 g	Calcium. . . . . 48 mg
Saturated fat . . . . 1.2 g	Sodium. . . . . 260 mg
Cholesterol. . . . . 0 mg	Iron . . . . 1.3 mg

SANDWICHES

Sweet-Treat Sandwich

Skill Level: Beginner   Serves 1

INGREDIENTS
- 2 slices raisin bread
- 2 tablespoons light cream cheese
- ¼ cup strawberries, hulled and sliced
- 1 tablespoon chopped pecans

EQUIPMENT
- measuring spoons
- spreader
- dry measuring cups
- cutting board
- small, sharp knife
- bread knife or serrated knife

1. Spread cream cheese on one slice of raisin bread.
2. Place strawberry slices over the cream cheese, then sprinkle with pecans.
3. Top with the second slice of raisin bread, then slice sandwich into halves or quarters to serve.

NUTRITIONAL INFORMATION

Calories per serving 239	**Fiber. . . . . 0.8 g**
Carbohydrate . . . . 31 g	Vitamin A. . . . . 219 IU
Protein . . . . 5 g	Vitamin C . . . . 21 mg
Total fat. . . . . 11 g	Calcium. . . . . 58 mg
Saturated fat . . . . *3.8 g*	*Sodium*. . . . . *224 mg*
Cholesterol. . . . . *15 mg*	Iron . . . . 1.1 mg

SANDWICHES

Tuna Pocket

Skill Level: Beginner Serves 3

INGREDIENTS
1 6½-ounce can tuna packed in water
2 tablespoons light mayonnaise
2 tablespoons plain low-fat yogurt
3 tablespoons chopped celery
2 hard-cooked egg whites, diced
2 teaspoons wine vinegar
¼ teaspoon pepper
3 mini pita breads
1 tomato, sliced
3 lettuce leaves

EQUIPMENT
mixing bowl
spoon
measuring spoons
cutting board
small, sharp knife
serrated knife
scissors

1. In a mixing bowl, stir tuna, mayonnaise, yogurt, celery, egg whites, vinegar, and pepper until well combined.
2. Using scissors, cut an opening halfway around the edge of the pita.
3. Layer tomato slices and lettuce inside the pitas. Add tuna filling. Serve.

NUTRITIONAL INFORMATION
Calories per serving 250
Carbohydrate .... 25 g
Protein............ 25 g
Total fat .... 5 g
Saturated fat .... 0.6 g
Cholesterol......... 39 mg
Fiber.............. 0.7 g
Vitamin A......... 674 IU
Vitamin C .... 15 mg
Calcium........... 76 mg
Sodium........... 318 mg
Iron .... 2.5 mg

SANDWICHES

Turkey Sandwich With Secret Sauce

Skill Level: Beginner Serves 2

INGREDIENTS
- 1 tablespoon light mayonnaise
- 1 teaspoon prepared mustard
- 2 teaspoons sweet and sour sauce
- ¼ teaspoon dry mustard
- 4 slices whole wheat or rye bread
- 4 ounces turkey, thinly sliced

EQUIPMENT
- measuring spoons
- small bowl
- spreader
- serrated knife or bread knife

1. To prepare secret sauce, combine mayonnaise, mustard, sweet and sour sauce, and dry mustard in a small bowl.
2. Spread one side of each whole wheat or rye bread slice with sauce. Top half the bread slices with turkey and place remaining bread slices on top to create sandwiches. Cut into halves.

NUTRITIONAL INFORMATION

Calories per serving 312	Fiber .... 0.3 g
Carbohydrate .... 27 g	Vitamin A .... 23 IU
Protein............. 21 g	Vitamin C .... 0 mg
Total fat............ 12 g	Calcium .... 65 mg
Saturated fat .... *2.3 g*	*Sodium*............ *533 mg*
Cholesterol .... *48 mg*	**Iron .... 2.0 mg**

SOUPS

Corny Chowder

Skill Level: Advanced   Serves 5

INGREDIENTS
- 2½ cups corn kernels (fresh or frozen)
- 3 cups low-fat (2%) milk, divided
- 1½ tablespoons margarine
- ½ medium-size white onion, chopped
- 2 tablespoons all-purpose flour
- ½ teaspoon salt
- ⅛ teaspoon cayenne pepper
- pinch of nutmeg
- ⅓ cup grated Parmesan cheese
- 3 tablespoons chopped green onion tops

EQUIPMENT
- small saucepan
- cutting board
- medium, sharp knife
- dry measuring cups
- liquid measuring cup
- hot pads
- wooden spoon
- large saucepan
- chef's knife
- measuring spoons
- blender or food processor
- rubber spatula
- ladle
- serving bowls
- grater
- small, sharp knife

1. In a small saucepan, simmer corn with 1 cup milk until tender, about 15 minutes.

2. Melt margarine over medium-high heat in a large saucepan. Add onion and sauté until soft, about 5 minutes.

3. Add flour and stir with a wooden spoon to coat onion.

4. Combine corn and onion in a blender or food processor. Puree until almost smooth, about 2 minutes.

5. Transfer corn puree to large saucepan, scraping sides of the blender or food processor container with a rubber spatula. Add 2 cups milk, salt, cayenne, and nutmeg. Heat soup over medium heat approximately 5 minutes.

6. Ladle hot soup into serving bowls. Sprinkle with grated Parmesan cheese and chopped green onion tops.

NUTRITIONAL INFORMATION	
Calories per serving 235	**Fiber**............... 0.7 g
Carbohydrate .... 28 g	**Vitamin A** .... 890 IU
Protein............. **11 g**	Vitamin C .... 11 mg
Total fat .... 9 g	**Calcium** .... **296 mg**
Saturated fat .... 3.5 g	Sodium............ 440 mg
Cholesterol.......... 16 mg	Iron.............. 0.9 mg

SOUPS

Fourth of July Strawberry Soup

Skill Level: Beginner   Serves 3

INGREDIENTS
- 1 pint strawberries, washed and hulled
- 3 tablespoons partially frozen apple juice concentrate
- ⅓ cup plain low-fat yogurt
- ⅔ cup low-fat (2%) milk
- 1 teaspoon sugar
- 3 tablespoons fresh blueberries (garnish)

EQUIPMENT
- blender or food processor
- measuring spoons
- dry measuring cups
- liquid measuring cup
- rubber spatula
- storage container
- serving cups or bowls

1. Puree half the strawberries in a blender or food processor. Add remaining strawberries and puree.
2. Add apple juice concentrate, yogurt, milk, and sugar to strawberries. Process until just blended, 10 to 30 seconds.
3. Transfer to storage container, then cover and chill several hours or overnight.
4. Pour into serving cups or bowls, and garnish with blueberries.

NUTRITIONAL INFORMATION

Calories per serving 108	**Fiber**............. **0.7 g**
Carbohydrate .... 20 g	Vitamin A......... 163 IU
Protein .... 4 g	**Vitamin C** .... **59 mg**
Total fat .... 2 g	Calcium .... 141 mg
Saturated fat........ *0.9 g*	Sodium .... 53 mg
Cholesterol.......... *6 mg*	Iron .... 0.6 mg

SOUPS

Homemade Chicken Stock

Skill Level: Advanced   Serves 8

INGREDIENTS
1   chicken, skinned, or 2½ pounds chicken wings, necks, and backs
1   onion, quartered
3   stalks celery, coarsely chopped
2   garlic cloves, mashed
2   carrots, coarsely chopped
1   bay leaf
2   quarts (8 cups) water

EQUIPMENT
large pot
cutting board
chef's knife
small, sharp knife
dough scraper
liquid measuring cup
hot pads
slotted spoon or skimmer
blender or food processor
rubber spatula
freezer containers

1. Combine all ingredients in a large pot and bring to a boil over high heat.
2. Reduce heat to low and simmer for 30 minutes.
3. Remove chicken, chicken bones, and vegetables from stock with a slotted spoon or skimmer.
4. Puree vegetables in a blender or food processor for about 30 seconds and return to broth.
5. Cover and refrigerate stock overnight to allow fat to float to surface. Skim fat off with a slotted spoon or skimmer.
6. Use stock in a recipe, or freeze it in 1-cup containers, plastic freezer bags, or ice cube trays. (Remove frozen cubes to plastic freezer bags for storage.)

NUTRITIONAL INFORMATION

Calories per serving..... 24	**Fiber.............. 0.6 g**
Carbohydrate .... 6 g	**Vitamin A....... 2110 IU**
Protein .... 1 g	Vitamin C.......... 8 mg
Total fat .... 0 g	Calcium........... 30 mg
Saturated fat......... 0 g	*Sodium* .... 68 mg
Cholesterol.......... 0 mg	Iron............. 0.4 mg

SOUPS

Smooth or Chunky Vegetable Soup

Skill Level: Advanced   Serves 8

INGREDIENTS
- 3 tablespoons margarine
- 1 leek (white part only), sliced
- 1 garlic clove, minced
- 2 Roma (plum) tomatoes, diced
- 1 zucchini, cut into rounds, then quartered
- 2 carrots, peeled and cut into rounds, then quartered
- 1 boiling potato, peeled and cubed
- ¾ cup green beans (ends removed), cut into ⅓-inch pieces
- 1 cup chopped broccoli florets
- 5 cups homemade chicken stock (page 117), divided
- 1 teaspoon sugar
- ¾ teaspoon salt
- ¼ teaspoon white pepper
- 1 tablespoon chopped parsley

EQUIPMENT
- large covered stockpot
- measuring spoons
- cutting board
- small, sharp knife
- dough scraper
- chef's knife
- wooden spoon
- hot pads
- serrated knife
- peeler
- dry measuring cups
- liquid measuring cup
- mezzaluna (optional)
- large spoon or ladle
- food processor or blender
- rubber spatula

1. In a large stockpot, melt margarine over medium heat; add leek and garlic, and sauté about 4 minutes.
2. Add tomatoes, zucchini, carrot, potato, green beans, broccoli, and 1 cup chicken stock; simmer on medium-low for about 20 minutes or until vegetables are soft.
3. Add remaining stock, sugar, salt, and pepper. Increase heat to high and bring mixture to a boil. Cover the pot, reduce heat to low, and simmer 10 minutes.
4. If serving soup chunky, sprinkle with parsley. If serving soup smooth, continue to step 5.

5. Let mixture stand until cool enough to handle. Using a large spoon or ladle, transfer vegetables, with a little broth, to food processor or blender and puree until smooth.

6. Return vegetables to broth. Reheat over medium heat. Sprinkle with parsley and serve.

NUTRITIONAL INFORMATION	
Calories per serving 118	**Fiber............. 1.3 g**
Carbohydrate .... 13 g	**Vitamin A........ 3487 IU**
Protein .... 6 g	**Vitamin C .... 57 mg**
Total fat .... 5 g	Calcium........... 69 mg
Saturated fat........ 0.9 g	*Sodium .... 73 mg*
Cholesterol.......... *0 mg*	Iron.............. 1.4 mg

SOUPS

Won Ton Soup

Skill Level: Advanced   Serves 8

INGREDIENTS
½ pound ground lean pork
2 tablespoons chopped green onion
2 tablespoons low-sodium soy sauce
2 tablespoons water
2 teaspoons cornstarch
¼ teaspoon peeled and grated ginger root
50 won ton wrappers
2 tablespoons water for sealing won tons
8 cups homemade chicken stock (see page 117)

EQUIPMENT
small mixing bowl
cutting board
small, sharp knife
grater
measuring spoons
small bowl
liquid measuring cup
large saucepan
hot pads
slotted spoon
ladle

1. In a small mixing bowl, combine pork, green onion, soy sauce, 2 tablespoons water, cornstarch, and ginger. Mix well with a spoon or your hand.
2. a. Place a won ton wrapper on a flat work surface so that it looks like a diamond. Place a small bowl of water near it.
   b. Put ¾ to 1 teaspoon of pork filling in the center of the won ton wrapper.
   c. Using your index finger, brush the top two edges of the diamond with water, then fold the dough over the filling so that it looks like a triangle. Press edges together.
   d. Using your index finger and thumb, press each edge and corner together. Bring opposite bottom corners together and press together.

   Repeat the process until all the won ton wrappers have been filled.

SOUPS

3. Bring chicken stock to a boil in a large saucepan over high heat. Carefully drop won tons into broth, and gently stir a few times with a slotted spoon. Return to a boil, then lower heat to medium and simmer 8 to 10 minutes.

4. Ladle soup into bowls and serve immediately.

NOTE: Ground turkey can be substituted for pork. You can also create your own ways of folding the won ton wrappers.

NUTRITIONAL INFORMATION	
Calories per serving 195	Fiber .... 0.4 g
Carbohydrate .... 15 g	**Vitamin A** .... **2143 IU**
Protein .... **9 g**	Vitamin C .... 1 mg
Total fat............ 11 g	Calcium........... 25 mg
Saturated fat .... *3.4 g*	*Sodium*........... *257 mg*
Cholesterol .... *30 mg*	Iron .... 1.2 mg

ENTREES

Beef and Snow Peas

Skill Level: Advanced   Serves 4

INGREDIENTS
- ¼ cup low-sodium soy sauce
- 1 tablespoon cornstarch
- 1 teaspoon sugar
- 1 pound flank steak, trimmed and thinly sliced against the grain (½-inch-wide slices, cut into 2-inch strips)
- 1 pound snow peas
- 2 tablespoons safflower oil, divided
- 2 ½-inch-thick slices peeled ginger root

EQUIPMENT
- liquid measuring cup
- measuring spoons
- large mixing bowl
- 2 wooden spoons
- cutting board
- medium-size sharp knife
- paper towels
- wok or large skillet
- hot pads
- plate
- small, sharp knife

1. Prepare marinade by combining soy sauce, cornstarch, and sugar in a large mixing bowl.
2. Add flank steak to marinade and toss to coat thoroughly. Let stand for 30 minutes or longer.
3. Wash snow peas, pat them dry with paper towels, then remove their tips and strings. To do so, hold each snow pea flat against your thumb, with your thumbnail pressing up to the end of snow pea. Grasp the stem of the snow pea between the index finger and thumb of your other hand and pull it toward you. The string will be attached to the stem.
4. Heat 1 tablespoon oil in wok or large skillet over medium-high heat. Add snow peas and stir-fry with a wooden spoon for 1 to 2 minutes. Transfer cooked snow peas to a plate.
5. Cool wok, then wipe it with a paper towel. Add remaining tablespoon of oil to wok. Heat wok over medium-high heat until hot. Add ginger root, then add flank steak after a few seconds. Stir-fry 3 minutes or until meat is no longer red. Discard ginger root.
6. Return snow peas to wok. Stir to combine with beef.

NOTE: Basic Boiled Rice (page 212) is a delicious and healthful accompaniment to Beef and Snow Peas.

NUTRITIONAL INFORMATION	
Calories per serving 336	**Fiber**............. **2.3 g**
Carbohydrate .... 20 g	**Vitamin A** .... **741 IU**
Protein............. **32 g**	Vitamin C .... 31 mg
Total fat............ 14 g	Calcium........... 46 mg
Saturated fat .... *3.7 g*	*Sodium*........... *602 mg*
Cholesterol......... *80 mg*	**Iron** .... **6.1 mg**

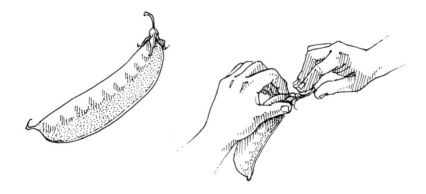

ENTREES

Beef With Chinese Barbecue Sauce

Skill Level: Advanced   Serves 6

INGREDIENTS

1½ pounds flank steak, trimmed and thinly sliced against the grain (½-inch-wide slices, cut into 2-inch strips)
1 teaspoon cornstarch
¼ cup water
1 large garlic clove
3 tablespoons safflower oil
2½ tablespoons Chinese barbecue sauce

Marinade

1 tablespoon safflower oil
3 tablespoons low-sodium soy sauce
1 tablespoon honey
1 teaspoon wine vinegar
1½ tablespoons water
1½ tablespoons cornstarch

EQUIPMENT

cutting board
small, sharp knife
large mixing bowl
whisk
measuring spoons
wooden spoons
liquid measuring cup
small bowl
dough scraper
wok or heavy skillet
hot pads

1. To make marinade, in a large mixing bowl whisk together 1 tablespoon oil, soy sauce, honey, vinegar, 1½ tablespoons water, and 1½ tablespoons cornstarch.
2. Add beef strips to marinade and toss to coat thoroughly. Marinate for at least 30 minutes or refrigerate for several hours.
3. Combine a few tablespoons of the water with the cornstarch in a small bowl and stir until smooth. Stir in remaining water. Set aside.
4. Press the flat side of a dough scraper against the garlic clove until clove is crushed and garlic skin can be easily removed. Peel the garlic.

5. Heat 3 tablespoons oil in a wok or heavy skillet over high heat. Add garlic. After a few seconds, add beef and stir constantly for 2 minutes, using wooden spoons, until cooked through.
6. Add barbecue sauce and stir-fry for 2 to 3 more minutes until coated with sauce. Discard garlic.
7. Continue stirring and add cornstarch mixture. Cook 1 minute to allow sauce to thicken. Serve.

NUTRITIONAL INFORMATION

Calories per serving 211	Fiber................ 0 g
Carbohydrate .... 6 g	Vitamin A .... 58 IU
Protein............. 25 g	Vitamin C .... 0 mg
Total fat .... 9 g	Calcium............ 17 mg
Saturated fat .... 3.3 g	Sodium............ 471 mg
Cholesterol......... 80 mg	**Iron .... 3.9 mg**

ENTREES

Father's Day Beef Kabobs

Skill Level: Advanced   Serves 6

INGREDIENTS
1   pound lean beef, cut into 1 to 1½-inch cubes

Marinade

2   tablespoons safflower oil
2   tablespoons fresh lemon juice
1   tablespoon Worcestershire sauce
1   garlic clove, chopped
½   teaspoon pepper

Vegetables

8   large whole mushrooms, wiped clean, stems trimmed
1   green pepper, seeded and cut into 1½-inch pieces
1   red pepper, seeded and cut into 1½-inch pieces
1   cucumber, cut into ½-inch slices
8   cherry tomatoes
1   onion, cut into 8 wedges

EQUIPMENT
large mixing bowl
measuring spoons
cutting board
serrated knife
juicer
dough scraper
chef's knife
mixing spoons
small, sharp knife
metal skewers
hot pads
long-handled basting brush

1. In large mixing bowl, combine oil, lemon juice, Worcestershire sauce, garlic, and pepper. Mix well. Add meat and stir to coat. Let stand for 2 hours, turning the meat every 20 minutes.
2. Prepare vegetables. After meat has been marinated for 2 hours, add vegetables to meat and toss to coat with marinade. Let meat and vegetables stand for 30 minutes, turning every 10 minutes.
3. Prepare the grill or fire.
4. Allow individuals to prepare their own kabobs, placing assorted vegetables and meat on the skewers according to taste.
5. Grill kabobs for 10 minutes over a medium fire, basting once with the remaining marinade. Turn the skewer and grill 8 more minutes, or until browned. (Time will vary depending on temperature of fire or coals.)

NOTE: Adult supervision is needed for grilling.

NUTRITIONAL INFORMATION	
Calories per serving 214	**Fiber.** .... **0.7 g**
Carbohydrate .... 2 g	Vitamin A. .... 106 IU
Protein. .... **25 g**	Vitamin C .... 11 mg
Total fat. .... 11 g	Calcium .... 18 mg
Saturated fat .... *3 g*	*Sodium* .... *76 mg*
Cholesterol .... *77 mg*	Iron .... 1 mg

ENTREES

Meatballs on Top of Spaghetti

Skill Level: Advanced   Serves 5

INGREDIENTS
- 1   28-ounce can tomatoes, drained in a colander
- ⅓   cup low-fat (2%) milk
- 1   slice whole wheat bread, crust removed
- 1   pound extra-lean ground beef
- 1   egg white
- 2   tablespoons grated Parmesan cheese
- 2   tablespoons grated onion
- ½   teaspoon salt
- ¼   teaspoon pepper
- ¼   teaspoon dried oregano
-     pinch of nutmeg
- 1   tablespoon safflower oil
- 10 ounces spaghetti, cooked according to directions on package

EQUIPMENT
- colander
- blender or food processor
- liquid measuring cup
- small bowl
- fork
- mixing bowl
- grater
- measuring spoons
- mixing spoons
- large, nonstick covered skillet
- metal spatula
- hot pads
- serving plate

1. Puree drained tomatoes in a blender or food processor until smooth. Set tomato puree aside.
2. Pour milk into a small bowl. Tear bread into several pieces and add to milk. Mash bread into milk with a fork until it is mushy.
3. In a mixing bowl, combine ground beef, egg white, Parmesan cheese, onion, salt, pepper, oregano, nutmeg, and milk-bread mixture. Use a mixing spoon or your hands to combine.
4. Roll the meat mixture into 1-inch balls using your hands.

5. In a large, nonstick skillet, heat safflower oil over medium-high heat. Put as many meatballs as will fit into the skillet without touching. Cook meatballs until browned on all sides, turning carefully with a metal spatula to prevent crumbling.
6. Remove browned meatballs from the skillet and place them on a plate covered with a paper towel to absorb the fat. Brown the remaining meatballs. Pour off any fat that has accumulated in the pan after cooking the meatballs.
7. Return all meatballs to the skillet. Add the tomato puree to the meatballs. Cover the skillet and cook over medium heat until tomato puree thickens, about 30 minutes.
8. Serve on spaghetti.

NUTRITIONAL INFORMATION

Calories per serving 963	**Fiber** . . . . **0.7 g**
Carbohydrate . . . . 53 g	**Vitamin A** . . . . **1496 IU**
Protein . . . . **29 g**	Vitamin C . . . . 28 mg
Total fat . . . . 14 g	Calcium . . . . 78 mg
Saturated fat . . . . *5.2 g*	*Sodium* . . . . *559 mg*
Cholesterol . . . . *67 mg*	**Iron** . . . . **5.7 mg**

ENTREES

Meaty Macaroni and Cheese

Skill Level: Advanced   Serves 8

INGREDIENTS
- 12 ounces macaroni
- 1 pound extra-lean ground beef
- ½ cup chopped onion
- 1 cup chopped carrot
- 2½ cups tomato sauce
- 1 cup plain low-fat yogurt
- 1 cup low-fat cottage cheese
- ¼ cup chopped parsley
- 4 ounces (1 cup) low-fat mozzarella cheese, grated

EQUIPMENT
- large pot or stockpot
- hot pads
- colander
- large mixing bowl
- skillet
- wooden spoon
- cutting board
- chef's knife
- dry measuring cups
- small, sharp knife
- mezzaluna (optional)
- rubber spatula
- 2½-quart deep casserole
- large spoon
- grater

1. Preheat oven to 350°F.
2. Half-fill a large pot or stockpot with water. Bring water to a boil over high heat. Add macaroni and cook until al dente (firm to bite) according to package instructions. Drain pasta in a colander and transfer to a large mixing bowl. Set aside.
3. In a skillet, stir beef and onion together with a wooden spoon over medium-high heat until beef is browned, about 5 minutes. Drain meat in a colander to remove fat, then return meat to the skillet.
4. Add carrot and tomato sauce to beef and simmer over low heat for 10 minutes, stirring occasionally.
5. Add yogurt, cottage cheese, and parsley to macaroni. Stir with a rubber spatula to coat all macaroni.

6. In a 2½-quart deep casserole, alternate layers of meat mixture and macaroni to make 4 layers, beginning with meat and ending with macaroni.
7. Top casserole with grated mozzarella.
8. Bake until lightly browned, about 30 minutes. Serve hot.

NOTE: In step 6, the meat and macaroni can be combined and spooned into the casserole dish instead of layered.

NUTRITIONAL INFORMATION	
Calories per serving 380	Fiber .... 0.3 g
Carbohydrate .... 44 g	**Vitamin A**....... **3117 IU**
Protein............ **28 g**	Vitamin C .... 11 mg
Total fat............ 10 g	**Calcium** .... **212 mg**
Saturated fat .... 5 g	Sodium........... 668 mg
Cholesterol......... 52 mg	**Iron** .... **3.6 mg**

ENTREES

 Mini Burgers

Skill Level: Intermediate   Serves 6

INGREDIENTS
- 1 pound lean ground beef
- 4 teaspoons Worcestershire sauce
- 1 tablespoon fresh lemon juice
- ½ teaspoon paprika
- ¼ teaspoon salt
- ¼ teaspoon pepper
- 12 slices whole wheat bread
- 1 tablespoon mustard
- 3 tablespoons light mayonnaise
- 6 lettuce leaves
- 1 tomato, sliced

EQUIPMENT
- mixing bowl
- measuring spoons
- cutting board
- serrated knife
- juicer
- skillet
- hot pads
- metal spatula
- large round cookie cutter (3 inches in diameter)
- spreader

1. Place ground beef in a mixing bowl, then add Worcestershire sauce, lemon juice, paprika, salt, and pepper. Combine the ingredients well with your hands.
2. Shape the meat mixture into 6 small patties.
3. Cook the patties in a skillet over medium-high heat about 4 minutes on each side until browned.
4. Using a large, round cookie cutter, cut the bread into circles. Spread mustard on 6 of the bread circles and mayonnaise on the other 6. Place a meat patty, lettuce, and a tomato slice on top of each of the 6 bread rounds with mustard, then top each with the remaining 6 rounds that are spread with mayonnaise.

NOTE: Meat patties can be grilled over a low fire to the desired doneness. Adult supervision is needed for grilling.

BEEF

NUTRITIONAL INFORMATION

Calories per serving 314	Fiber.............. **0.5 g**
Carbohydrate .... 29 g	Vitamin A......... 401 IU
Protein.............. **20 g**	Vitamin C .... 15 mg
Total fat............. 13 g	Calcium........... 67 mg
Saturated fat........ 4.2 g	Sodium............ 500 mg
Cholesterol......... 53 mg	**Iron** .... **3.6 mg**

ENTREES

 # Sloppy Muffin

Skill Level: Intermediate Serves 6
Microwave Method

INGREDIENTS

- 1 pound extra-lean ground beef
- ½ cup chopped onion
- ½ cup chopped celery
- ½ cup grated carrot
- 1 6-ounce can tomato paste
- 1 cup water
- 1 tablespoon chili powder
- ¼ teaspoon dry mustard
- ¼ teaspoon salt
- 3 whole wheat English muffins, split and toasted
- 3 ounces (¾ cup) grated low-fat mozzarella cheese

EQUIPMENT

- plastic colander
- large microwave-safe bowl
- dry measuring cups
- cutting board
- chef's knife
- small, sharp knife
- grater
- 2 wooden spoons
- hot pads
- paper towels
- liquid measuring cup
- measuring spoons
- microwave-safe plastic wrap
- toaster
- 6 serving plates

1. Place a plastic colander into a large microwave-safe bowl.
2. Crumble ground beef into the colander, then add onion, celery, and carrot. Stir mixture together with a wooden spoon.
3. Microwave on high (100%) power for 3 minutes. Stir meat well to break up any chunks.
4. Microwave on high for 3 minutes, or until meat is no longer pink. Remove bowl and colander from the microwave, then stir the ground beef mixture again. Carefully remove the colander from the bowl, then throw away the fat and juices that have accumulated in the bowl. Wipe out the bowl with paper towels.
5. Pour the meat mixture into the bowl.
6. Stir tomato paste, water, chili powder, dry mustard, and salt into the cooked meat.
7. Cover the bowl with plastic wrap. Microwave the ground beef mixture on high 4 minutes, then stir well.

8. Replace plastic wrap and microwave 4 minutes on high. Let mixture stand an additional 4 minutes.
9. Place toasted English muffin halves on serving plates, then top with the ground beef. Sprinkle each with grated cheese, then serve.

NUTRITIONAL INFORMATION

Calories per serving 276	**Fiber**................ **0.5 g**
Carbohydrate .... 22 g	**Vitamin A**........ **2395 IU**
Protein............. **23 g**	Vitamin C .... 17 mg
Total fat.............. 11 g	Calcium .... 173 mg
Saturated fat .... 5 g	Sodium........... 375 mg
Cholesterol .... 61 mg	**Iron**............. **4.3 mg**

ENTREES

 **Soft Tacos**

Skill Level: Intermediate   Serves 4

INGREDIENTS
- 1 pound extra-lean ground beef
- ½ cup chopped onion
- ½ teaspoon chopped garlic
- 1½ teaspoons chili powder
- ½ teaspoon dried oregano
- ½ teaspoon paprika
- ¼ teaspoon cumin
- ¼ teaspoon salt
- ¼ cup tomato paste
- 1 cup water
- 1 tablespoon safflower oil
- 8 corn tortillas
- ½ cup shredded lettuce
- ½ cup diced tomatoes
- 2 ounces grated low-fat mozzarella cheese (½ cup)

EQUIPMENT
- large, nonstick skillet
- cutting board
- chef's knife
- dry measuring cups
- dough scraper
- measuring spoons
- hot pads
- wooden spoon
- colander
- liquid measuring cup
- small skillet
- basting brush
- tongs
- serrated knife
- cheese grater

1. Crumble ground beef into a large nonstick skillet. Add onion and garlic to the beef. Over medium-high heat, brown the meat until it is no longer pink.
2. Transfer meat to a colander to drain off excess fat. Return meat to skillet.
3. Add chili powder, oregano, paprika, cumin, salt, tomato paste, and water to beef. Stir well.
4. Simmer for 30 minutes over medium-low heat, stirring occasionally.
5. At serving time, brush a small skillet with oil, and lightly brush both sides of each tortilla with oil. Over medium-high heat, heat the tortilla about 30 seconds on first side, then turn with tongs and heat an additional 30 seconds until soft and flexible. Repeat this process for each tortilla.

6. Spoon seasoned beef into each tortilla, and top with lettuce, tomato, and cheese. Fold tortilla around mixture. Serve.

NUTRITIONAL INFORMATION	
Calories per serving 427	**Fiber............. 1.1 g**
Carbohydrate .... 34 g	**Vitamin A .... 909 IU**
Protein............. 32 g	Vitamin C .... 16 mg
Total fat............ 18 g	**Calcium .... 253 mg**
Saturated fat .... 7.2 g	*Sodium............ 367 mg*
Cholesterol .... 88 mg	**Iron .... 6.2 mg**

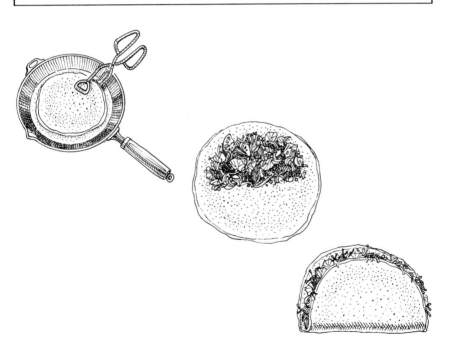

ENTREES

Spaghetti Pie

Skill Level: Advanced Serves 6

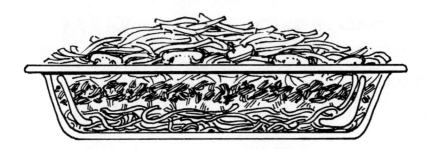

INGREDIENTS
nonstick vegetable cooking spray
6 ounces spaghetti
⅓ cup low-fat (2%) milk
1 egg
1 egg white
½ pound extra-lean ground beef
½ cup chopped onion
1 garlic clove, chopped
1¼ cups homemade tomato sauce (page 205)
½ cup cottage cheese
1 cup sliced mushrooms
1¼ cups (5 ounces) grated low-fat mozzarella cheese

EQUIPMENT
9-inch pie pan
large pot or stockpot
hot pads
colander
large mixing bowl
liquid measuring cup
whisk
nonstick skillet
cutting board
chef's knife
dry measuring cups
dough scraper
2 wooden spoons
rubber spatula
small, sharp knife
grater

1. Preheat oven to 350°F. Coat a 9-inch pie pan with nonstick vegetable cooking spray.

2. Half-fill a large pot or stockpot with water. Bring water to a boil over high heat. Add spaghetti and cook until al dente (firm to bite) according to package instructions. Drain the spaghetti in a colander.

3. While waiting for the water to come to a boil, whisk the milk, egg, and egg white together in a large mixing bowl. Set aside.
4. Combine ground beef, onion, and garlic in a nonstick skillet and cook over medium-high heat until meat is no longer pink, stirring often.
5. Add tomato sauce to meat and simmer over medium-low heat until the sauce thickens, about 5 minutes.
6. Add cooked spaghetti to egg mixture and toss to coat. Spread mixture evenly in prepared pie pan.
7. Cover spaghetti with cottage cheese. Spread tomato and meat sauce over the cottage cheese. Sprinkle the spaghetti pie with sliced mushrooms and grated mozzarella.
8. Bake for 20 minutes. Let stand 5 to 10 minutes before cutting.

NUTRITIONAL INFORMATION

Calories per serving 364	**Fiber**............. 0.9 g
Carbohydrate .... 37 g	**Vitamin A**....... 1897 IU
Protein............. **25 g**	**Vitamin C**........... 34 mg
Total fat............. 14 g	**Calcium**.......... 243 mg
Saturated fat........ 5.1 g	Sodium........... 577 mg
Cholesterol........ 87 mg	**Iron**............. 3.5 mg

ENTREES

Easter Brunch Lamb Chops

Skill Level: Advanced   Serves 6

INGREDIENTS
- 2   large garlic cloves, chopped
- 3½ tablespoons chopped mint
- 2   teaspoons olive oil
- 6   4-ounce lamb chops about 1 inch thick, trimmed of all visible fat (about 2½ ounces each actual meat)

EQUIPMENT
- cutting board
- chef's knife
- mezzaluna (optional)
- small bowl
- spoon
- measuring spoons
- baking pan fitted with a broiling rack
- hot pads
- tongs

1. Combine chopped garlic and mint in a small bowl. Stir them together to blend.
2. Rub olive oil on the lamb chops.
3. Rub lamb chops with the mint and garlic, then let stand about 30 minutes at room temperature.
4. Preheat broiler.
5. Place lamb chops on broiler rack in a baking pan. Broil for about 8 to 12 minutes, turning once with tongs during cooking.
6. Serve hot.

NOTE: These Lamb Chops are wonderful grilled over hot coals. Adult supervision is needed for grilling.

NUTRITIONAL INFORMATION

Calories per serving 194	Fiber .... 0 g
Carbohydrate .... 0 g	Vitamin A .... 0 IU
Protein............ 10 g	Vitamin C .... 0 mg
Total fat............. 17 g	Calcium........... 6 mg
Saturated fat........ 8.7 g	Sodium .... 35 mg
Cholesterol.......... 58 mg	Iron .... 0.7 mg

LAMB

St. Patrick's Day Irish Stew

Skill Level: Intermediate   Serves 8

INGREDIENTS
- 4 medium-size boiling potatoes, peeled, halved and sliced into ⅓-inch thick pieces
- 2 pounds lean leg of lamb, cut into 1-inch cubes, with all visible fat trimmed
- 2 medium onions, peeled, halved, and cut into ⅓-inch-thick slices
- 4 carrots, peeled and cut into ⅓-inch-thick slices
- 1 cup frozen peas
- 2½ cups water
- 1 teaspoon salt
- ¼ teaspoon pepper
- 2 tablespoons chopped fresh parsley

EQUIPMENT
- large covered pot
- cutting board
- peeler
- chef's knife
- medium, sharp knife
- small, sharp knife
- dry measuring cups
- liquid measuring cup
- hot pads
- measuring spoons
- mezzaluna (optional)

1. Layer potatoes, lamb, onions, carrots, and peas in a large pot with a tight-fitting lid, starting and finishing with potatoes. Add water, salt, and pepper.
2. Cover and cook over medium heat. When liquid begins to boil, reduce heat to low and cook slowly for about 1½ hours until vegetables and meat are cooked through.
3. Sprinkle with parsley before serving.

NUTRITIONAL INFORMATION

Calories per serving.... 257	**Fiber**............ **1.4 g**
Carbohydrate........ 21 g	**Vitamin A**....... **4177 IU**
Protein............ **28 g**	Vitamin C......... 25 mg
Total fat............ 6 g	Calcium........... 49 mg
Saturated fat........ 3.4 g	Sodium........... 351 mg
Cholesterol......... 67 mg	**Iron**............ **3.2 mg**

ENTREES

Grilled Pork Loin With Lime Spread

Skill Level: Advanced   Serves 8
Oven and Grilling Methods

INGREDIENTS

1½ pounds boneless pork loin, trimmed of all visible fat

Marinade

- 3 tablespoons fresh lime juice
- 1 teaspoon grated peeled ginger root
- 2 tablespoons chopped cilantro
- 2 teaspoons Dijon-style mustard
- 2 tablespoons safflower oil
- ¼ teaspoon pepper

Lime Spread

- 3 tablespoons margarine
- 2 teaspoons chopped cilantro
- 2 teaspoons chopped parsley
- 1 teaspoon fresh lime juice
- ¼ teaspoon white pepper

EQUIPMENT

cutting board
small, sharp knife
juicer
measuring spoons
grater
chef's knife or mezzaluna
mixing bowl
spoon
blender or food processor
rubber spatula
wax paper or plastic wrap
roasting pan
meat thermometer
hot pads

1. Combine marinade ingredients in a mixing bowl. Add pork loin and marinate for at least 1 hour.
2. Combine all ingredients for lime spread in a blender or food processor until well blended, about 1 minute.
3. Transfer lime spread to wax paper or plastic wrap and shape into cylinder; refrigerate. At serving time, remove wax paper from lime spread and slice it into rounds.

PORK

Grilling Method

Grill pork over hot coals for 15 minutes on each side or until the internal temperature of the meat is 170°F. Slice pork and serve with lime spread.

Oven Method

Preheat oven to 350°F. Place pork loin in a roasting pan and bake for about 1½ hours, until the internal temperature of the meat is 170°F. Slice pork and serve with lime spread.

NOTE: Adult supervision is needed for grilling.

NUTRITIONAL INFORMATION

Calories per serving	178	Fiber	0 g
Carbohydrate	1 g	Vitamin A	315 IU
Protein	**12 g**	Vitamin C	6 mg
Total fat	14 g	Calcium	10 mg
Saturated fat	*3.0 g*	Sodium	*111 mg*
Cholesterol	*55 mg*	Iron	0.9 mg

ENTREES

 # Honey-Mustard Pork Tenderloin

Skill Level: Intermediate Serves 6

INGREDIENTS
1½ pounds pork tenderloin (1 large or 2 small)
¼ cup fresh orange juice
4 teaspoons honey
1 tablespoon prepared mustard
2 tablespoons safflower oil
2 tablespoons low-sodium soy sauce
½ teaspoon chopped garlic
¾ cup apple butter

EQUIPMENT
toothpicks
deep bowl
measuring spoons
liquid measuring cup
cutting board
serrated knife
juicer
dough scraper
chef's knife
roasting pan fitted with a rack
hot pads
meat thermometer
slicing knife
dry measuring cups

1. Fold thin end of tenderloin over and secure with toothpicks.
2. In a deep bowl, combine orange juice, honey, mustard, oil, soy sauce, and garlic. Add pork and marinate for at least 1 hour.
3. Preheat oven to 450°F.
4. Place tenderloin on a rack in a roasting pan. Roast for 20 minutes. Reduce heat to 350°F and roast 15 minutes. Test for doneness by using a meat thermometer, which should read 170°F.
5. Slice into rings and serve with 2 tablespoons apple butter on the side.

NUTRITIONAL INFORMATION

Calories per serving 329	Fiber . . . . 0.4 g
Carbohydrate . . . . 22 g	Vitamin A . . . . 28 IU
Protein . . . . **12 g**	Vitamin C . . . . 5 mg
Total fat . . . . 21 g	Calcium . . . . 12 mg
Saturated fat . . . . *7 g*	*Sodium* . . . . *85 mg*
Cholesterol . . . . *55 mg*	Iron . . . . 1.0 mg

PORK

Rob's Grilled Pork Chops

Skill Level: Advanced   Serves 4

INGREDIENTS
- 4 teaspoons fresh lemon juice
- 2 teaspoons Worcestershire sauce
- 1 teaspoon rubbed sage
- ¼ teaspoon pepper
- 2 8-ounce, butterfly-cut 1-inch-thick pork chops, well trimmed

EQUIPMENT
- serrated knife
- cutting board
- juicer
- small bowl
- measuring spoons
- 11×8×2-inch baking pan
- long-handled tongs
- hot pads

1. Combine lemon juice, Worcestershire sauce, sage, and pepper in a small bowl.
2. Place pork chops in an 11×8×2-inch baking pan.
3. Rub lemon juice mixture into pork chops. Marinate at least 30 minutes, or several hours in the refrigerator.
4. Prepare grill.
5. Place pork chops on grilling rack over hot coals and grill about 8 minutes on each side until cooked through. Turn with long-handled tongs.
6. Serve warm.

NOTE: Adult supervision is needed for grilling.

NUTRITIONAL INFORMATION

Calories per serving 258	Fiber................ 0 g
Carbohydrate .... 0 g	Vitamin A .... 16 IU
Protein............. **17 g**	Vitamin C .... 5 mg
Total fat............. 20 g	Calcium............ 7 mg
Saturated fat........ 7.2 g	Sodium .... 76 mg
Cholesterol......... 65 mg	Iron .... 0.8 mg

ENTREES

Grilled Veal Chops

Skill Level: Advanced   Serves 6

INGREDIENTS
- 6 veal chops, 4 ounces each, well trimmed
- 1 garlic clove, crushed
- 2 tablespoons fresh lemon juice
- 1½ teaspoons chopped fresh rosemary or ½ teaspoon dried rosemary
- ¼ teaspoon pepper

EQUIPMENT
- platter
- dough scraper
- cutting board
- serrated knife
- juicer
- measuring spoons
- chef's knife or mezzaluna
- long-handled tongs

1. Place veal chops on a platter and rub with crushed garlic.
2. Combine lemon juice, rosemary and pepper in a small bowl. Rub this mixture on veal chops. Set chops aside.
3. Prepare grill.
4. Cook veal chops on grill over hot coals until cooked to medium doneness, about 6 to 8 minutes on each side. Turn chops over once during cooking with long-handled tongs.

NOTE: Adult supervision is needed for grilling.

NUTRITIONAL INFORMATION

Calories per serving 204	Fiber................ 0 g
Carbohydrate .... 0 g	Vitamin A .... 1 IU
Protein............ 22 g	Vitamin C .... 2 mg
Total fat............. 18 g	Calcium........... 10 mg
Saturated fat........ 8.7 g	Sodium .... 39 mg
Cholesterol......... 75 mg	**Iron .... 2.8 mg**

VEAL

Veal Scallopini With Potatoes

Skill Level: Advanced   Serves 6

INGREDIENTS
- 6 pieces of veal butt or veal top round, 5 ounces each
- 2 tablespoons safflower oil, divided
- 2 Idaho potatoes, peeled
- 3 tablespoons fresh lemon juice
- 2 tablespoons chopped parsley
- 1 tablespoon margarine

EQUIPMENT
- wax paper
- flat meat pounder
- peeler
- cutting board
- medium-size sharp knife
- measuring spoons
- large nonstick skillet
- metal spatula
- hot pads
- ovenproof platter
- tongs
- serrated knife
- juicer
- chef's knife or mezzaluna
- wooden spoons

1. Pound each piece of veal between 2 sheets of wax paper with a meat pounder until ¼ inch thick. Set aside.
2. Preheat oven to warm.
3. Cut peeled potatoes in half lengthwise with medium-size sharp knife, then place flat side down and slice into thin semicircles. You should have about 3½ cups.
4. Heat 1½ tablespoons safflower oil in a large nonstick skillet. Add potatoes and sauté over medium-high heat 15 to 20 minutes until lightly browned, turning potatoes frequently with a metal spatula.
5. Transfer cooked potatoes to ovenproof platter. Arrange around edge in a thick border. Place platter in a warm oven.
6. Add 1½ teaspoons safflower oil to skillet. Add veal slices and cook over medium-high heat for 1 minute, then turn meat over with tongs and cook about 1 minute, or until cooked through.

Continued on next page

ENTREES

7. Remove platter from oven and place veal slices in the center.
8. Add lemon juice and parsley to skillet. Remove from heat and stir margarine into juice.
9. Pour sauce over veal.

NUTRITIONAL INFORMATION

Calories per serving 302
Carbohydrate . . . . 7 g
Protein . . . . **30 g**
Total fat . . . . 29 g
Saturated fat . . . . 12.0 g
Cholesterol . . . . 100 mg
Fiber . . . . 0 g
Vitamin A . . . . 66 IU
Vitamin C . . . . 10 mg
Calcium . . . . 16 mg
Sodium . . . . 54 mg
Iron . . . . **4.6 mg**

"Always A Favorite" Chicken Salad

Skill Level: Beginner   Serves 8

INGREDIENTS
- 4 cups shredded, cooked chicken, skinned
- 1¼ cups diced celery
- 3 tablespoons light mayonnaise
- 3 tablespoons plain low-fat yogurt
- ½ teaspoon salt
- ¼ teaspoon pepper
- ½ cup slivered almonds

EQUIPMENT
- medium mixing bowl
- cutting board
- small, sharp knife
- dry measuring cups
- small mixing bowl
- measuring spoons
- 2 mixing spoons

1. Combine chicken and celery in a medium mixing bowl.
2. Combine mayonnaise, yogurt, salt, and pepper in a small mixing bowl. Stir together until well mixed.
3. Add mayonnaise mixture to chicken and celery, gently stirring to coat chicken. Stir in almonds. Serve or chill.

NOTE: "Always A Favorite" Chicken Salad can be served either on lettuce or whole grain bread as a meal or on wheat crackers or in Tiny Tart Shells (page 64) for a snack.

NUTRITIONAL INFORMATION

Calories per serving 221	Fiber .... 0 g
Carbohydrate .... 3 g	Vitamin A .... 111 IU
Protein .... **21 g**	Vitamin C .... 2 mg
Total fat .... 14 g	Calcium .... 50 mg
Saturated fat .... 2.5 g	Sodium .... 240 mg
Cholesterol .... 65 mg	Iron .... 1.4 mg

ENTREES

Barbecued Chicken

Skill Level: Advanced   Serves 4

INGREDIENTS

4	chicken breasts (2 pounds), skinned

Marinade

½	cup apple cider vinegar
½	cup water
¼	cup tomato paste
2	tablespoons ketchup
4	teaspoons Worcestershire sauce
1	tablespoon brown sugar
½	teaspoon dry mustard
½	teaspoon paprika
¼	teaspoon cayenne pepper

EQUIPMENT

small saucepan
dry measuring cups
measuring spoons
liquid measuring cup
wooden spoon
mixing bowl
2 spoons
13×9×2-inch baking pan fitted with a broiling rack
foil
basting brush
hot pads
tongs

1. Combine all marinade ingredients in a small saucepan. Bring to a boil over high heat, then reduce heat to low and simmer sauce 20 minutes.
2. Put chicken breasts in a mixing bowl, then pour sauce over them. Toss with 2 spoons to coat. Cover and refrigerate at least 3 hours or overnight.
3. Preheat oven to broil.
4. Line a 13×9×2-inch pan with foil. Place broiling rack on foil.
5. Place chicken breasts bone side up on broiling rack, and baste with sauce. Broil 10 minutes.
6. Turn chicken breasts over using tongs, and baste chicken with sauce. Broil 25 to 30 minutes until chicken is cooked through.

NOTE: Chicken can be barbecued outside over a grill. Baste 3 to 4 times during cooking. Adult supervision is needed for grilling.

NUTRITIONAL INFORMATION	
Calories per serving 238	Fiber . . . . 0.2 g
Carbohydrate . . . . 11 g	**Vitamin A** . . . . **756 IU**
Protein . . . . **24 g**	Vitamin C . . . . 19 mg
Total fat . . . . 11 g	Calcium . . . . 28 mg
Saturated fat . . . . *3.0 g*	*Sodium* . . . . *205 mg*
Cholesterol . . . . *72 mg*	**Iron** . . . . **2.1 mg**

ENTREES

Chicken Drumsticks

Skill Level: Intermediate   Serves 6

INGREDIENTS
nonstick vegetable cooking spray
6   chicken legs
12   unsalted soda crackers
⅔   cup plain low-fat yogurt
¼   teaspoon salt
⅛   teaspoon cayenne pepper

EQUIPMENT
11×7×1½-inch baking dish
paper towel or cloth
heavy plastic bag
meat pounder (optional)
shallow bowl
dry measuring cups
measuring spoons
spoon
hot pads

1. Preheat oven to 375°F.
2. Spray an 11×7×1½-inch baking dish with nonstick vegetable cooking spray.
3. Remove skin from chicken by pulling skin from top of leg inside out over narrow end of leg, holding skin with a cloth or paper towel to prevent slipping.
4. Crush crackers by placing them in a heavy plastic bag and pounding them with a meat pounder or your fist.
5. In a shallow bowl, stir yogurt, salt, and cayenne pepper together.
6. Dip each chicken leg into the yogurt mixture one at a time to coat, and then into cracker crumbs to coat evenly.
7. Place in prepared pan. Bake for 45 minutes or until browned.

NUTRITIONAL INFORMATION

Calories per serving 135	Fiber. . . . . 0 g
Carbohydrate . . . . 6 g	Vitamin A . . . . 81 IU
Protein. . . . . 10 g	Vitamin C . . . . 1 mg
Total fat . . . . 8 g	Calcium. . . . . 52 mg
Saturated fat . . . . 2.1 g	*Sodium. . . . . 203 mg*
Cholesterol . . . . 39 mg	Iron . . . . 0.5 mg

CHICKEN

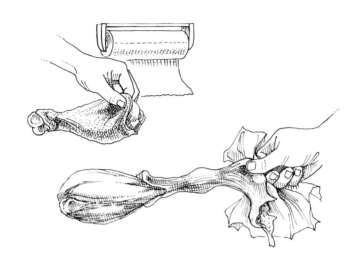

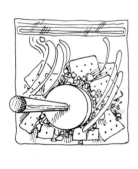 

ENTREES

 Chicken Enchiladas

Skill Level: Advanced   Serves 6

INGREDIENTS
nonstick vegetable cooking spray
3   tablespoons safflower oil, divided
3   tablespoons all-purpose flour
1½ tablespoons chili powder
2   teaspoons cumin
2   garlic cloves, crushed
½   teaspoon salt
2⅔ cups hot water
2½ cups (12 ounces) cooked shredded chicken
1 to 2 fresh green chilies, to taste
1   cup (4 ounces) grated low-fat mozzarella cheese
12 corn tortillas

EQUIPMENT
11×9×2-inch baking dish
small saucepan
measuring spoons
cutting board
dough scraper
chef's knife
wooden spoons
liquid measuring cup
hot pads
mixing bowl
dry measuring cups
small, sharp knife
small skillet
tongs
paper towels
grater

1. Lightly coat an 11×9×2-inch baking dish with nonstick vegetable cooking spray.
2. In a small saucepan, combine 2 tablespoons safflower oil with flour, chili powder, cumin, garlic, and salt. Stir well with a wooden spoon.
3. To prepare enchilada sauce, gradually add water to flour mixture over low heat, stirring constantly. If flour begins to lump, remove from heat and stir until lumps are gone. Place over heat again and continue adding water a little at a time. Simmer gently for about 30 minutes over medium heat, stirring occasionally, until thickened.
4. Preheat oven to 300°F.
5. Combine chicken and green chilies in a mixing bowl, tossing with 2 spoons. Add ½ cup enchilada sauce, and toss with spoons to coat chicken.
6. Heat 1 tablespoon safflower oil in a small skillet over medium heat. Cook each tortilla for about 10 seconds on one

side in the oil, then use tongs to flip it and cook for 10 seconds longer. Remove tortilla with tongs. The tortillas should be flexible, not crisp. Drain the tortillas on paper towels.
7. Place 3 heaping tablespoons of chicken mixture along the center of each tortilla, and roll up the mixture inside the tortilla. Put the enchiladas in a baking dish folded side down, placing them close to each other.
8. Pour remaining hot enchilada sauce over enchiladas and sprinkle with grated cheese.
9. Bake about 12 minutes or until cheese melts and enchiladas are heated through. Serve immediately.

NUTRITIONAL INFORMATION	
Calories per serving 357	**Fiber**.............. 0.6 g
Carbohydrate .... 31 g	Vitamin A.......... 246 IU
Protein.............. **27 g**	**Vitamin C**............ **36 mg**
Total fat............. 13 g	**Calcium** .... **254 mg**
Saturated fat .... *3.1 g*	*Sodium*............ *375 mg*
Cholesterol .... *57 mg*	**Iron** .... **2.5 mg**

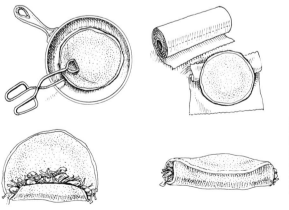

ENTREES

 # Chicken "Nuggets" With Dipping Sauce

Skill Level: Intermediate   Serves 5

Chicken "Nuggets"

INGREDIENTS
3½ cups cornflakes
1 teaspoon Italian seasoning
¼ teaspoon pepper
3 tablespoons margarine, melted
1 pound chicken breast, skinned and cut into 1-inch squares
nonstick vegetable cooking spray

EQUIPMENT
dry measuring cups
heavy plastic bag
rolling pin (optional)
measuring spoons
small bowl
serrated knife
cutting board
tongs
15×10×1-inch baking sheet
hot pads

1. Preheat oven to 350°F.
2. Place cornflakes in a heavy plastic bag. Seal bag and crush cornflakes into fine crumbs using hands or a rolling pin.
3. Add Italian seasoning and pepper to crumbs. Close the bag and shake it to mix well.
4. Pour melted margarine into a small bowl.
5. Dip chicken nuggets in margarine, then place in the bag. Close the bag and shake until the nuggets are well coated.
6. Coat a baking sheet with nonstick vegetable cooking spray, then place the chicken on it.
7. Bake for 15 minutes or until nuggets are golden.
8. Serve hot nuggets with Dipping Sauce (recipe follows).

CHICKEN

Dipping Sauce

INGREDIENTS
¼ cup ketchup
1 tablespoon pineapple juice
2 teaspoons brown sugar
1½ teaspoons wine vinegar
¼ teaspoon chili powder

EQUIPMENT
dry measuring cups
measuring spoons
small bowl
spoon

Stir all ingredients together in a small bowl.

NUTRITIONAL INFORMATION	
Calories per serving 276	Fiber .... 0.2 g
Carbohydrate .... 20 g	**Vitamin A .... 755 IU**
Protein............ 17 g	Vitamin C .... 9 mg
Total fat............ 14 g	Calcium........... 18 mg
Saturated fat........ 3.3 g	Sodium........... 427 mg
Cholesterol......... 46 mg	Iron............. 1.1 mg

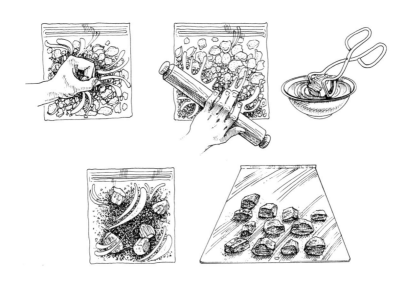

ENTREES

 # Chicken on a Skewer

Skill Level: Advanced   Serves 4

INGREDIENTS
nonstick vegetable cooking spray
1 pound boneless chicken breasts skinned and cut into 1-inch cubes

Marinade

3 tablespoons low-sodium soy sauce
2 tablespoons brown sugar
1 tablespoon safflower oil
1 teaspoon red wine or balsamic vinegar
1 garlic clove, chopped
¼ teaspoon pepper

EQUIPMENT
mixing bowl
measuring spoons
cutting board
dough scraper
chef's knife
2 spoons
15×10×1-inch baking sheet
4 metal skewers
hot pads
basting brush

1. To prepare marinade, combine all ingredients except chicken in a mixing bowl.
2. Add chicken to marinade and toss with 2 spoons to coat. Marinate for 30 minutes.
3. Preheat broiler.
4. Coat a shallow baking sheet with nonstick vegetable cooking spray.
5. Skewer chicken pieces with metal skewers. Place on baking sheet. Save remaining marinade.
6. Broil chicken for 5 minutes. Using hot pads, remove baking sheet from oven carefully. Turn each skewer over and brush chicken with remaining marinade. Broil an additional 5 minutes until chicken is no longer pink in center.

7. Cool 3 to 5 minutes before removing chicken from skewers.

NUTRITIONAL INFORMATION

Calories per serving 219	Fiber .... 0 g
Carbohydrate .... 8 g	Vitamin A .... 76 IU
Protein .... 20 g	Vitamin C .... 1 mg
Total fat .... 12 g	Calcium .... 19 mg
Saturated fat .... 2.8 g	Sodium .... 573 mg
Cholesterol .... 58 mg	Iron .... 1.1 mg

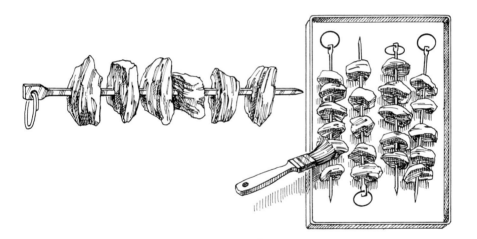

CHICKEN

Hidden Lemon Chicken

Skill Level: Intermediate   Serves 6

INGREDIENTS
- 1   3½-pound chicken
- ½   teaspoon pepper
- 2   small whole lemons
- 2   sprigs fresh rosemary or 1 teaspoon dried rosemary

EQUIPMENT
- paper towels
- measuring spoon
- toothpicks
- roasting pan
- hot pads
- carving knife
- cutting board

1. Preheat oven to 400°F.
2. Wash the chicken in cold water, both inside and out. Remove all bits of fat. Dry it well with paper towels.
3. Sprinkle pepper on the chicken. Rub the pepper over the entire inside and outside surface of the chicken with fingertips.
4. Roll lemons back and forth several times on a work surface to soften them. Make 35 to 40 holes in each lemon with a toothpick.
5. Place both lemons and the rosemary in the cavity of the chicken and close it with toothpicks.
6. Place the chicken in a roasting pan with the breast facing up. Bake for 1 hour and 15 minutes. Test for doneness by pricking thigh; if juices are clear, the chicken is done.
7. Ask an adult to carve the chicken, and serve it.

NUTRITIONAL INFORMATION

Calories per serving 220	Fiber............. 0.7 g
Carbohydrate .... 6 g	Vitamin A......... 473 IU
Protein............. **15 g**	**Vitamin C** .... **53 mg**
Total fat............. 15 g	Calcium........... 30 mg
Saturated fat........ 5.0 g	Sodium .... 91 mg
Cholesterol.......... 45 mg	**Iron** .... **2.9 mg**

ENTREES

Pan-Fried Chicken With Lemon

Skill Level: Advanced   Serves 4

INGREDIENTS
- 4 boned and skinned chicken breasts (about 4 ounces each)
- 2 egg whites
- ¾ cup dry, unseasoned bread crumbs (preferably homemade)
- 3 teaspoons margarine, divided
- 3 teaspoons safflower oil, divided
- ⅛ teaspoon salt
- ¼ teaspoon pepper
- ½ lemon, cut into 4 wedges

EQUIPMENT
- wax paper
- meat pounder (optional)
- 2 shallow bowls
- small whisk or fork
- dry measuring cups
- measuring spoons
- large nonstick skillet
- metal spatula
- hot pads
- serrated knife
- cutting board

1. Place chicken between 2 sheets of wax paper and pound lightly with your fist or a meat pounder.
2. In a shallow bowl, beat egg whites using a small whisk or a fork until frothy. Set aside.
3. Spread bread crumbs on the bottom of a second bowl.
4. Dip each chicken breast into egg whites, and then coat with bread crumbs.
5. Heat 2 teaspoons margarine and 2 teaspoons safflower oil in a large nonstick skillet over medium-high heat. Add coated chicken breasts and cook about 5 minutes until bottom of chicken is brown and crisp. Add remaining 1 teaspoon each of margarine and safflower oil to skillet. Turn chicken over with a metal spatula and cook through for about 7 minutes.
6. Season with salt and pepper. Serve with lemon wedges.

NUTRITIONAL INFORMATION

Calories per serving 295	Fiber . . . . 0.1 g
Carbohydrate . . . . 15 g	Vitamin A. . . . . 195 IU
Protein. . . . . **23 g**	Vitamin C . . . . 5 mg
Total fat. . . . . 16 g	Calcium. . . . . 38 mg
Saturated fat . . . . *3.5 g*	*Sodium*. . . . . *317 mg*
Cholesterol . . . . *58 mg*	Iron . . . . 1.4 mg

ENTREES

Rosemary Grilled Chicken

Skill Level: Advanced   Serves 4

INGREDIENTS
- 4 chicken breasts on the bone, skin removed, 6 ounces each
- 1 garlic clove, crushed
- 2 tablespoons fresh lemon juice
- 2 teaspoons balsamic vinegar
- 1 tablespoon chopped fresh rosemary or 1 teaspoon dried rosemary
- ¼ teaspoon pepper

EQUIPMENT
- platter
- cutting board
- dough scraper
- serrated knife
- juicer
- measuring spoons
- chef's knife or mezzaluna
- long-handled tongs
- hot pads

1. Place chicken on a platter.
2. Rub crushed garlic over breast meat of chicken.
3. Combine lemon juice and balsamic vinegar in a small bowl. Rub mixture into chicken.
4. Rub rosemary and pepper into chicken. Set chicken aside for at least 30 minutes.
5. Prepare grill.
6. Cook chicken over hot charcoal for about 15 to 20 minutes until cooked through, turn over once during cooking with long-handled tongs.

NOTE: Leftover Rosemary Grilled Chicken can be combined with green salad, pasta, or rice for a delicious main-course salad. Adult supervision is needed for grilling.

NUTRITIONAL INFORMATION

Calories per serving 276	Fiber . . . . 0 g
Carbohydrate . . . . 0 g	Vitamin A . . . . 183 IU
Protein . . . . 31 g	Vitamin C . . . . 1 mg
Total fat . . . . 16 g	Calcium . . . . 17 mg
Saturated fat . . . . 4.3 g	Sodium . . . . 93 mg
Cholesterol . . . . 100 mg	Iron . . . . 1.4 mg

CHICKEN

Warm Chicken Salad Vinaigrette

Skill Level: Intermediate   Serves 5

INGREDIENTS

- 1 chicken, about 3½ pounds
- 1 carrot, peeled and halved
- 1 onion, peeled and quartered
- 2 bay leaves
- 1 stalk celery, halved
- 2 green onions, chopped
- ¼ cup diced red pepper

Salad Dressing

- 2 tablespoons olive oil
- 1 tablespoon red wine vinegar
- 1 tablespoon water
- ½ teaspoon Worcestershire sauce
- 1 garlic clove, chopped
- 2 teaspoons Dijon-style mustard
- ¼ teaspoon salt
- ¼ teaspoon pepper

EQUIPMENT

- large saucepan, covered
- cutting board
- peeler
- small, sharp knife
- chef's knife
- hot pads
- small jar
- measuring spoons
- dough scraper
- large mixing bowl
- serving spoons

1. Place the chicken, breast side down, in a large saucepan. Add carrot, onion, bay leaves, celery, and enough water to cover chicken. Bring to a boil over high heat. Cover with a lid, reduce heat to medium-low, and simmer 30 minutes. Remove saucepan from stove and set aside to allow chicken to cool in broth for 30 minutes.
2. While chicken is cooling, combine all ingredients for dressing in a small jar. Cover and shake to combine.
3. Remove chicken from broth. Pick the meat off the bones, discarding the skin and bones. Shred the meat into bite-size pieces with your hands, then transfer to a large mixing bowl. Add green onions and red pepper to chicken.

Continued on next page

ENTREES

4. Shake dressing again and add to chicken mixture. Toss with serving spoons to coat chicken.

NUTRITIONAL INFORMATION

Calories per serving 280	Fiber . . . . 0.3 g
Carbohydrate . . . . 2 g	Vitamin A. . . . . 408 IU
Protein. . . . . 32 g	Vitamin C . . . . 9 mg
Total fat. . . . . 16 g	Calcium. . . . . 30 mg
Saturated fat . . . . 4.3 g	*Sodium. . . . . 231 mg*
Cholesterol . . . . 100 mg	Iron . . . . 1.8 mg

TURKEY

Homemade Turkey Sausage

Skill Level: Intermediate   Serves 6

INGREDIENTS
- 2 pounds ground turkey
- ½ teaspoon salt
- ¼ teaspoon dried thyme
- ¼ teaspoon dried savory
- ¼ teaspoon pepper
- ¼ teaspoon marjoram
- 1 tablespoon chopped cilantro
- 1 teaspoon paprika
- ⅛ teaspoon fennel seed
- 1 garlic clove, minced

EQUIPMENT
- large mixing bowl
- mixing spoon
- measuring spoons
- cutting board
- dough scraper
- mezzaluna (optional)
- chef's knife
- nonstick skillet
- hot pads
- metal spatula
- paper towels

1. In a large mixing bowl, using a mixing spoon or your hands, combine all ingredients.
2. Make 1-inch meatballs by rolling the turkey sausage mixture in your hands. Flatten the meatballs with the palm of your hand to form patties.
3. Place sausage patties in a nonstick skillet. Cook over medium heat until they are browned on the bottom. Turn patties with a metal spatula and cook thoroughly. Remove sausage and drain on paper towels. Serve.

NUTRITIONAL INFORMATION

Calories per serving 158	Fiber . . . . 0 g
Carbohydrate . . . . 0 g	Vitamin A . . . . 0 IU
Protein . . . . **21 g**	Vitamin C . . . . 0 mg
Total fat . . . . 7 g	Calcium . . . . 21 mg
Saturated fat . . . . *2.1 g*	*Sodium* . . . . *229 mg*
Cholesterol . . . . *62 mg*	Iron . . . . 1.4 mg

ENTREES

 Mama Mia Pizza

Skill Level: Advanced   Serves 6

INGREDIENTS

- 1⅓ cups all-purpose flour, divided
- ¾ cup whole wheat flour
- ½ cup oat bran
- 1 ¼ ounce package rapid-rise yeast
- 1 teaspoon sugar
- ½ teaspoon salt
- ¾ cup hot water (130°F)
- 2 tablespoons olive oil
- 1½ tablespoons cornmeal

Toppings

- 1 recipe (1¼ cups) tomato sauce (page 205)
- ½ cup grated zucchini
- ½ cup sliced mushrooms
- ½ red pepper, sliced
- 4 ounces turkey sausage, cubed
- 1½ cups (6 ounces) grated low-fat mozzarella cheese

EQUIPMENT

- food processor
- dry measuring cups
- measuring spoons
- liquid measuring cup
- mixing bowl
- damp cloth
- 15-inch pizza pan
- rolling pin
- serving spoon
- cutting board
- grater
- small, sharp knife
- hot pads
- cooling rack
- 2 spatulas
- scissors or pizza wheel

1. In the bowl of a food processor, combine 1 cup of the all-purpose flour, whole wheat flour, oat bran, yeast, sugar, and salt. Process until blended.

2. With the food processor running, add the hot water to the flour mixture, then add the olive oil. Keep processing until the dough forms a ball, about 30 seconds to 1 minute.

3. Turn the food processor off. If dough is sticky, add more flour, 1 tablespoon at a time, processing for 10 to 15 seconds between additions until dough is smooth, not sticky.

4. Sprinkle 1 tablespoon flour on a flat work surface, and sprinkle 2 teaspoons flour into a mixing bowl. Transfer dough from the food processor to a floured work surface. Knead gently with the palms of your hands. Add more flour to work surface if dough sticks to it. Knead about 3 minutes, until dough springs back when indented with a fingertip.

5. Put dough in the floured bowl, cover it with a damp cloth, and let it rise until it has doubled in size, about 45 minutes.
6. Preheat oven to 425°F. Sprinkle cornmeal on pizza pan.
7. Lightly flour the work surface and a rolling pin. Punch dough down and shape it into a mound. Place the dough on the floured work surface, then roll it into a flat circle. Be careful not to roll over the edges of the dough.

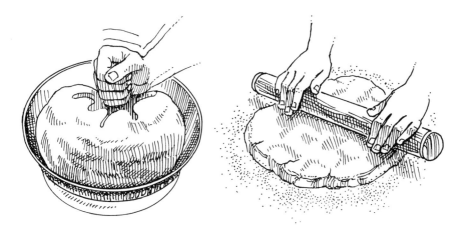

8. Wrap dough around rolling pin, then unroll it onto prepared pizza pan.
9. Spread tomato sauce on pizza dough, then add zucchini, mushrooms, pepper slices, and turkey sausage. Top with mozzarella cheese.
10. Bake until crust is golden, about 20 minutes.
11. Cool pizza about 8 minutes on a cooling rack.

Continued on next page

ENTREES

12. Use 2 spatulas to transfer the pizza to a cutting board, then cut it into wedges with scissors or a pizza wheel.

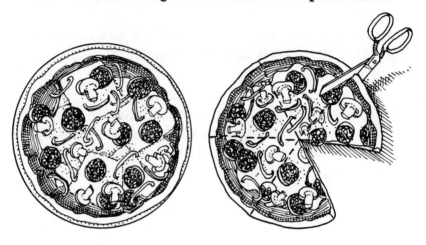

NUTRITIONAL INFORMATION	
Calories per serving 402	Fiber............. 1.3 g
Carbohydrate .... 46 g	**Vitamin A**....... 1891 IU
Protein............ **19 g**	**Vitamin C** .... 43 mg
Total fat............. 17 g	Calcium .... 223 mg
Saturated fat........ *5.1 g*	*Sodium*........... *760 mg*
Cholesterol......... *32 mg*	**Iron** .... **2.2 mg**

Roast Beef and Turkey Roll-Ups

Skill Level: Beginner   Serves 4

INGREDIENTS
- 1 tablespoon light mayonnaise
- 1 teaspoon Dijon-style mustard
- 1 teaspoon low-fat (2%) milk
- 4 1-ounce slices lean roast beef
- 4 1-ounce slices baked turkey breast

EQUIPMENT
- small bowl
- measuring spoons
- spoon
- spreader
- toothpicks

1. Stir together mayonnaise, mustard, and milk in a small bowl to make a sauce.
2. Place roast beef slices on a work surface. Spread sauce on beef slices, then cover each one with a turkey slice.
3. Roll up each stack, then secure the roll with a toothpick.

NUTRITIONAL INFORMATION

Calories per serving 168	Fiber .... 0 g
Carbohydrate .... 0 g	Vitamin A .... 28 IU
Protein .... 13 g	Vitamin C .... 0 mg
Total fat .... 12 g	Calcium .... 11 mg
Saturated fat .... 5 g	*Sodium .... 61 mg*
Cholesterol .... 40 mg	Iron .... 1.0 mg

ENTREES

 # Roasted Turkey Breast

Skill Level: Advanced   Serves 12

INGREDIENTS
nonstick vegetable cooking spray
1   5-pound turkey breast, completely thawed
2   onions, quartered
1   cup water

EQUIPMENT
12×9×2-inch baking dish
paper towels
cutting board
chef's knife
hot pads
liquid measuring cup
basting brush
cooling rack

1. Preheat oven to 325°F.
2. Coat a 12×9×2-inch baking dish with nonstick vegetable cooking spray.
3. Wash turkey, then pat dry with paper towels.
4. Place the turkey breast skin side up in prepared dish. Separate quartered onions into pieces and place around turkey. Add water to baking dish.
5. Bake turkey for about 2½ hours, basting with liquid every 30 minutes using a basting brush. If liquid cooks away, add more water. The meat should be slightly pink to white when cooked.
6. Remove turkey from oven, then place the baking dish on a cooling rack. Let the turkey stand for about 15 minutes before transferring turkey to a cutting board to carve.

NUTRITIONAL INFORMATION

Calories per serving 253	Fiber . . . . 0.2 g
Carbohydrate . . . . 2 g	Vitamin A . . . . 21 IU
Protein. . . . . 31 g	Vitamin C . . . . 3 mg
Total fat. . . . . 12 g	Calcium. . . . . 30 mg
Saturated fat . . . . 3.4 g	*Sodium. . . . . 101 mg*
Cholesterol . . . . 103 mg	**Iron . . . . 2.3 mg**

Turkey and Rice Combo

Skill Level: Advanced   Serves 8

INGREDIENTS	EQUIPMENT
1 tablespoon safflower oil	large nonstick skillet
1 onion, chopped	measuring spoons
½ cup chopped celery	cutting board
1 garlic clove, chopped	chef's knife
1 pound ground turkey	dry measuring cups
1 28-ounce can tomatoes, chopped, juice reserved	small, sharp knife
	dough scraper
¼ teaspoon cayenne pepper	hot pads
1 tablespoon chopped fresh oregano or 1 teaspoon dried oregano	wooden spoon
	mezzaluna (optional)
	liquid measuring cup
1 tablespoon chopped fresh basil or 1 teaspoon dried basil	mixing bowl
	grater
1½ cups low-fat cottage cheese	mixing spoon
2 egg whites	13×9×2-inch baking dish
6 ounces (1½ cups) low-fat mozzarella cheese, grated, divided	
nonstick vegetable cooking oil	
3 cups cooked rice (page 212)	

1. Add oil, onion, celery, and garlic to a large nonstick skillet. Sauté over medium-high heat until tender, about 4 minutes.
2. Add turkey and continue cooking, stirring frequently, until turkey is no longer pink, about 8 minutes.
3. Add tomatoes, reserved tomato juice, cayenne pepper, oregano, and basil to turkey mixture. Simmer over medium-low heat for 30 minutes. If mixture begins to dry out, add water, ¼ cup at a time.
4. Preheat oven to 350°F.
5. In a mixing bowl, combine cottage cheese, egg whites, and 1 cup grated mozzarella with a mixing spoon. Set aside.

Continued on next page

6. Coat a 13×9×2-inch baking dish with nonstick vegetable cooking spray.
7. Spread half of the turkey mixture on bottom of prepared baking dish. Spread half of the rice over the turkey, then spread half of the cottage cheese over the rice. Repeat the process to create 3 more layers, then sprinkle with remaining mozzarella cheese.
8. Bake for 30 to 35 minutes until heated through and top has browned.

NOTE: Turkey and Rice Combo can be prepared ahead of time, stored in the refrigerator, or frozen. Bake just before serving for 35 to 45 minutes (if frozen, thaw before baking).

NUTRITIONAL INFORMATION	
Calories per serving 309	**Fiber** . . . . **0.7 g**
Carbohydrate . . . . 24 g	**Vitamin A** . . . . **1108 IU**
Protein . . . . **27 g**	Vitamin C . . . . 20 mg
Total fat . . . . 11 g	**Calcium** . . . . **224 mg**
Saturated fat . . . . 4.3 g	Sodium . . . . 484 mg
Cholesterol . . . . 53 mg	**Iron** . . . . **2.1 mg**

Turkey Salad

Skill Level: Beginner   Serves 6

INGREDIENTS
- ½ cup low-fat cottage cheese
- 2 tablespoons light mayonnaise
- 2 tablespoons chutney
- ¼ teaspoon curry powder
- 1 pound cooked turkey, cubed
- ¼ cup chopped celery
- 1 large apple, cored and diced
- 6 lettuce leaves
- 2 tablespoons chopped peanuts

EQUIPMENT
- food processor or blender
- dry measuring cups
- measuring spoons
- rubber spatula
- small, sharp knife
- cutting board
- apple corer and slicer
- mixing bowl
- 2 mixing spoons

1. Blend cottage cheese, mayonnaise, chutney, and curry powder in a food processor or blender until smooth.
2. Combine turkey, celery, and apple in a mixing bowl. Add cottage cheese mixture, then toss with 2 mixing spoons until well combined. Cover and chill until serving time.
3. At serving time, place lettuce leaves on plate, then top with a scoop of turkey salad. Sprinkle chopped peanuts over salad.

NUTRITIONAL INFORMATION

Calories per serving	191	Fiber	0.3 g
Carbohydrate	11 g	Vitamin A	127 IU
Protein	**19 g**	Vitamin C	2 mg
Total fat	8 g	Calcium	27 mg
Saturated fat	*2.2 g*	*Sodium*	*158 mg*
Cholesterol	*33 mg*	Iron	0.5 mg

ENTREES

Baked Fish

Skill Level: Advanced   Serves 4

INGREDIENTS
- ½ cup plain low-fat yogurt
- ¼ cup light mayonnaise
- 1 teaspoon fresh lime juice
- ½ teaspoon dry mustard
- 4 5-ounce skinless white fish fillets
- nonstick vegetable cooking spray
- ½ teaspoon paprika

EQUIPMENT
- dry measuring cups
- cutting board
- serrated knife
- juicer
- measuring spoons
- mixing bowl
- mixing spoon
- 12×8×2-inch baking dish
- hot pads

1. Combine yogurt, mayonnaise, lime juice, and dry mustard in a mixing bowl.
2. Add fillets to yogurt sauce and marinate for at least 30 minutes.
3. Preheat oven to 500°F. Coat a 12×8×2-inch baking dish with nonstick vegetable cooking spray.
4. Place fish fillets in the prepared baking dish. Sprinkle with paprika.
5. Bake for 8 minutes, then increase heat to broil. Broil fillets for about 6 minutes, until lightly browned and fish flakes easily. Serve.

NUTRITIONAL INFORMATION

Calories per serving 221	Fiber .... 0 g
Carbohydrate .... 2 g	Vitamin A .... 81 IU
Protein .... **28 g**	Vitamin C .... 5 mg
Total fat .... 11 g	Calcium .... 118 mg
Saturated fat .... *1.5 g*	*Sodium* .... *192 mg*
Cholesterol .... *2 mg*	Iron .... 1.5 mg

SEAFOOD

Fish Bites

Skill Level: Intermediate   Serves 4

INGREDIENTS
nonstick vegetable cooking spray
3   large shredded wheat biscuits
1   teaspoon paprika
2   egg whites
1   pound fresh halibut, cut into 1-inch cubes
3   tablespoons ketchup
1   lemon, quartered

EQUIPMENT
baking sheet
food processor or blender
2 shallow bowls
measuring spoons
spoon
fork
hot pads
cutting board
small, sharp knife
serrated knife

1. Preheat oven to 500°F. Coat a baking sheet with nonstick vegetable cooking spray.
2. Place shredded wheat biscuits in food processor or blender and process into fine crumbs. Place wheat crumbs in a shallow bowl. Add paprika and stir to mix.
3. In a second shallow bowl, beat egg whites with a fork until slightly frothy.
4. Dip fish cubes in egg whites, and then dip them in the crushed shredded wheat to coat.
5. Place cubes on prepared baking sheet. Bake for 10 minutes or until lightly browned.
6. Serve fish bites with ketchup and lemon wedges.

NUTRITIONAL INFORMATION
Calories per serving 223
Carbohydrate . . . . 21 g
Protein . . . . **26 g**
Total fat . . . . 4 g
Saturated fat . . . . 0.5 g
Cholesterol . . . . 0 mg
Fiber . . . . **0.5 g**
Vitamin A . . . . 196 IU
Vitamin C . . . . 13 mg
Calcium . . . . 68 mg
Sodium . . . . 251 mg
Iron . . . . **2.2 mg**

ENTREES

 # Our Favorite Fish Fillets

Skill Level: Advanced   Serves 4

INGREDIENTS
nonstick vegetable cooking spray
4   skinless trout fillets, 6 ounces each
½   onion, diced
2   tomatoes, diced
2   tablespoons olive oil
3   tablespoons fresh lemon juice
¼   teaspoon cayenne pepper
2   tablespoons chopped parsley
1   lemon, quartered

EQUIPMENT
12×8×2-inch baking dish
cutting board
chef's knife
serrated knife
measuring spoons
juicer
mezzaluna (optional)
hot pads
fork

1. Preheat oven to 450°F. Coat a 12×8×2-inch baking dish with nonstick vegetable cooking spray.
2. Place fillets in baking dish in a single layer. Sprinkle fish with onion, tomatoes, olive oil, lemon juice, cayenne pepper and parsley.
3. Bake for 10 minutes or just until fish flakes with a fork.
4. Increase heat to broil. Broil fish 2 minutes.
5. Serve fish with lemon wedges.

NUTRITIONAL INFORMATION

Calories per serving 288	Fiber............. 0.7 g
Carbohydrate .... 7 g	Vitamin A....... 1245 IU
Protein............. **38 g**	Vitamin C .... 32 mg
Total fat............. 12 g	Calcium........... 55 mg
Saturated fat........ *2.2 g*	*Sodium* .... *72 mg*
Cholesterol......... *93 mg*	**Iron** .... **2.4 mg**

SEAFOOD

Snapper Kabobs

Skill Level: Intermediate Serves 4
Microwave Method

INGREDIENTS
- 4 teaspoons safflower oil
- 2 tablespoons fresh lemon juice
- 1 teaspoon Worcestershire sauce
- 1 10-ounce snapper fillet or two 5-ounce fillets
- 2 small zucchini, cut into 8 rounds each

EQUIPMENT
- mixing bowl
- measuring spoons
- serrated knife
- cutting board
- juicer
- small, sharp knife
- 2 spoons
- 16 toothpicks
- microwave-safe 10-inch flat round dish or quiche pan
- microwave-safe plastic wrap
- hot pads

1. In a mixing bowl, combine oil, lemon juice, and Worcestershire sauce.
2. Using a small, sharp knife, cut snapper into ½-inch cubes. Add snapper pieces and zucchini rounds to oil mixture and toss to coat with 2 spoons.
3. Skewer 2 fish cubes on each toothpick, placing a zucchini round in between the fish cubes.
4. Arrange kabobs like spokes of a wheel on a 10-inch flat dish or quiche pan. Cover the dish tightly with microwave-safe plastic wrap.
5. Cook kabobs on high (100%) power for 3 to 4 minutes or until fish is cooked through.
6. Uncover and serve hot.

NUTRITIONAL INFORMATION

Calories per serving 126	Fiber . . . . 0.2 g
Carbohydrate . . . . 2 g	Vitamin A. . . . . 160 IU
Protein. . . . . 14 g	Vitamin C . . . . 15 mg
Total fat . . . . 7 g	Calcium. . . . . 43 mg
Saturated fat . . . . 0.7 g	Sodium . . . . 79 mg
Cholesterol . . . . 26 mg	Iron . . . . 0.9 mg

ENTREES

Trout Parmesan

Skill Level: Advanced   Serves 6

INGREDIENTS

- ¾ cup bread crumbs
- ¼ cup grated Parmesan cheese
- ¼ teaspoon paprika
- ¼ teaspoon pepper
- 2 teaspoons chopped fresh oregano or ¾ teaspoon dried oregano
- 1½ tablespoons chopped parsley
- 1½ tablespoons all-purpose flour
- 1½ tablespoons whole wheat flour
- 3 egg whites
- 4 fillets of trout (6 ounces each)
- 2 tablespoons margarine
- 1 tablespoon olive oil
- 1 lemon, cut into sixths

EQUIPMENT

- 3 pie plates or shallow dishes
- dry measuring cups
- grater
- measuring spoons
- chef's knife or mezzaluna
- cutting board
- small whisk or fork
- large, nonstick skillet
- hot pads
- wooden spoon
- wide spatula
- serrated knife

1. In a pie plate or shallow dish, combine bread crumbs, Parmesan cheese, paprika, pepper, oregano, and parsley.
2. In a second pie plate or shallow dish, combine the all-purpose flour and whole wheat flour.
3. In a third pie plate or shallow dish, beat egg whites until frothy with a small whisk or fork.
4. Dust fillets with flour and dip in beaten egg whites, then dip in seasoned bread crumbs, coating thoroughly.
5. Heat margarine and oil in a large, nonstick skillet over medium heat and stir until combined. Cook fish until golden on one side, about 5 minutes. Turn carefully with a wide spatula and brown on other side (about 3 to 4 minutes). Test for doneness; fish should be white and flaky.
6. Serve with lemon wedges.

NUTRITIONAL INFORMATION

Calories per serving 363	Fiber .... 0.1 g
Carbohydrate .... 13 g	Vitamin A......... 432 IU
Protein............. 30 g	Vitamin C .... 7 mg
Total fat............. 21 g	Calcium........... 92 mg
Saturated fat .... 3 g	*Sodium........... 269 mg*
Cholesterol......... 65 mg	Iron.............. 1.9 mg

SEAFOOD

Breaded Shrimp

Skill Level: Advanced   Serves 6
Grilling and Conventional Method

INGREDIENTS
- 1½ pounds large fresh shrimp
- 1½ tablespoons olive oil
- 2 tablespoons safflower oil
- ⅔ cup bread crumbs
- 1 garlic clove, finely chopped
- 3 tablespoons chopped cilantro or parsley
- ¼ teaspoon pepper
- nonstick vegetable cooking spray
- 1 lemon, cut into 6 wedges
- 1 lime, cut into 6 wedges

EQUIPMENT
- shrimp peeler or small, sharp knife
- paper towels
- large mixing bowl
- measuring spoons
- dry measuring cups
- cutting board
- dough scraper
- chef's knife
- mezzaluna (optional)
- 2 mixing spoons
- shallow grilling basket or 13×9×2-inch baking dish
- hot pads
- metal spatula
- serrated knife

Grilling Method

1. Peel and devein shrimp with a shrimp peeler or remove shell from shrimp, then use a small, sharp knife to cut down the back of the shrimp and remove vein. Rinse shrimp in water and pat dry with paper towels.
2. In a large mixing bowl, combine shrimp, olive oil, safflower oil, bread crumbs, garlic, cilantro or parsley, and pepper and toss together with 2 mixing spoons until shrimp are coated evenly.
3. Set shrimp aside for 30 minutes to 2 hours.
4. Prepare grill.
5. Coat a shallow grilling basket with nonstick vegetable cooking spray.
6. Place breaded shrimp in basket.
7. Grill about 3 minutes on each side until shrimp are pink and have a crisp crust.

Continued on next page

ENTREES

8. Serve shrimp with lemon and lime wedges.

Conventional Method

Follow steps 1-3 as for grilling method.

4. Place oven rack on second shelf from top of oven. Preheat broiler.
5. Spread shrimp in a single layer in baking dish.
6. Broil the shrimp for 3 minutes. Carefully remove baking pan from oven and turn all shrimp over once. Return shrimp to oven and continue broiling 1 to 3 minutes more depending on size of shrimp. Broil until shrimp are pink and have a crisp crust.
7. Serve with lemon and lime wedges.

NOTE: Adult supervision is needed for grilling.

NUTRITIONAL INFORMATION

Calories per serving 211	Fiber .... 0.1 g
Carbohydrate .... 11 g	Vitamin A. .... 173 IU
Protein............ 22 g	Vitamin C .... 11 mg
Total fat .... 8 g	Calcium........... 91 mg
Saturated fat........ 0.9 g	*Sodium........... 241 mg*
Cholesterol .... 159 mg	**Iron .... 2.4 mg**

SEAFOOD

Hickory Smoked Shrimp

Skill Level: Advanced   Serves 2

INGREDIENTS
- 10 shrimp
- 1 tablespoon margarine, melted
- 2 teaspoons Worcestershire sauce
- 2 teaspoons fresh lemon juice
- ½ lemon, cut into 4 wedges

EQUIPMENT
- shrimp peeler or small sharp knife
- paper towels
- cutting board
- small bowl
- measuring spoons
- serrated knife
- juicer
- spoon or small whisk
- pastry brush
- baking pan fitted with broiling rack
- hot pads

1. Peel and devein shrimp with a shrimp peeler or remove shell from shrimp, then use a small, sharp knife to cut down the back of the shrimp and remove vein. Rinse shrimp in water and pat dry with paper towels.
2. Preheat oven to broil.
3. Blend margarine, Worcestershire sauce, and lemon juice in a small bowl with a spoon or whisk.
4. Using a pastry brush, brush mixture on shrimp, then place them on a broiling rack in a baking pan.
5. Broil shrimp until just pink and opaque, about 6 to 8 minutes.
6. Serve shrimp with lemon wedges.

NUTRITIONAL INFORMATION	
Calories per serving 107	Fiber .... 0.1 g
Carbohydrate .... 5 g	Vitamin A. .... 285 IU
Protein .... 8 g	**Vitamin C .... 38 mg**
Total fat .... 6 g	Calcium........... 48 mg
Saturated fat .... 1.1 g	*Sodium. .... 274 mg*
Cholesterol .... 60 mg	*Iron............. 1.7 mg*

ENTREES

 # Shrimp Peel

Skill Level: Advanced   Serves 6

INGREDIENTS

- 2 tablespoons pickling spice
- 3 quarts water
- 1¼ pounds extra-large shrimp (in shells)

Red Sauce

- ½ cup ketchup
- 1 tablespoon fresh lemon juice
- 2 teaspoons prepared horseradish
- 1 teaspoon Worcestershire sauce

EQUIPMENT

measuring spoons
6-inch cheesecloth square
string
covered stockpot
hot pads
mixing bowl
colander
small bowl
spoon
dry measuring cups
cutting board
serrated knife
juicer

1. Place pickling spice in a 6-inch square of cheesecloth. Gather the edges of the cheesecloth, and tie it closed with a string.
2. Place the pickling spice bundle into a stockpot with water. Bring the water to a boil, then cover and cook 15 minutes to season water.
3. Add shrimp to boiling seasoned water and cook for 2 to 3 minutes, until they are pink and opaque.
4. Meanwhile, half-fill a mixing bowl with ice water.
5. Drain the shrimp in a colander, then transfer them to the ice water to cool for 15 minutes.
6. In a small bowl, stir together ketchup, lemon juice, horseradish, and Worcestershire sauce.

7. Drain shrimp in a colander.
8. When serving, each person peels his or her own shrimp, and the red sauce is for dipping.

NUTRITIONAL INFORMATION

Calories per serving 109	Fiber .... 0.1 g
Carbohydrate .... 7 g	Vitamin A. .... 293 IU
Protein............. 18 g	Vitamin C .... 7 mg
Total fat .... 1 g	Calcium........... 65 mg
Saturated fat .... *0.3 g*	*Sodium*. .... *348 mg*
Cholesterol .... *132 mg*	Iron............. 1.7 mg

VEGETABLES

Cauliflower With Lemon "Butter"

Skill Level: Advanced   Serves 6
Conventional and Microwave Methods

Conventional Method

INGREDIENTS
1¼ pound cauliflower head
2 tablespoons margarine
1 tablespoon fresh lemon juice
pinch of pepper

EQUIPMENT
small, sharp knife
cutting board
saucepan
hot pads
colander
small saucepan
serrated knife
juicer
measuring spoons
wooden spoon

1. Trim away all outer leaves from cauliflower.
2. Remove core by cutting about a 1-inch cone-shaped wedge around the base of the cauliflower with a small, sharp knife. Wash cauliflower well, and shake off water.
3. Place cauliflower in a saucepan and cover with water.
4. Bring water to a boil over high heat. Boil cauliflower until tender, about 5 minutes.
5. Transfer cauliflower to a colander and allow to drain for 1 minute.
6. Melt margarine with lemon juice and pepper in a small saucepan over medium heat.
7. Place cauliflower on a plate and drizzle with lemon sauce.
8. Using a serrated knife, cut cauliflower head into wedges, as you would a pie. Serve.

VEGETABLES

Microwave Method

EQUIPMENT
small, sharp knife
cutting board
microwave-safe 8-inch round
    baking dish
microwave-safe plastic wrap
hot pads
microwave-safe small bowl
serrated knife
juicer
measuring spoons

1. Follow Steps 1 and 2 of conventional method.
2. Place cauliflower stem side down on microwave-safe 8-inch round baking dish. Cover tightly with microwave-safe plastic wrap.
3. Microwave cauliflower on high (100%) power 6 to 7 minutes until tender. Let stand 3 minutes.
4. Remove cauliflower from microwave. Melt margarine with lemon juice and pepper in a microwave-safe small bowl at medium-high (70%) power for 1 minute.
5. Continue with Step 7 of conventional method.

NUTRITIONAL INFORMATION

Calories per serving 60	Fiber . . . . 1.0 g
Carbohydrate . . . . 5 g	Vitamin A . . . . 212 IU
Protein . . . . 3 g	**Vitamin C . . . . 75 mg**
Total fat . . . . 4 g	Calcium . . . . 25 mg
Saturated fat . . . . 0.6 g	*Sodium . . . . 14 mg*
Cholesterol . . . . 0 mg	Iron . . . . 1.0 mg

VEGETABLES

Cheese Sauce For Vegetables

Skill Level: Intermediate   Yields 2 cups; serves 6

INGREDIENTS
- 1 cup low-fat cottage cheese
- 1 5-ounce can evaporated milk
- 1 cup (4 ounces) grated low-fat cheddar cheese
- ⅛ teaspoon pepper

EQUIPMENT
- dry measuring cups
- blender or food processor
- rubber spatula
- small saucepan
- hot pads
- wooden spoon
- grater

1. Combine cottage cheese and milk in a blender or food processor. Process until smooth.
2. Transfer mixture to a small saucepan, then heat over medium-low heat, stirring constantly with a wooden spoon.
3. Add cheddar cheese and pepper to sauce; stir until cheese melts.

NOTE: Cheese Sauce can also be served on cooked pasta.

NUTRITIONAL INFORMATION	
Calories per serving 100	Fiber .... 0 g
Carbohydrate .... 6 g	Vitamin A .... 254 IU
Protein .... 10 g	Vitamin C .... 0 mg
Total fat .... 4 g	**Calcium .... 221 mg**
Saturated fat .... 2.0 g	Sodium .... 446 mg
Cholesterol .... 12 mg	Iron .... 0.1 mg

VEGETABLES

Corn Fritters

Skill Level: Intermediate   Yield: 16   1 serving = four 2-inch fritters

INGREDIENTS
- 2 cups fresh corn, cut from the cob, or thawed frozen corn
- 1 egg, lightly beaten
- 2 egg whites, stiffly beaten
- 2 tablespoons all-purpose flour
- 1 teaspoon baking powder
- ¼ teaspoon salt
- ¼ teaspoon pepper
- 2 teaspoons safflower oil (for coating pan)

EQUIPMENT
- cutting board
- small, sharp knife
- dry measuring cups
- 2 mixing bowls
- electric mixer
- measuring spoons
- large spoon
- large, nonstick skillet
- hot pads
- metal spatula

Toppings

- ¼ cup honey *or*
- ¼ cup plain low-fat yogurt *and*
- ½ cup chopped green onion tops

1. Combine corn, egg, egg whites, flour, baking powder, salt, and pepper in a mixing bowl. Stir together.
2. Coat a nonstick skillet with oil. Heat over medium-high heat.
3. Spoon the batter by generous tablespoons onto skillet. Cook until lightly browned, about 1 minute. Turn over, using a metal spatula, and cook second side about 1 minute.
4. Serve corn fritters with honey, or with yogurt and green onions.

NOTE: Analysis does not include toppings.

NUTRITIONAL INFORMATION

Calories per serving 129	**Fiber.............. 0.6 g**
Carbohydrate .... 19 g	Vitamin A......... 395 IU
Protein .... 6 g	Vitamin C.......... 6 mg
Total fat .... 5 g	Calcium........... 13 mg
Saturated fat........ 0.6 g	*Sodium........... 284 mg*
Cholesterol......... 69 mg	Iron............... 0.9 mg

VEGETABLES

Green Beans Parmesan

Skill Level: Advanced   Serves 6

INGREDIENTS
- 1 pound green beans
- 2 tablespoons margarine
- 3 tablespoons grated Parmesan cheese
- ¼ teaspoon salt

EQUIPMENT
- stockpot or large saucepan
- hot pads
- colander
- measuring spoons
- large skillet
- wooden spoon
- grater

1. Snap both ends off the beans, removing any strings. Snap beans into 2-inch pieces.
2. Fill a large saucepan or stockpot ⅔ full with water. Bring water to a boil. Drop in the green beans and return water to a boil. Cook beans for 4 to 8 minutes until crisp-tender. Drain beans in a colander.
3. Melt margarine in a large skillet over medium-high heat. Add green beans and sauté for 3 minutes or until heated through, stirring with a wooden spoon. Turn heat off, then add Parmesan cheese and salt. Toss beans until lightly coated. Serve hot.

NUTRITIONAL INFORMATION

Calories per serving..... 70	Fiber............. 0.8 g
Carbohydrate .... 6 g	Vitamin A......... 628 IU
Protein .... 2 g	Vitamin C .... 14 mg
Total fat .... 5 g	Calcium........... 79 mg
Saturated fat........ 1.2 g	Sodium........... 185 mg
Cholesterol.......... 2 mg	Iron............. 0.6 mg

Green Beans Sesame

Skill Level: Advanced Serves 4
Conventional and Microwave Methods

Conventional Method

INGREDIENTS
- ½ pound fresh green beans
- 2 teaspoons margarine, melted
- 2 teaspoons toasted sesame seeds

EQUIPMENT
- covered saucepan fitted with steamer
- hot pads
- measuring spoons
- wooden spoons

1. Snap ends off green beans with your hands, then snap beans into 1½-inch pieces.
2. Put enough water in a saucepan so that it almost touches the bottom of the steamer. Place green beans in the steamer. Cover the saucepan and steam green beans over high heat until crisp-tender, about 6 to 8 minutes.
3. Remove green beans from steamer. Remove steamer and pour water out of saucepan.
4. Return green beans to the saucepan, and place it on the stove over medium-high heat. Add margarine and toss the green beans with a wooden spoon to coat, about 2 minutes.
5. Sprinkle green beans with toasted sesame seeds.

Microwave Method

EQUIPMENT
- two 12-inch squares microwave-safe plastic wrap
- hot pads
- serving bowl
- measuring spoons
- serving spoons

1. Follow Step 1 as in conventional method.

Continued on next page

VEGETABLES

2. Place half of green beans on each 12-inch square of microwave-safe plastic wrap. Sprinkle beans with water. Wrap plastic wrap tightly around beans, folding ends of wrap under to secure.
3. Microwave on high (100%) power for 4 to 4½ minutes.
4. Carefully open the plastic wrap, and transfer beans to a serving dish. Toss with melted margarine and sesame seeds.

NOTE: To toast sesame seeds, place seeds in a nonstick skillet. Stir them over medium-high heat until lightly browned.

NUTRITIONAL INFORMATION

Calories per serving	59	**Fiber**	**0.8 g**
Carbohydrate	6 g	Vitamin A	558 IU
Protein	2 g	Vitamin C	14 mg
Total fat	4 g	Calcium	46 mg
Saturated fat	*0.7 g*	*Sodium*	*35 mg*
Cholesterol	*0 mg*	Iron	0.7 mg

Mashed Sweet Potato With Thanksgiving Garnish

Skill Level: Advanced   Serves 6

Sweet Potatoes

INGREDIENTS
5 medium-size sweet potatoes, scrubbed
nonstick vegetable cooking spray
2½ tablespoons margarine
¼ cup low-fat (2%) milk
¼ teaspoon dried thyme
¼ teaspoon nutmeg
¼ teaspoon salt
pepper to taste

EQUIPMENT
stockpot
hot pads
fork
colander
peeler
2-quart baking dish or 8×8×2-inch baking dish
measuring spoons
large mixing bowl
electric mixer
liquid measuring cup
rubber spatula
foil
serving spoon

1. Place sweet potatoes in a stockpot and cover them with water. Bring water to a boil and cook potatoes until fork tender, about 25 minutes after water boils.
2. Drain the potatoes in a colander, and let them cool so that they can be peeled. Peel potatoes.
3. Preheat oven to 350°F. Coat 2-quart or 8×8×2-inch baking dish with nonstick vegetable cooking spray.
4. Place potatoes in a large mixing bowl and add margarine, milk, thyme, nutmeg, salt, and pepper. Beat with an electric mixer until fluffy, about 2 minutes.
5. Place mixture in baking dish and cover with foil. Bake about 25 minutes. Prepare garnish.

Continued on next page

VEGETABLES

Garnish

INGREDIENTS
6 thin slices whole wheat bread
1 teaspoon margarine

EQUIPMENT
pencil
paper
ruler
scissors
measuring spoons
baking sheet
hot pads

1. Preheat oven to 350°F.
2. Draw a pattern of a turkey's head and one of a tail on a piece of paper. The patterns should be about 3 inches tall. Cut out the patterns with scissors.
3. Dab each pattern with margarine and stick onto a slice of bread. Cut around the outline of the pattern using scissors. Repeat for each slice of bread.
4. Place the bread designs on a baking sheet, and bake for 20 minutes or until the bread is crisp.
5. Spoon a mound of the sweet potatoes onto each plate. Place a toasted turkey head and tail on either side of each mound of sweet potatoes. Serve.

NUTRITIONAL INFORMATION

Calories per serving 255	**Fiber**. . . . . **1.5 g**
Carbohydrate . . . . 45 g	**Vitamin A**. . . . . . . **7922 IU**
Protein . . . . 5 g	Vitamin C . . . . 21 mg
Total fat . . . . 7 g	Calcium. . . . . 80 mg
Saturated fat . . . . *1.3 g*	*Sodium*. . . . . *318 mg*
Cholesterol. . . . . *1 mg*	Iron . . . . 1.6 mg

VEGETABLES

Miniature Corn Medley

Skill Level: Advanced   Serves 4

INGREDIENTS
- 4 teaspoons safflower oil
- ½ cup celery, cut into ½-inch diagonal slices
- 1 15-ounce can miniature corn, drained and rinsed
- ½ red pepper, cut into 2-inch thin strips
- 1 tablespoon fresh lime juice
- ¼ teaspoon pepper

EQUIPMENT
- measuring spoons
- nonstick skillet
- cutting board
- small, sharp knife
- hot pads
- dry measuring cups
- wooden spoon
- serrated knife
- juicer

1. Heat oil over medium-high heat in a nonstick skillet. Add celery, and sauté 2 minutes.
2. Add corn and red pepper to celery, and sauté about 5 minutes or until all vegetables are cooked.
3. Remove from heat, then season with lime juice and pepper.

NUTRITIONAL INFORMATION

Calories per serving 138	Fiber............. 1.1 g
Carbohydrate .... 23 g	Vitamin A......... 470 IU
Protein .... 3 g	Vitamin C .... 21 mg
Total fat .... 5 g	Calcium........... 12 mg
Saturated fat........ *0.4 g*	*Sodium*........... *279 mg*
Cholesterol......... *0 mg*	Iron.............. 0.7 mg

VEGETABLES

Mr. McGregor's Baby Cabbage Patch

Skill Level: Advanced   Serves 6

INGREDIENTS
- 1 pound Brussels sprouts
- 2 tablespoons margarine, melted
- 2 teaspoons fresh lemon juice
- 1 teaspoon Dijon-style mustard
- 3 tablespoons grated Parmesan cheese

EQUIPMENT
- cutting board
- small, sharp knife
- large saucepan
- hot pads
- colander
- small bowl
- small whisk
- measuring spoons
- serrated knife
- juicer
- 2 serving spoons
- grater

1. Wash and trim off the stem of each Brussels sprout. Cut an "X" in the stem of each sprout with a small, sharp knife.
2. Half fill a large saucepan with water. Bring water to a boil. Gently add sprouts, then return water to a boil and cook for about 6 to 8 minutes, until sprouts are tender. Drain sprouts in a colander, then return them to the pan.
3. Whisk melted margarine, lemon juice, and mustard together in a small bowl.
4. Add margarine mixture to Brussels sprouts; toss to coat. Sprinkle with Parmesan cheese.

NUTRITIONAL INFORMATION	
Calories per serving..... 81	**Fiber............. 1.2 g**
Carbohydrate .... 6 g	Vitamin A......... 589 IU
Protein .... 5 g	**Vitamin C........... 78 mg**
Total fat .... 5 g	Calcium........... 64 mg
Saturated fat........ 1.2 g	*Sodium........... 112 mg*
Cholesterol.......... 2 mg	Iron............. 1.2 mg

VEGETABLES

New Potatoes In Their Jackets

Skill Level: Intermediate   Serves 4

INGREDIENTS
- 12 small new potatoes
- 4 teaspoons olive oil
- ¼ teaspoon pepper

EQUIPMENT
- foil
- ruler
- scissors
- measuring spoons
- baking sheet
- hot pads
- fork

1. Preheat oven to 450°F.
2. Cut foil into 4 sheets, each 6×12 inches.
3. Place 3 potatoes on each piece of foil. Sprinkle potatoes with olive oil and pepper. Turn potatoes to coat with olive oil.
4. Fold foil around potatoes, and wrap securely.
5. Place foil packets on a baking sheet, and bake for 35 to 40 minutes, or until potatoes are tender when pierced with a fork. Serve.

NOTE: Sprigs of fresh herbs can be added to the potatoes before cooking to enhance the flavor. Try dill, thyme, or rosemary.

NUTRITIONAL INFORMATION

Calories per serving 104	Fiber .... 0.4 g
Carbohydrate .... 15 g	Vitamin A .... 0 IU
Protein .... 2 g	Vitamin C .... 17 mg
Total fat .... 5 g	Calcium............ 6 mg
Saturated fat .... *0.6 g*	*Sodium* .... *3 mg*
Cholesterol.......... *0 mg*	Iron .... 0.5 mg

VEGETABLES

Oriental Broccoli

Skill Level: Advanced   Serves 6

INGREDIENTS
- 2 teaspoons cornstarch
- ¾ cup homemade chicken stock (page 117)
- 2 tablespoons safflower oil
- 1 pound broccoli florets
- 1 teaspoon Oriental sesame seed oil

EQUIPMENT
- small bowl
- measuring spoons
- liquid measuring cup
- spoon
- wok or heavy nonstick skillet
- 2 wooden spoons
- hot pads

1. Combine cornstarch with a little of the chicken stock in a small bowl and stir until smooth. Add remaining stock and set aside.
2. Heat safflower oil over medium-high heat in a wok or heavy nonstick skillet.
3. Add broccoli and stir constantly with wooden spoons for 3 minutes.
4. Add chicken stock mixture and sesame oil. Cook about 3 minutes or until sauce is thickened and broccoli is crisp-tender.

NUTRITIONAL INFORMATION

Calories per serving..... 79	**Fiber**............... **0.6 g**
Carbohydrate .... 6 g	**Vitamin A**....... **2150 IU**
Protein .... 3 g	**Vitamin C** .... **86 mg**
Total fat .... 5 g	Calcium........... 81 mg
Saturated fat .... *0.5 g*	*Sodium* .... *20 mg*
Cholesterol.......... *0 mg*	Iron.............. 0.9 mg

VEGETABLES

Parmesan Potato Sticks

Skill level: Advanced   Serves 4

INGREDIENTS
- 2 large baking potatoes, scrubbed
- 4 teaspoons olive oil
- 2 tablespoons grated Parmesan cheese
- ⅛ teaspoon salt

EQUIPMENT
- cutting board
- chef's knife
- 15×10×1-inch baking sheet
- measuring spoons
- hot pads
- metal spatula
- grater

1. Preheat oven to 425°F.

2. On cutting board, cut potatoes in half, lengthwise. Place potato halves flat side down, and cut each into 4 sticks.

3. Place potato sticks on a baking sheet and sprinkle with olive oil. Toss lightly with hands to coat potato sticks.

4. Bake for 35 minutes, turning the potato sticks over once after 15 minutes with a metal spatula.

5. Sprinkle potato sticks with cheese and salt, then return them to the oven for 2 minutes, or until a light golden brown. Serve hot.

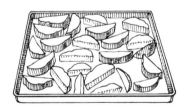

NUTRITIONAL INFORMATION

Calories per serving	124	**Fiber**	**0.6 g**
Carbohydrate	16 g	Vitamin A	18 IU
Protein	3 g	Vitamin C	16 mg
Total fat	5 g	Calcium	71 mg
Saturated fat	*1.1 g*	*Sodium*	*113 mg*
Cholesterol	*2 mg*	Iron	0.6 mg

VEGETABLES

Pinto Beans With A Hidden Ingredient

Skill Level: Intermediate   Serves 10

INGREDIENTS
- 1 pound dried pinto beans
- 8 cups water
- ¾ cup chopped onion
- ½ cup chopped green or red pepper
- 2 tablespoons margarine
- 1 teaspoon chopped garlic
- 1 tablespoon creamy natural peanut butter
- 2 tablespoons chopped cilantro

EQUIPMENT
- colander
- bean pot or large covered saucepan
- liquid measuring cup
- measuring spoons
- cutting board
- dough scraper
- chef's knife
- dry measuring cups
- small, sharp knife
- wooden spoon
- hot pad
- mezzaluna (optional)

1. Wash pinto beans very well in a colander, and remove any small pebbles by hand.
2. Place beans in a bean pot or large saucepan.
3. Add water, onion, pepper, margarine, and garlic to beans. Stir with a wooden spoon.
4. Bring water to a boil. Reduce heat so that the water continues to simmer, and cover the pan.
5. Cook beans at a low simmer for about 3½ hours, or until beans are soft and skins are broken. Stir well every hour.
6. Stir in peanut butter and cilantro.
7. Simmer for 10 more minutes and serve.

NUTRITIONAL INFORMATION

Calories per serving 165	Fiber............. 3.8 g
Carbohydrate .... 26 g	Vitamin A.......... 117 IU
Protein .... 8 g	Vitamin C.......... 9 mg
Total fat .... 4 g	Calcium........... 50 mg
Saturated fat........ 0.6 g	*Sodium .... 14 mg*
Cholesterol.......... 0 mg	**Iron .... 2.5 mg**

VEGETABLES

Quick Corn-On-The-Cob

Skill Level: Intermediate   Serves 2
Microwave Method

INGREDIENTS
- 2 ears of corn in the husk, with silks
- 2 teaspoons margarine
- ¼ teaspoon pepper

EQUIPMENT
- hot pads
- measuring spoons
- spreader

1. Place ears of corn in microwave oven and cook on high (100%) power for 3 minutes. Let rest 1 minute and, using a hot pad, turn over each ear of corn.

2. Microwave on high power 3 more minutes. Remove ears from oven, using a hot pad. Let corn cool just until cool enough to handle. Remove and discard husk and silks.

3. Spread with margarine and season with pepper. Serve.

NUTRITIONAL INFORMATION

Calories per serving 104	Fiber............. 1.0 g
Carbohydrate .... 16 g	Vitamin A......... 466 IU
Protein .... 2 g	Vitamin C .... 7 mg
Total fat .... 4 g	Calcium............ 3 mg
Saturated fat........ *0.7 g*	*Sodium* .... *45 mg*
Cholesterol.......... *0 mg*	Iron.............. 0.5 mg

VEGETABLES

Stir-Fried Snow Peas and Carrots

Skill Level: Advanced   Serves 4

INGREDIENTS
- 5 carrots
- 2 cups snow peas
- 1 teaspoon cornstarch
- 5 tablespoons homemade chicken stock, divided (see page 117)
- 1 tablespoon olive oil
- ½ teaspoon salt

EQUIPMENT
- peeler
- small, sharp knife
- cutting board
- paper towels or dish cloth
- dry measuring cups
- measuring spoons
- small bowl
- spoon
- wok or nonstick skillet
- 2 wooden spoons
- hot pads

1. Wash carrots, then peel them with a peeler. Cut diagonally into ½-inch slices.

2. Wash snow peas, pat them dry, then remove their tips and strings. To do so, hold each snow pea flat against your thumb, with your thumbnail pressing up to the end of snow pea. Grasp the stem of the snow pea between the index finger and thumb of your other hand and pull it toward you. The string will be attached to the stem.

3. To prepare thickening sauce, combine cornstarch with 2 tablespoons chicken stock in a small bowl. Stir to dissolve cornstarch. Set aside.

4. In a wok or nonstick skillet, heat oil over medium-high heat. Add carrots to oil and stir-fry 3 minutes.

5. Add 3 tablespoons chicken stock, snow peas, and salt to carrots. Stir-fry 2 minutes.

6. Add cornstarch mixture and stir over heat until thickened. Serve.

NOTE: If fresh snow peas are not available, frozen snow peas can be used. Shorten cooking time to 1 minute, or until heated through.

NUTRITIONAL INFORMATION

Calories per serving 133	**Fiber............. 2.5 g**
Carbohydrate .... 20 g	**Vitamin A...... 10375 IU**
Protein .... 6 g	Vitamin C .... 27 mg
Total fat .... 4 g	Calcium........... 54 mg
Saturated fat........ 0.5 g	*Sodium........... 133 mg*
Cholesterol.......... 0 mg	Iron............. 1.3 mg

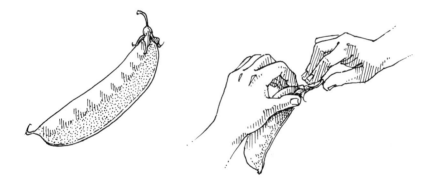

VEGETABLES

Stop-Light Peppers

Skill Level: Advanced   Serves 6

INGREDIENTS	EQUIPMENT
1 large red pepper	cutting board
1 large yellow pepper	small, sharp knife
1 large green pepper	measuring spoons
4 teaspoons margarine	large nonstick skillet
1 tablespoon chopped fresh basil, or 1 teaspoon dried basil	wooden spoon
	hot pads
¼ teaspoon ground pepper	chef's knife or mezzaluna

1. Place each pepper on its side. Use a small, sharp knife to cut a circle about an inch all the way around the stem but not through it. With your fingers, grasp under the cut rim and turn the stem to loosen it. Pull the stem away from the pepper along with the core attached to it.

2. Cut each cored pepper in half, then remove the white ribs with your fingers. Cut peppers into julienne strips about ¼ inch wide, always cutting with the flat side of the pepper against the work surface.

3. Heat margarine in a large nonstick skillet. Add the peppers and sauté over medium heat until cooked but still slightly crisp, about 5 minutes.

4. Add basil and ground pepper to skillet, toss to combine. Serve.

NUTRITIONAL INFORMATION

Calories per serving	32	**Fiber**	**0.6 g**
Carbohydrate	2 g	Vitamin A	274 IU
Protein	1 g	**Vitamin C**	**51 mg**
Total fat	3 g	Calcium	4 mg
Saturated fat	*0.5 g*	*Sodium*	*35 mg*
Cholesterol	*0 mg*	Iron	0.3 mg

VEGETABLES

Stuffed Potato Boats

Skill Level: Intermediate   Serves 4

INGREDIENTS
- 2 large russet potatoes
- ¼ cup low-fat (2%) milk
- ¼ cup low-fat cottage cheese
- 3 tablespoons plain low-fat yogurt
- 6 green onions, tops only, chopped
- ⅛ teaspoon salt
- ⅛ teaspoon pepper
- 4 tablespoons grated Parmesan cheese, divided

EQUIPMENT
- hot pads
- fork
- cooling rack
- cutting board
- small, sharp knife
- spoon
- mixing bowl
- liquid measuring cup
- dry measuring cups
- measuring spoons
- grater
- electric mixer
- baking pan

1. Preheat oven to 400°F.
2. Place potatoes in the oven and bake for 50 to 60 minutes, until center is soft when tested with a fork. Transfer potatoes to a cooling rack.
3. Lower oven temperature to 350°F.
4. To form boats, cut cooled baked potatoes in half lengthwise. Carefully scoop out potato flesh with a spoon to avoid tearing the skins. Reserve skins.
5. In a mixing bowl, combine potato flesh with milk, cottage cheese, yogurt, green onions, salt, pepper, and 2 tablespoons Parmesan cheese. Beat on medium speed with an electric mixer until well combined.
6. Spoon the potato mixture into the reserved potato skins and sprinkle with remaining Parmesan cheese.
7. Place stuffed potatoes in a baking pan and bake for 20 to 25 minutes, until heated through and lightly browned. Serve hot.

NOTE: These can be prepared ahead of time and baked just before serving.

Continued on next page

VEGETABLES

NUTRITIONAL INFORMATION

Calories per serving 130	Fiber . . . . 0.4 g
Carbohydrate . . . . 19 g	Vitamin A. . . . . 466 IU
Protein . . . . 7 g	Vitamin C . . . . 14 mg
Total fat . . . . 3 g	Calcium . . . . 143 mg
Saturated fat . . . . *1.6 g*	*Sodium*. . . . . *252 mg*
Cholesterol. . . . . *8 mg*	Iron . . . . 0.5 mg

Tomato Sauce

Skill Level: Advanced Yield: 1¼ cups 1 serving = ¼ cup

INGREDIENTS
- 2 28-ounce cans Italian-style peeled tomatoes
- 4 teaspoons olive oil
- 1 cup chopped onion
- ¾ teaspoon chopped garlic
- 1 tablespoon chopped fresh basil or 1 teaspoon dried basil
- 1 tablespoon chopped fresh oregano or 1 teaspoon dried oregano
- ¼ teaspoon salt
- ½ teaspoon pepper
- 2 tablespoons tomato paste

EQUIPMENT
- colander
- mixing bowl
- large saucepan
- hot pads
- measuring spoons
- cutting board
- chef's knife
- dough scraper
- dry measuring cups
- wooden spoon
- mezzaluna (optional)

1. Drain liquid from peeled tomatoes. Place tomatoes in a mixing bowl and, using your hands, break tomatoes into small pieces.
2. In a large saucepan, heat olive oil over medium heat. Add onion and garlic and sauté for 5 minutes, or until onion is limp.
3. Slowly add the crushed tomatoes, stirring well.
4. Add basil, oregano, salt, pepper, and tomato paste. Mix well and simmer for 30 minutes, stirring the sauce several times.

NOTE: This is a great sauce for pizza, pasta, or any recipe that requires tomato sauce. For a smooth sauce, puree in blender or food processor.

NUTRITIONAL INFORMATION

Calories per serving..... 77	Fiber............. 0.8 g
Carbohydrate .... 10 g	Vitamin A....... 1652 IU
Protein .... 2 g	Vitamin C.......... 32 mg
Total fat .... 4 g	Calcium........... 16 mg
Saturated fat........ 0.5 g	Sodium........... 317 mg
Cholesterol.......... 0 mg	Iron............. 1.1 mg

PASTA

Fettuccine With Parmesan

Skill Level: Advanced   Serves 4

INGREDIENTS
- 6 ounces fettuccine
- 2 tablespoons margarine
- ¼ teaspoon nutmeg
- ¼ teaspoon pepper
- 2 tablespoons grated Parmesan cheese

EQUIPMENT
- large pot or stockpot
- hot pads
- colander
- small, sharp knife
- cutting board
- large skillet
- 2 wooden spoons
- measuring spoons
- grater

1. Half-fill a large pot with water and bring it to a boil over high heat. Add fettuccine and cook according to package instructions until al dente (firm to bite). Drain in a colander.
2. Melt margarine in a large skillet over medium heat.
3. Add fettuccine and toss with wooden spoons to coat with margarine.
4. Sprinkle with nutmeg and pepper; toss to coat.
5. Sprinkle with Parmesan cheese. Mix lightly and serve.

NUTRITIONAL INFORMATION
Calories per serving 201	Fiber................ 0 g
Carbohydrate .... 28 g	Vitamin A......... 252 IU
Protein .... 6 g	Vitamin C .... 0 mg
Total fat .... 7 g	Calcium........... 47 mg
Saturated fat........ 1.6 g	Sodium........... 114 mg
Cholesterol.......... 2 mg	Iron .... 1.1 mg

Noodle Kugel

Skill Level: Advanced   Serves 12

INGREDIENTS
- 8 ounces wide noodles
- nonstick vegetable cooking spray
- 1 cup low-fat cottage cheese
- 4 ounces light cream cheese
- 2 tablespoons margarine
- ⅓ cup sugar
- 1 egg
- 3 egg whites
- 1¼ cups low-fat (2%) milk
- ⅓ cup plain low-fat yogurt
- ⅓ cup golden raisins
- ½ teaspoon vanilla
- ½ teaspoon cinnamon

EQUIPMENT
- stockpot
- hot pads
- colander
- 13×9×2-inch baking dish
- 2 mixing bowls
- measuring spoons
- dry measuring cups
- 2 mixing spoons
- fork
- liquid measuring cup

1. Fill a stockpot half-full with water. Bring water to boil over high heat. Cook noodles according to package instructions until al dente (firm to bite). Drain noodles in a colander.
2. Preheat oven to 350°F. Coat a 13×9×2-inch baking dish with nonstick vegetable cooking spray.
3. Transfer warm noodles to mixing bowl. Add cottage cheese, cream cheese, margarine, and sugar and toss together with 2 mixing spoons until noodles are well coated.
4. Combine egg and egg whites in a mixing bowl and beat together with a fork until mixed. Stir in milk, yogurt, raisins, vanilla, and cinnamon.
5. Add egg mixture to noodles and stir to combine. Transfer mixture to prepared baking dish. Bake for about 50 minutes or until noodles are golden.

NUTRITIONAL INFORMATION

Calories per serving 174	Fiber................ 0 g
Carbohydrate .... 25 g	Vitamin A.......... 250 IU
Protein .... 7 g	Vitamin C .... 0 mg
Total fat .... 6 g	Calcium........... 43 mg
Saturated fat........ 2.8 g	*Sodium*........... 150 mg
Cholesterol........ 35 mg	Iron.............. 0.9 mg

PASTA

Olive Oyl's Pasta Salad

Skill Level: Advanced   Serves 4

INGREDIENTS
- 6 ounces wagon wheel pasta
- 3 tablespoons olive oil
- 1 cup shredded fresh spinach
- ¼ teaspoon chopped garlic
- ½ teaspoon salt
- ¼ teaspoon pepper
- 3 tablespoons grated Parmesan cheese

EQUIPMENT
- large pot or stockpot
- hot pads
- colander
- large mixing bowl
- measuring spoons
- 2 serving spoons
- cutting board
- dough scraper
- chef's knife
- dry measuring cups
- grater

1. Half-fill a large pot or stockpot with water. Bring water to boil over high heat. Add pasta and cook according to package instructions until al dente (firm to bite). Drain in a colander and transfer to large mixing bowl.

2. Add olive oil, and toss with 2 serving spoons to coat pasta. Add spinach, garlic, salt, and pepper, and toss to coat. Sprinkle with Parmesan cheese, and toss to coat. Serve at room temperature or chilled.

NUTRITIONAL INFORMATION

Calories per serving 278	**Fiber**. . . . . **0.5 g**
Carbohydrate . . . . 33 g	**Vitamin A** . . . . **966 IU**
Protein . . . . 7 g	Vitamin C . . . . 5 mg
Total fat. . . . . 12 g	Calcium. . . . . 79 mg
Saturated fat . . . . *2.1 g*	*Sodium*. . . . . *349 mg*
Cholesterol. . . . . *3 mg*	Iron . . . . 1.7 mg

Pasta Primavera Salad

Skill Level: Advanced   Serves 8

INGREDIENTS
- 3 carrots, peeled and sliced
- 1½ cup green beans, cut into ⅓-inch pieces
- 8 ounces rotelle (pasta spirals)
- 1 recipe Seasoned Salad Dressing (about 1 cup), divided (page 228)
- ½ cup chopped red pepper
- 3 tablespoons diced purple onion
- ½ teaspoon salt

EQUIPMENT
- stockpot or large saucepan
- hot pads
- cutting board
- peeler
- small, sharp knife
- slotted spoon or skimmer
- colander fitted in a bowl
- small mixing bowl
- dry measuring cups
- large serving bowl
- measuring spoons
- liquid measuring cup
- mixing spoons

1. Half-fill a stockpot or large saucepan with water. Bring water to a boil.
2. Add carrots to boiling water and cook until crisp-tender, 3 to 5 minutes. Remove carrots from water with a slotted spoon or skimmer, and drain them in a colander fitted in a bowl. Transfer drained carrots to a small mixing bowl.
3. Add green beans to water carrots were boiled in. Cook until crisp-tender, about 4 to 5 minutes.
4. Remove green beans from water with the slotted spoon or skimmer, and drain them in the colander. Add drained green beans to carrots.
5. Return water to a boil. Add pasta and cook according to package instructions until al dente (firm to bite).
6. Place colander in the sink and drain pasta in it.

Continued on next page

7. Place pasta in a large serving bowl. Add 3 tablespoons Seasoned Salad Dressing and toss to coat. Add carrots, green beans, red pepper, and purple onion to pasta. Add remaining dressing and salt. Toss to coat well.
8. Refrigerate pasta salad several hours or, even better, overnight.

NOTE: If you want to serve Pasta Primavera Salad as a main course, add shredded chicken from Rosemary Grilled Chicken (page 162).

NUTRITIONAL INFORMATION

Calories per serving 158	**Fiber** .... 0.6 g
Carbohydrate .... 27 g	**Vitamin A** .... 3119 IU
Protein .... 4 g	Vitamin C .... 13 mg
Total fat .... 4 g	Calcium .... 32 mg
Saturated fat .... 0.5 g	Sodium .... 215 mg
Cholesterol .... 0 mg	Iron .... 1.2 mg

Power-Packed Pasta

Skill Level: Advanced   Serves 6

INGREDIENTS
nonstick vegetable cooking spray
8   ounces pasta shells
1   cup part-skim ricotta cheese
½   cup plain low-fat yogurt
⅓   cup grated Parmesan cheese
2   tablespoons margarine, melted
⅛   teaspoon nutmeg

EQUIPMENT
1½-quart casserole dish
large pot or stockpot
hot pads
colander
large mixing bowl
dry measuring cups
measuring spoons
grater
mixing spoon

1. Preheat oven to 300°F. Coat a 1½-quart casserole dish with nonstick vegetable cooking spray.
2. Half-fill a large pot or stockpot with water. Bring water to a boil over high heat. Cook pasta according to package directions until al dente (firm to bite). Drain pasta in a colander.
3. In a large mixing bowl, combine ricotta cheese, yogurt, Parmesan cheese, margarine and nutmeg. Stir until well combined. Add pasta and toss to coat. Spoon mixture into the prepared casserole dish. Bake for 45 minutes, or until lightly browned. Serve hot.

NOTE: To further lower fat content, low-fat cottage cheese can be substituted for ricotta cheese.

NUTRITIONAL INFORMATION	
Calories per serving 262	Fiber . . . . 0 g
Carbohydrate . . . . 32 g	Vitamin A . . . . 376 IU
Protein . . . . **12 g**	Vitamin C . . . . 0 mg
Total fat . . . . 9 g	**Calcium** . . . . **218 mg**
Saturated fat . . . . 3.8 g	Sodium . . . . 192 mg
Cholesterol . . . . 17 mg	Iron . . . . 1.3 mg

RICE

Basic Rice

Skill Level: Intermediate   Serves 6
Conventional and Microwave Methods

Conventional Method

INGREDIENTS
1 cup uncooked rice
1¾ cups homemade chicken stock
  (page 117)

EQUIPMENT
dry measuring cups
liquid measuring cup
medium covered saucepan
hot pads
wooden spoon
fork

1. Combine rice and chicken stock in a medium saucepan.
2. Bring to a boil over high heat; stir once.
3. Cover and reduce heat to low. Simmer for 15 minutes until all liquid has been absorbed.
4. Remove from heat and let stand 5 minutes longer before uncovering. Fluff with a fork.

Microwave Method

EQUIPMENT
dry measuring cups
liquid measuring cup
deep 2-quart microwave-safe
  container
wooden spoon
plastic wrap
hot pads
fork

1. Combine rice and chicken stock in a deep 2-quart microwave-safe container. Cover with a lid, or cover with plastic wrap, folding back the wrap at one corner to serve as a vent for the steam created during cooking.
2. Microwave on high (100%) power for 5 minutes.
3. Reduce setting to medium (50%) power, and microwave for 15 minutes. Fluff rice with a fork.

NUTRITIONAL INFORMATION

Calories per serving 145
Carbohydrate . . . . 29 g
Protein . . . . 3 g
Total fat . . . . 2 g
Saturated fat . . . . 0.4 g
Cholesterol . . . . 3 mg
Fiber . . . . 0.5 g
Vitamin A . . . . 633 IU
Vitamin C . . . . 2 mg
Calcium . . . . 22 mg
Sodium . . . . 46 mg
Iron . . . . 1.2 mg

Fried Rice

Skill Level: Advanced   Serves 6

INGREDIENTS
- 3 cups cooked rice (1 cup uncooked)
- 2 egg whites
- 1 egg
- 2 tablespoons safflower oil
- 3 green onions, chopped (green portion only)
- ½ cup frozen green peas
- 2 tablespoons low-sodium soy sauce

EQUIPMENT
- small bowl
- fork
- measuring spoons
- large, nonstick skillet or wok
- small, sharp knife
- cutting board
- dry measuring cups
- wooden spoon
- hot pads

1. See Basic Rice recipe on page 212 to cook rice.
2. In a small bowl, beat egg whites and egg lightly with a fork.
3. Heat oil in a large, nonstick skillet or wok over medium-high heat. Add eggs, green onions, and peas. Stir with a wooden spoon for 20 seconds.
4. Add rice and soy sauce. Stir-fry until well combined and heated through. Serve immediately.

NUTRITIONAL INFORMATION

Calories per serving	159	Fiber	0.6 g
Carbohydrate	31 g	**Vitamin A**	**1096 IU**
Protein	8 g	Vitamin C	11 mg
Total fat	1 g	Calcium	34 mg
Saturated fat	*0.3 g*	*Sodium*	*288 mg*
Cholesterol	*45 mg*	Iron	1.7 mg

RICE

Gratinéed Rice

Skill Level: Advanced   Serves 6

INGREDIENTS
- 3 tablespoons margarine
- 6 green onions, chopped
- 3 cups cooked brown rice (1 cup uncooked)
- 1 cup grated (4 ounces) white or yellow low-fat cheddar cheese
- nonstick vegetable cooking spray
- 1 egg
- 1 egg white
- 1 cup low-fat (2%) milk
- ½ teaspoon salt
- ¼ teaspoon white pepper
- ¼ teaspoon nutmeg

EQUIPMENT
- saucepan
- cutting board
- small, sharp knife
- hot pads
- wooden spoon
- dry measuring cups
- grater
- 2-quart rectangular baking dish
- large mixing bowl
- liquid measuring cup
- measuring spoons
- electric mixer
- rubber spatula

1. Melt margarine in a saucepan over medium heat. Add green onions and sauté until soft, about 5 minutes, stirring with a wooden spoon.
2. Remove saucepan from heat. Stir in cooked rice and cheese until well combined with the green onion and margarine.
3. Preheat oven to 350°F.
4. Coat a 2-quart rectangular baking dish with nonstick vegetable cooking spray.
5. In a large mixing bowl, combine egg, egg white, milk, salt, white pepper, and nutmeg. Beat with an electric mixer on medium-high until ingredients are mixed, about 1 minute.
6. Stir rice mixture into egg mixture with rubber spatula.
7. Spoon into prepared baking dish, spreading evenly.
8. Bake for 30 minutes until cooked through and lightly browned on top.

NOTE: To prepare Gratinéed Rice ahead of time, follow steps 1 through 7. Cover and refrigerate; bake for 30 to 40 minutes, then serve.

NUTRITIONAL INFORMATION

Calories per serving 291	**Fiber**............. **0.5 g**
Carbohydrate .... 30 g	**Vitamin A** .... **894 IU**
Protein .... **11 g**	Vitamin C .... 6 mg
Total fat............ 14 g	**Calcium** .... **221 mg**
Saturated fat .... *5.8 g*	*Sodium*........... *343 mg*
Cholesterol .... *69 mg*	Iron .... 1 mg

RICE

Rice Pilaf

Skill Level: Intermediate   Serves 6

INGREDIENTS
- 2 cups homemade chicken stock (page 117)
- 1 cup uncooked white rice
- 1 cup chopped celery
- 1 cup grated carrot
- ¾ cup chopped onion
- 3 tablespoons margarine, cubed

EQUIPMENT
11¾ × 7½ × 1¾-inch baking dish
dry measuring cups
grater
cutting board
chef's knife
small, sharp knife
liquid measuring cup
large spoon
hot pads

1. Preheat oven to 325°F.
2. In the baking dish stir all ingredients together.
3. Bake for 1 hour, stirring once after 30 minutes.

NOTE: If rice seems dry during cooking, add more stock or water.

NUTRITIONAL INFORMATION

Calories per serving 203	**Fiber............. 0.6 g**
Carbohydrate .... 32 g	**Vitamin A....... 2938 IU**
Protein .... 5 g	Vitamin C .... 6 mg
Total fat .... 6 g	Calcium........... 34 mg
Saturated fat........ 1.2 g	*Sodium........... 302 mg*
Cholesterol.......... 0 mg	Iron............. 1.6 mg

Risotto With Celery

Skill Level: Intermediate Serves 6
Microwave Method

INGREDIENTS
- 4 teaspoons margarine, divided
- 1 tablespoon safflower oil
- ½ cup diced yellow onion
- 1 cup finely chopped celery
- 1 cup arborio rice
- 3 cups homemade chicken stock (page 117)
- ¼ cup grated Parmesan cheese
- ½ teaspoon salt

EQUIPMENT
- measuring spoons
- 12×8×2-inch microwave-safe baking dish
- cutting board
- chef's knife
- small, sharp knife
- dry measuring cups
- wooden spoons
- hot pads
- liquid measuring cup
- grater

1. In microwave oven heat 2 teaspoons margarine and oil in a 12×8×2-inch glass baking dish at high (100%) power for 1 minute.
2. Add onion and celery to dish and stir to coat. Cook on high power for 3½ minutes.
3. Add rice and stir to coat. Cook, uncovered, for 3 minutes more.
4. Stir in stock. Cook, uncovered, on high power for 10 minutes. Stir well and cook for 10 minutes more.
5. Remove rice from oven. Let stand 5 minutes for rice to absorb remaining liquid, stirring several times. Stir in remaining 2 teaspoons margarine, Parmesan cheese, and salt. Cook, uncovered, on high power for 1 minute. Serve.

NUTRITIONAL INFORMATION

Calories per serving.... 218	**Fiber**............. **0.5 g**
Carbohydrate........ 30 g	**Vitamin A**....... **2296 IU**
Protein............. 6 g	Vitamin C.......... 3 mg
Total fat........... 8 g	Calcium............ 76 mg
Saturated fat........ *1.9 g*	*Sodium*............ *341 mg*
Cholesterol......... *3 mg*	Iron............... 1.3 mg

SALADS

Caesar Salad

Skill Level: Intermediate   Serves 6

INGREDIENTS

Caesar Dressing

- 1 garlic clove, crushed and peeled
- 2 teaspoons Dijon-style mustard
- 1 teaspoon anchovy paste
- 2 tablespoons fresh lemon juice
- 1 tablespoon balsamic or red wine vinegar
- ¼ teaspoon pepper
- 1 egg
- 3 tablespoons olive oil
- 2 tablespoons grated Parmesan cheese

Salad

- 6 cups torn romaine lettuce
- ½ cup croutons

EQUIPMENT

cutting board
dough scraper
chef's knife
salad bowl
measuring spoons
serrated knife
juicer
whisk
small, sharp knife
hot pads
small saucepan
slotted spoon
liquid measuring cup
grater
wooden spoons

1. Rub garlic around the bottom of a salad bowl, leaving a few small pieces. Add mustard, anchovy paste, lemon juice, vinegar, and pepper. Whisk together until well blended.

2. Bring a small saucepan of water to a boil. Turn heat off and place whole egg in water for 4 minutes to coddle it (partially cooking the egg until it is barely set). Remove egg with a slotted spoon.

3. Gradually whisk olive oil into mixture in the salad bowl until it reaches a thick consistency.

4. Crack egg and whisk coddled egg into mixture. Add Parmesan cheese. Stir to combine.
5. Add torn lettuce to dressing. Add croutons, and toss with dressing to coat lettuce. Serve.

NUTRITIONAL INFORMATION	
Calories per serving 117	Fiber . . . . 0.4 g
Carbohydrate . . . . 6 g	**Vitamin A. . . . . . . 1105 IU**
Protein . . . . 4 g	Vitamin C . . . . 12 mg
Total fat . . . . 9 g	Calcium . . . . 67 mg
Saturated fat . . . . 1.5 g	*Sodium.* . . . . *120 mg*
Cholesterol . . . . 47 mg	Iron . . . . 1.1 mg

SALADS

Citrus And Spinach Salad

Skill Level: Beginner   Serves 8

INGREDIENTS
- 2 10-ounce packages fresh spinach
- 1 orange, peeled and sectioned
- 1 grapefruit, peeled and sectioned
- 3 ounces slivered almonds
- ½ cup "Good for Fruit" Salad Dressing (page 224)

EQUIPMENT
- paper towels or dish cloth
- salad bowl
- cutting board
- serrated knife
- liquid measuring cup
- salad tongs

1. Wash spinach very well in several changes of water to get rid of sand. Pat dry. Tear spinach into bite-sized pieces, and place in a salad bowl.
2. Add orange sections, grapefruit sections, and almonds to spinach.
3. Pour dressing over salad and toss lightly.

NOTE: Analysis includes salad dressing.

NUTRITIONAL INFORMATION	
Calories per serving 176	Fiber............. 0.8 g
Carbohydrate .... 13 g	Vitamin A....... 5864 IU
Protein .... 5 g	Vitamin C .... 57 mg
Total fat............. 13 g	Calcium .... 100 mg
Saturated fat........ 1.1 g	Sodium........... 339 mg
Cholesterol.......... 0 mg	Iron .... 2.7 mg

SALADS

Italian Romas

Skill Level: Beginner   Serves 4

INGREDIENTS
- 8 lettuce leaves
- 4 ripe Roma (plum) tomatoes, sliced
- 6 fresh basil leaves
- 1 tablespoon olive oil
- 1 tablespoon red wine vinegar
- 1/8 teaspoon pepper

EQUIPMENT
- serving platter or 4 salad plates
- cutting board
- serrated knife
- scissors
- measuring spoons

1. On a serving platter or on each of 4 salad plates, arrange lettuce leaves.
2. Arrange tomato slices on lettuce leaves.
3. Roll basil leaves up into little cylinders, then cut them crosswise into thin strips with scissors. Sprinkle basil on tomatoes.
4. Drizzle olive oil and vinegar on tomatoes.
5. Sprinkle tomatoes with pepper. Serve.

NUTRITIONAL INFORMATION

Calories per serving..... 53	**Fiber**............. **0.6 g**
Carbohydrate .... 5 g	**Vitamin A**....... **1018 IU**
Protein .... 1 g	Vitamin C .... 23 mg
Total fat .... 4 g	Calcium........... 19 mg
Saturated fat........ *0.4 g*	*Sodium* .... *4 mg*
Cholesterol.......... *0 mg*	Iron.............. 0.9 mg

SALADS

Lettuce And Cucumber Salad With Creamy Garlic Dressing

Skill Level: Beginner   Serves 6

INGREDIENTS
Garlic Dressing

- ¼ cup light mayonnaise
- 2 tablespoons plain low-fat yogurt
- 2 tablespoons low-fat (2%) milk
- 1 tablespoon apple cider vinegar
- ⅛ teaspoon garlic powder

Salad

- 3 cups shredded lettuce
- 1 cucumber, peeled and thinly sliced

EQUIPMENT
dry measuring cups
measuring spoons
small bowl
spoon
6 salad plates
peeler
small, sharp knife
cutting board

1. Combine all dressing ingredients in a small bowl. Stir well.
2. Arrange shredded lettuce on salad plates and top with sliced cucumber. Spoon dressing on top of each salad and serve.

NUTRITIONAL INFORMATION

Calories per serving..... 46	Fiber .... 0.3 g
Carbohydrate .... 2 g	Vitamin A. .... 335 IU
Protein .... 1 g	Vitamin C .... 4 mg
Total fat .... 4 g	Calcium............ 31 mg
Saturated fat .... 0.5 g	*Sodium* .... *36 mg*
Cholesterol........... *1 mg*	Iron.............. 0.8 mg

French Dressing

Skill Level: Beginner   Yield: ½ cup   1 serving = 1 tablespoon

INGREDIENTS	EQUIPMENT
1 to 2 tablespoons fresh lemon juice	measuring spoons
1 teaspoon balsamic vinegar	serrated knife
1 teaspoon red wine vinegar	cutting board
1 teaspoon Dijon-style mustard	juicer
1 teaspoon sugar	covered bottle
½ teaspoon paprika	liquid measuring cup
½ teaspoon salt	
¼ cup olive oil	
¼ cup safflower oil	

1. Combine lemon juice, balsamic vinegar, red wine vinegar, mustard, sugar, paprika, and salt in bottle. Cover tightly and shake well until ingredients are blended.
2. Add olive oil and safflower oil to mixture, then shake bottle again until well blended. Store dressing in refrigerator. Shake before serving.

NUTRITIONAL INFORMATION

Calories per serving 123	Fiber . . . . 0 g
Carbohydrate . . . . 1 g	Vitamin A . . . . 1 IU
Protein . . . . 0 g	Vitamin C . . . . 2 mg
Total fat . . . . 14 g	Calcium . . . . 2 mg
Saturated fat . . . . 1.6 g	*Sodium* . . . . 130 mg
Cholesterol . . . . 0 mg	Iron . . . . 0 mg

SALADS

"Good For Fruit" Salad Dressing

Skill Level: Beginner   Yield: 1½ cups   1 serving = 1 tablespoon

INGREDIENTS	EQUIPMENT
½ cup sugar	dry measuring cups
⅓ cup apple cider vinegar	measuring spoons
1 teaspoon dry mustard	liquid measuring cup
½ teaspoon salt	blender or food processor
¾ cup safflower oil	rubber spatula
	covered container

1. Combine sugar, vinegar, dry mustard, and salt in a blender or food processor.
2. With machine running, slowly add oil.
3. Store dressing in a covered container in the refrigerator.

NOTE: For a variation on this dressing, add 1 tablespoon of poppy seeds before adding the oil.

NUTRITIONAL INFORMATION

Calories per serving..... 77	Fiber............... 0 g
Carbohydrate .... 4 g	Vitamin A .... 0 IU
Protein .... 0 g	Vitamin C .... 0 mg
Total fat .... 7 g	Calcium............ 0 mg
Saturated fat........ 0.6 g	*Sodium .... 0 mg*
Cholesterol.......... 0 mg	Iron .... 0 mg

Sweet And Sour Salad Dressing

Skill Level: Beginner   Yield: ½ cup   1 serving = 1 tablespoon

INGREDIENTS
- 3 tablespoons safflower oil
- 2 tablespoons wine vinegar
- 2 tablespoons ketchup
- 1 garlic clove, crushed and peeled
- 1 teaspoon honey
- ¾ teaspoon mixed dried herbs
- ½ teaspoon paprika

EQUIPMENT
- measuring spoons
- pastry scraper
- cutting board
- covered jar

1. Combine all ingredients in a jar. Cover and shake well to mix.
2. Chill. At serving time, shake again and discard garlic clove.

NUTRITIONAL INFORMATION

Calories per serving..... 59	Fiber................ 0 g
Carbohydrate .... 2 g	Vitamin A .... 50 IU
Protein .... 0 g	Vitamin C .... 0 mg
Total fat .... 6 g	Calcium............ 1 mg
Saturated fat........ 0.9 g	Sodium............ 109 mg
Cholesterol.......... 0 mg	Iron .... 0 mg

SALADS

Tangy Buttermilk Dressing

Skill Level: Beginner Yield: 1¾ cups
1 serving = 1 generous tablespoon

INGREDIENTS
- 1 cup buttermilk
- ½ cup low-fat cottage cheese
- 2 tablespoons light mayonnaise
- 1 tablespoon fresh lemon juice
- 1 tablespoon chopped parsley
- ¼ teaspoon garlic powder
- ¼ teaspoon salt
- ¼ teaspoon pepper

EQUIPMENT
- liquid measuring cup
- dry measuring cups
- measuring spoons
- food processor or blender
- rubber spatula
- serrated knife
- cutting board
- juicer
- chef's knife or mezzaluna

1. Combine buttermilk, cottage cheese, and mayonnaise in a food processor or blender and blend until smooth. Push dressing from side of container with a rubber spatula.
2. Add lemon juice, parsley, garlic powder, salt, and pepper to buttermilk mixture. Blend for about 30 seconds until the ingredients are well combined.
3. Serve. Store leftover dressing in the refrigerator.

NUTRITIONAL INFORMATION

Calories per serving..... 30	Fiber............ 0.1 mg
Carbohydrate......... 2 g	Vitamin A......... 86 IU
Protein.............. 2 g	Vitamin C.......... 2 mg
Total fat............ 2 g	Calcium........... 32 mg
Saturated fat....... 0.4 g	Sodium........... 114 mg
Cholesterol......... 2 mg	Iron............. 0.1 mg

Thousand Island Dressing

Skill Level: Beginner   Yield: 1 cup   1 serving = 2 tablespoons

INGREDIENTS
- ⅓ cup plain low-fat yogurt
- ⅓ cup light mayonnaise
- ¼ cup ketchup
- 2 tablespoons apple cider vinegar
- 2 tablespoons low-fat (2%) milk
- ¼ teaspoon dry mustard

EQUIPMENT
- dry measuring cups
- measuring spoons
- container with lid

1. Combine all ingredients in a container with a tight-fitting lid. Cover and shake until well combined.
2. Serve. Store leftover dressing in the refrigerator.

NUTRITIONAL INFORMATION

Calories per serving..... 50	Fiber............... 0 g
Carbohydrate......... 3 g	Vitamin A......... 132 IU
Protein............. 1 g	Vitamin C.......... 1 mg
Total fat............ 4 g	Calcium............ 25 mg
Saturated fat....... *0.5 g*	*Sodium*........... *113 mg*
Cholesterol......... *1 mg*	Iron............. 0.1 mg

SALADS

Seasoned Salad Dressing

Skill Level: Intermediate   Yield: 1 cup   1 serving = 2½ tablespoons

INGREDIENTS
- 2 tablespoons olive oil
- 1 garlic clove, chopped
- ½ teaspoon dried oregano, crumbled
- ½ teaspoon paprika
- ¼ teaspoon salt
- ¼ teaspoon pepper
- ⅛ teaspoon cayenne pepper
- ⅔ cup water
- 1½ teaspoons cornstarch
- 2 tablespoons plus 1 teaspoon wine vinegar

EQUIPMENT
- small bowl
- small whisk
- measuring spoons
- cutting board
- dough scraper
- chef's knife
- small saucepan
- liquid measuring cup
- wooden spoon
- hot pads
- covered glass jar

1. In a small bowl, whisk together oil, garlic, oregano, paprika, salt, pepper, and cayenne. Set aside.
2. Combine a few tablespoons of the water with cornstarch in a small saucepan and stir until smooth with a wooden spoon. Stir in remaining water and vinegar. Place over medium-high heat and bring mixture to a boil.
3. Add oil mixture to the saucepan and stir with the wooden spoon for 1 minute. Remove from heat. Cool.
4. Transfer mixture to a glass jar, cover and chill.

NUTRITIONAL INFORMATION

Calories per serving	44	Fiber	0 g
Carbohydrate	1 g	Vitamin A	0 IU
Protein	0 g	Vitamin C	0 mg
Total fat	5 g	Calcium	1 mg
Saturated fat	*0.6 g*	*Sodium*	*89 mg*
Cholesterol	*0 mg*	Iron	0 mg

FRUITS

Ape Over Apples And Grapes

Skill Level: Beginner   Serves 3

INGREDIENTS
- 1 apple
- 1 tablespoon fresh lemon juice
- ½ cup seedless grapes
- 3 tablespoons low-fat vanilla custard-style yogurt

EQUIPMENT
- apple corer and slicer
- cutting board
- small, sharp knife
- serrated knife
- juicer
- bowl
- measuring spoons
- spoons
- dry measuring cups

1. Core apple and cut into wedges with apple corer and slicer. Dice apple slices into chunks with small, sharp knife, then place the chunks in a bowl.
2. Add lemon juice to the bowl, and toss so that apple chunks are coated to prevent browning.
3. Slice grapes in half, then add to apple chunks.
4. Add yogurt to the fruit, and toss to coat.
5. Chill.

NUTRITIONAL INFORMATION

Calories per serving 56	**Fiber............. 0.5 g**
Carbohydrate .... 12 g	Vitamin A .... 60 IU
Protein .... 2 g	Vitamin C .... 6 mg
Total fat .... 1 g	Calcium........... 58 mg
Saturated fat .... 0.3 g	Sodium .... 21 mg
Cholesterol.......... 2 mg	Iron .... 0.2 mg

FRUITS

Apple Cartwheels

Skill Level: Intermediate   Serves 8

INGREDIENTS
- 8 medium-size Red Delicious apples
- 1 cup natural peanut butter
- ¼ cup unsweetened cocoa powder
- ¼ cup raisins
- 3 tablespoons honey

EQUIPMENT
- apple corer
- dry measuring cups
- measuring spoons
- small mixing bowl
- spoon
- rubber spatula
- plastic wrap
- small, sharp knife
- cutting board

1. Remove core from each apple, leaving a hole 1 inch in diameter.
2. Combine peanut butter, cocoa, raisins, and honey in a small mixing bowl. Stir together with a spoon.
3. Using a rubber spatula, fill the center of each apple with the peanut butter mixture.
4. Wrap the apple in plastic wrap, then chill in a refrigerator for at least 2 hours.
5. When ready to serve, slice the apples crosswise into ½-inch slices.

NUTRITIONAL INFORMATION

Calories per serving 334	**Fiber**. . . . . **1.8 g**
Carbohydrate . . . . 39 g	Vitamin A . . . . 76 IU
Protein . . . . **9 g**	Vitamin C . . . . 8 mg
Total fat. . . . . 17 g	Calcium. . . . . 35 mg
Saturated fat . . . . *3.4 g*	*Sodium*. . . . . *197 mg*
Cholesterol. . . . . *0 mg*	Iron . . . . 1.0 mg

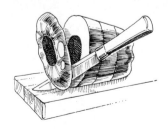

FRUITS

Apple Strudel

Skill Level: Advanced   Yield: 2 strudels; serves 12

INGREDIENTS
- 2 pounds apples (Red Delicious, Rome Beauty, Granny Smith, or a combination)
- ⅓ cup raisins
- ⅓ cup sugar
- 1 teaspoon cinnamon
- nonstick vegetable cooking spray
- 8 sheets phyllo dough
- 6 tablespoons margarine, melted and cooled
- 1 egg white, slightly beaten
- 6 tablespoons graham cracker crumbs, divided

EQUIPMENT
- peeler
- cutting board
- apple corer and slicer
- small, sharp knife
- large bowl
- dry measuring cups
- measuring spoons
- mixing spoon
- baking sheet
- 3 dish towels
- small bowl
- spoon
- pastry brush
- hot pads

1. Peel apples with a peeler, then core and slice them with an apple corer and slicer. Cut apple slices into small chunks using a small, sharp knife.
2. In a large bowl, combine apple chunks, raisins, sugar, and cinnamon.
3. Preheat oven to 375°F. Coat a baking sheet with nonstick vegetable cooking spray.
4. Unfold sheets of phyllo dough on work surface, and keep it covered with a damp dish towel to prevent it from drying out.
5. Combine margarine with egg white in a small bowl. Stir together.
6. Lay out a clean dish towel on work surface. Place one sheet of phyllo dough lengthwise on the towel. Using a pastry brush, lightly brush entire surface of dough with margarine mixture, and sprinkle with 1 tablespoon graham cracker crumbs. Repeat process 2 more times, ending with a fourth layer of phyllo dough.

Continued on next page

FRUITS

7. Spread half the apple mixture along the bottom quarter of the dough, leaving 1½ inches uncovered on sides and bottom.
8. Fold sides of phyllo dough inward over apples. Roll dough up into a cylinder about 3 inches wide, lifting the edge of the dish towel to help it fold. Brush the seam with margarine, and roll strudel onto prepared baking sheet. Brush remaining surface of strudel with margarine. Cover it with a damp cloth while making the second apple strudel.
9. Bake for 20 to 25 minutes, or until golden brown. Slice each strudel into sixths and serve warm.

NUTRITIONAL INFORMATION

Calories per serving 165	**Fiber. . . . . 0.7 g**
Carbohydrate . . . . 27 g	Vitamin A. . . . . 275 IU
Protein . . . . 1 g	Vitamin C . . . . 4 mg
Total fat . . . . 7 g	Calcium. . . . . 14 mg
Saturated fat . . . . 1.3 g	Sodium. . . . . 132 mg
Cholesterol. . . . . 0 mg	Iron . . . . 0.4 mg

FRUITS

Baked Apple Chunks

Skill Level: Advanced   Serves 8

INGREDIENTS
- 1 quart water (for apple slices)
- 2 teaspoons fresh lemon juice
- 6 Rome Beauty apples
- 3 tablespoons brown sugar
- ⅓ cup peach jam
- ¼ cup water (for glaze)

EQUIPMENT
- large mixing bowl
- liquid measuring cup
- cutting board
- serrated knife
- juicer
- measuring spoons
- apple corer and slicer
- small, sharp knife
- 11×8×2-inch baking dish
- dry measuring cups
- 2 wooden spoons
- hot pads
- small saucepan

1. Preheat oven to 400°F.
2. Combine 1 quart water with lemon juice in a large mixing bowl.
3. Core and slice apples with apple corer and slicer.
4. Cut apple wedges into ½-inch chunks. As they are cut, place apple chunks in lemon water to prevent them from turning brown.
5. Remove apple chunks from water and place in an 11×8×2-inch baking dish. Add brown sugar and toss apples to coat using 2 wooden spoons.
6. Bake for about 20 minutes or until apples are tender and edges are lightly browned.
7. While apples are cooking, combine the jam and ¼ cup water in a small saucepan. Place saucepan over low heat and stir with a wooden spoon for about 5 minutes or until mixture thins.

Continued on next page

FRUITS

8. After removing the apple chunks from the oven, drizzle the peach glaze over them, then toss to coat with wooden spoons. Serve hot.

NUTRITIONAL INFORMATION

Calories per serving 117	**Fiber............. 0.9 g**
Carbohydrate .... 30 g	Vitamin A .... 57 IU
Protein .... 0 g	Vitamin C .... 8 mg
Total fat .... 0 g	Calcium........... 15 mg
Saturated fat .... *0 g*	*Sodium* .... *4 mg*
Cholesterol.......... *0 mg*	Iron .... 0.5 mg

Charoses

Skill Level: Beginner Serves 10

INGREDIENTS
- ¾ cup white grape juice
- 5 large apples
- ¾ cup chopped pecans
- ¼ cup sugar
- 1 teaspoon cinnamon

EQUIPMENT
- liquid measuring cup
- mixing bowl
- apple corer and slicer
- small, sharp knife
- cutting board
- 2 mixing spoons
- dry measuring cups
- measuring spoons

1. Pour grape juice into a mixing bowl.
2. Core and slice apples with an apple corer and slicer. With a small, sharp knife, cut apples into small chunks. Add apples to grape juice, then toss to coat with mixing spoons.
3. Add nuts, sugar, and cinnamon. Toss to combine.
4. Cover and chill before serving.

NOTE: Charoses is a traditional Passover dish.

NUTRITIONAL INFORMATION

Calories per serving 127	Fiber .... 0.7 g
Carbohydrate .... 20 g	Vitamin A .... 49 IU
Protein .... 1 g	Vitamin C .... 4 mg
Total fat .... 6 g	Calcium .... 13 mg
Saturated fat .... 0.5 g	Sodium .... 1 mg
Cholesterol .... 0 mg	Iron .... 0.4 mg

FRUITS

Cranberry Orange Sauce

Skill Level: Intermediate   Serves 12
Conventional and Microwave Methods

INGREDIENTS
12 ounces cranberries, washed
1 cup sugar
½ cup water
½ cup fresh orange juice
½ cup slivered almonds

Conventional Method

EQUIPMENT
colander
dry measuring cups
liquid measuring cup
serrated knife
cutting board
juicer
saucepan
wooden spoon
hot pads

1. Combine cranberries, sugar, water, and orange juice in a saucepan.
2. Cook over high heat until the berry skins pop open, about 10 minutes.
3. Skim foam off the surface. Remove saucepan from heat. Add the almonds and cool. See note to mold Cranberry Orange Sauce or just store it in the refrigerator.

Microwave Method

EQUIPMENT
colander
dry measuring cups
liquid measuring cup
serrated knife
cutting board
juicer
8-cup microwave-safe measure, or deep, 2-quart microwave-safe bowl
wooden spoon
hot pads

1. Stir cranberries, sugar, water, and orange juice together in an 8-cup measure or 2-quart bowl.
2. Cook cranberries uncovered on high (100%) power for 10 minutes.
3. Remove cranberries from microwave. Stir almonds into mixture. See note to mold Cranberry Orange Sauce or just store it in the refrigerator.

NOTE: Cranberry Orange Sauce can be molded in a festive mold. Coat mold lightly with nonstick vegetable cooking spray. Pour mixture into mold, cover, and chill for at least 5 hours. Loosen sides of mold by guiding a knife around the edge. Place a serving plate over the mold, then carefully invert the mold onto the plate.

NUTRITIONAL INFORMATION

Calories per serving 118	**Fiber............ 0.5 g**
Carbohydrate .... 22 g	Vitamin A .... 34 IU
Protein .... 3 g	Vitamin C .... 9 mg
Total fat .... 3 g	Calcium........... 17 mg
Saturated fat........ *0.3 g*	*Sodium* .... *1 mg*
Cholesterol.......... *0 g*	Iron.............. 0.4 mg

FRUITS

Fresh Fruit Salad

Skill Level: Intermediate   Serves 8

INGREDIENTS
1   orange, peeled
½   grapefruit, peeled
½   pound seedless grapes
1   cup blueberries
½   cantaloupe, seeds removed
1   cup strawberries
½   pineapple, peeled and cored
½   watermelon
fresh mint sprigs

EQUIPMENT
cutting board
sharp knife
large bowl
paper towels or dish cloth
melon baller
small, sharp knife
serrated knife
ballpoint pen or toothpick
large spoon

1. Divide orange and grapefruit into sections and place in a large bowl.

2. Wash grapes and blueberries and pat dry with a paper towel or dishcloth. Add to orange and grapefruit.

3. Use a melon baller to make cantaloupe balls.

4. Wash strawberries, pat dry and remove their stems. Cut each in half and add to fruit.

5. Place pineapple half flat side down on cutting board. Use a serrated knife to cut pineapple into long sticks, then cut pineapple sticks into chunks. Add to bowl of fruit.

6. With adult supervision, carve watermelon serving bowl by outlining a design on the outside rind with a ballpoint pen or toothpick. Cut rind pattern with a small, sharp knife. Remove watermelon seeds, then make cubes or balls from

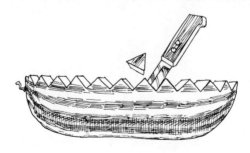

the watermelon. Add to the bowl of fruit. Mix the fruits together with a large spoon.
7. Fill watermelon bowl with fruit. Garnish with mint.

NUTRITIONAL INFORMATION	
Calories per serving 249	**Fiber............. 2.4 g**
Carbohydrate .... 53 g	**Vitamin A....... 2969 IU**
Protein .... 4 g	**Vitamin C .... 94 mg**
Total fat .... 3 g	Calcium........... 59 mg
Saturated fat .... *0 g*	*Sodium* .... *15 mg*
Cholesterol.......... *0 mg*	Iron............. 1.2 mg

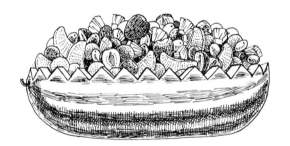

FRUITS

Melon Melody

Skill Level: Beginner   Serves 12

INGREDIENTS
½ cantaloupe
½ honeydew melon
½ watermelon
6 sprigs fresh mint

EQUIPMENT
cutting board
large knife
spoon
melon baller
large mixing bowl

1. Clean out the seeds of the cantaloupe and honeydew melon with a spoon.
2. Using a melon baller, scoop out balls of cantaloupe and honeydew. Combine in a large mixing bowl.
3. Remove as many seeds as possible from the watermelon. Scoop out watermelon balls, and combine with the cantaloupe and honeydew.
4. Garnish with fresh mint.

NUTRITIONAL INFORMATION

Calories per serving 128
Carbohydrate . . . . 30 g
Protein . . . . 2 g
Total fat . . . . 1 g
Saturated fat . . . . 0 g
Cholesterol . . . . 0 mg
Fiber . . . . **1.4 g**
Vitamin A . . . . **1913 IU**
Vitamin C . . . . **54 mg**
Calcium . . . . 31 mg
Sodium . . . . 14 mg
Iron . . . . 0.6 mg

FRUITS

Strawberry Soufflé

Skill Level: Intermediate   Serves 6

INGREDIENTS
1½ teaspoons margarine
3   tablespoons sifted powdered sugar, divided
2   10-ounce packages frozen sweetened strawberries, thawed, divided
1   tablespoon cornstarch, divided
5   egg whites
⅛   teaspoon salt
pinch of cream of tartar
2   tablespoons sugar

EQUIPMENT
7-inch soufflé dish
measuring spoons
blender or food processor
rubber spatula
small saucepan
hot pads
wooden spoons
large mixing bowl
electric mixer
rubber spatula

1. Preheat oven to 350°F.
2. Coat a 7-inch soufflé dish with margarine and dust with 2 tablespoons powdered sugar.
3. Puree 1 package strawberries in a blender or food processor. With machine running, add 1½ teaspoons cornstarch to the strawberries.
4. In a small saucepan, cook strawberry mixture over low heat until thick and frothy, about 9 minutes. Cool.
5. Combine egg whites, salt, and cream of tartar in a dry, large mixing bowl and beat with an electric mixer on high speed until soft peaks form. Slowly add sugar and beat just until stiff peaks form.
6. Gently fold egg whites into strawberries, using a rubber spatula.
7. Transfer strawberry mixture to the prepared soufflé dish. Bake for 20 minutes.

Continued on next page

FRUITS

8. While soufflé is baking, repeat steps 3 and 4 to make sauce to serve with soufflé.
9. Spoon sauce onto serving plates. As soon as soufflé is removed from oven, spoon soufflé on top of sauce and serve.

NUTRITIONAL INFORMATION

Calories per serving 131	**Fiber.............. 0.6 g**
Carbohydrate .... 29 g	Vitamin A .... 65 IU
Protein .... 3 g	**Vitamin C .... 37 mg**
Total fat .... 1 g	Calcium............ 15 mg
Saturated fat........ 0.2 g	*Sodium .... 98 mg*
Cholesterol.......... 0 mg	Iron.............. 0.5 mg

Summer Peach Crisp

Skill Level: Advanced   Serves 9

INGREDIENTS
nonstick vegetable cooking spray
5   large, ripe peaches (4 cups slices)
1   teaspoon fresh lemon juice
1   cup rolled oats
½   cup brown sugar
¼   cup all-purpose flour
¼   cup toasted wheat germ
1   teaspoon cinnamon
¼   cup margarine, melted

EQUIPMENT
8×8×2-inch baking pan
small saucepan
hot pads
3 mixing bowls
slotted spoon
small, sharp knife
cutting board
serrated knife
juicer
measuring spoons
dry measuring cups
mixing spoon

1. Preheat oven to 350°F. Coat an 8×8×2-inch baking pan with nonstick vegetable cooking spray.
2. To peel peaches, bring a small saucepan of water to a boil, and fill a mixing bowl with ice water. Place a peach on a slotted spoon, then gently lower it into boiling water for 30 seconds to 1 minute. Use the slotted spoon to transfer peach to mixing bowl with ice water. Repeat with remaining peaches. Remove cooled peaches from water. Slip off the skins with gentle fingertip pressure.
3. Use a small, sharp knife to slice peaches. Place peach slices in a second mixing bowl, then toss them with lemon juice to prevent browning. Set aside.
4. Combine oats, brown sugar, flour, wheat germ, and cinnamon in a third mixing bowl. Use a mixing spoon to stir the ingredients. Add margarine to oat mixture and stir until well blended.

Continued on next page

FRUITS

5. Spread peaches in prepared pan. Cover evenly with oat mixture.
6. Bake 30 to 35 minutes or until lightly browned.
7. Serve warm.

NUTRITIONAL INFORMATION	
Calories per serving 169	Fiber .... 0.4 g
Carbohydrate .... 27 g	Vitamin A .... 467 IU
Protein .... 3 g	Vitamin C .... 3 mg
Total fat .... 6 g	Calcium .... 21 mg
Saturated fat .... *1 g*	*Sodium* .... *63 mg*
Cholesterol .... *0 mg*	Iron .... 1.1 mg

FRUITS

Sweet and Tart Pineapple

Skill Level: Advanced   Serves 6

INGREDIENTS
nonstick vegetable cooking spray
1   fresh pineapple
¼   cup brown sugar or honey

EQUIPMENT
baking sheet
cutting board
sharp knife
small, sharp knife
measuring spoons
hot pads

1. Preheat oven to 300°F. Lightly coat a baking sheet with nonstick vegetable cooking spray.
2. Lay the pineapple on its side and cut a thick slice from each end using a sharp knife. Stand the pineapple upright on a cutting board. Cut the peel off by slicing along the edge from the top downward with a sharp knife, continuing around the entire pineapple. Remove any "eyes" in the pineapple with a small, sharp knife. Place pineapple on its side and slice it into 1-inch rounds. Cut each round in half, then cut a triangular wedge from the center to remove the core.
3. Place pineapple wedges on prepared baking sheet. Sprinkle each with brown sugar or honey.
4. Bake for 12 minutes. Serve warm.

NUTRITIONAL INFORMATION

Calories per serving..... 82	Fiber .... 0.4 g
Carbohydrate .... 21 g	Vitamin A .... 17 IU
Protein .... 0 g	Vitamin C .... 12 mg
Total fat .... 0 g	Calcium............ 6 mg
Saturated fat .... *0 g*	*Sodium* .... *1 mg*
Cholesterol......... *0 mg*	Iron............. 0.4 mg

CAKES

"Full Of Surprises" Chocolate Cake (Halloween)

Skill Level: Intermediate   Serves 24

INGREDIENTS
- 2 cups sugar
- 1½ cups all-purpose flour
- 1½ cups whole wheat flour
- ½ cup unsweetened cocoa powder
- 2 teaspoons baking soda
- 1 teaspoon salt
- 2 cups water
- 1 cup safflower oil
- 2 tablespoons white vinegar
- 2 teaspoons vanilla
- ¼ cup powdered sugar for decoration
- raisins

EQUIPMENT
- 24 1½-inch paper squares
- 24 1½-inch foil squares
- ballpoint pens
- coins or a dollar bill (optional)
- sifter
- large mixing bowl
- dry measuring cups
- measuring spoons
- liquid measuring cup
- spoon
- 13×9×2-inch baking pan
- hot pads
- cake tester
- parchment paper
- scissors

1. Preheat oven to 350°F.
2. Write messages (Boo!, Happy Halloween!, etc.) or draw pictures (ghosts, pumpkins, witches) on squares of paper. Fold into smaller squares and wrap in foil. For bonus surprises, wrap coins or a dollar bill into a foil square.
3. In a large mixing bowl, sift together sugar, all-purpose flour, whole wheat flour, cocoa, baking soda, and salt.
4. Add water, oil, vinegar, and vanilla to the sifted ingredients. Stir with a spoon to combine. Add secret messages and stir to distribute evenly.
5. Pour batter into a 13×9×2-inch baking pan and submerge all the packets.

CAKES

6. Bake for 40 to 45 minutes, or until a cake tester inserted into the center comes out clean.
7. Cool cake in the baking pan on a cooling rack.
8. On a 13×9-inch piece of parchment paper, draw a large ghost or a few small ghosts. Cut out the ghost shape(s) with scissors to create a stencil. (See illustration.)
9. Place stencil over the cooled cake. Sift powdered sugar over the cut-out ghost(s). (See illustration.)
10. Carefully remove stencil to reveal ghostly pattern. Use raisins to make eyes for the ghost(s). Serve directly from the cake pan.

NUTRITIONAL INFORMATION

Calories per serving 208	Fiber 0.2g
Carbohydrate .... 30 g	Vitamin A .... 0 IU
Protein .... 2 g	Vitamin C .... 0 mg
Total fat .... 9 g	Calcium............ 6 mg
Saturated fat........ *0.8 g*	*Sodium*............ *232 mg*
Cholesterol.......... *0 mg*	Iron .... 0.6 mg

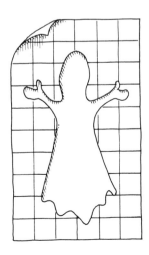

CAKES

Gingerbread

Skill Level: Intermediate   Serves 10

INGREDIENTS
nonstick vegetable cooking spray
½   cup whole wheat flour
½   cup all-purpose flour
1   teaspoon baking powder
¼   teaspoon baking soda
¼   teaspoon salt
1   teaspoon ground ginger
½   teaspoon cinnamon
¼   teaspoon nutmeg
⅓   cup safflower oil
⅓   cup apple juice
⅓   cup "lite" maple syrup
⅓   cup sugar
2   egg whites, slightly beaten
2   tablespoons powdered sugar

EQUIPMENT
8-inch round cake pan
2 mixing bowls
dry measuring cups
measuring spoons
rubber spatula
liquid measuring cup
whisk
hot pads
cake tester
cooling rack
serving plate
paper doily

1. Preheat oven to 350°F. Coat an 8-inch round cake pan with nonstick vegetable cooking spray.
2. In a mixing bowl, stir together whole wheat flour, all-purpose flour, baking powder, baking soda, salt, ginger, cinnamon, and nutmeg with a rubber spatula. Set aside.
3. In a second mixing bowl, stir oil, apple juice, and syrup together with a whisk. Add sugar and egg whites and whisk until well combined.
4. Stir dry ingredients into wet mixture using a rubber spatula until well combined.
5. Pour batter into prepared pan. Bake for 25 minutes or until tester inserted into cake comes out clean.
6. Place pan on cooling rack for about 5 minutes. Invert cake onto serving plate.

7. Place a paper doily on top of the cake. Dust top with powdered sugar. Gently press powdered sugar into the doily's spaces using fingertips. Carefully remove doily to reveal powdered sugar pattern on cake.
8. Serve warm or at room temperature.

NUTRITIONAL INFORMATION

Calories per serving 174	**Fiber** .... 1.2 g
Carbohydrate .... 26 g	Vitamin A .... 0 IU
Protein .... 2 g	Vitamin C .... 0 mg
Total fat .... 7 g	Calcium .... 10 mg
Saturated fat .... *0.7 g*	*Sodium* .... *113 mg*
Cholesterol .... *0 mg*	Iron .... 0.7 mg

CAKES

Happy Birthday Cake (White Cake)

Skill Level: Advanced   Serves 12

INGREDIENTS
nonstick vegetable cooking spray
2½ cups pastry flour
2 teaspoons baking powder
¼ teaspoon salt
1 cup sugar, divided
½ cup margarine
1½ teaspoons vanilla
1¼ cups water
4 egg whites

Icing

1 cup powdered sugar
¼ cup margarine
1 tablespoon low-fat (2%) milk
¼ cup all-fruit strawberry jam

EQUIPMENT
two 8-inch round cake pans
sifter
dry measuring cups
measuring spoons
3 mixing bowls
large mixing bowl
electric mixer
liquid measuring cup
rubber spatula
hot pads
cooling racks
2 dull knives or spreaders

1. Preheat oven to 350°F.
2. Coat two 8-inch round cake pans with nonstick vegetable cooking spray.
3. Sift flour, baking powder, and salt together into a mixing bowl. Set aside.
4. In a large mixing bowl, cream together ½ cup sugar, margarine, and vanilla with an electric mixer on high speed, about 1 minute or until fluffy.
5. Alternate adding ⅓ of the flour mixture and ⅓ of the water to creamed mixture, beginning with flour, mixing well after each addition. Push batter from sides with rubber spatula. Set aside.
6. In a dry mixing bowl, beat egg whites with electric mixer while gradually adding ½ cup sugar, until stiff peaks form, about 2 minutes.

CAKES

7. Gently fold egg whites into batter using a spatula.
8. Pour batter into prepared pans.
9. Bake for 20 to 27 minutes or until tester inserted in middle comes out clean.
10. Cool cakes in pans about 5 minutes, then invert them onto cooling racks.
11. To prepare icing, combine powdered sugar, margarine, and milk in a mixing bowl. Beat with an electric mixer on low speed until combined. Then increase power to medium and beat about 30 seconds until fluffy.
12. Place one cake layer on a serving plate. Spread strawberry jam on top of it with a dull knife or spreader.
13. Place the second cake layer on top. Spread top and sides with icing. Serve.

NUTRITIONAL INFORMATION

Calories per serving	300	Fiber	0 g
Carbohydrate	47 g	Vitamin A	468 IU
Protein	3 g	Vitamin C	0 mg
Total fat	12 g	Calcium	18 mg
Saturated fat	1.8 g	Sodium	271 mg
Cholesterol	0 mg	Iron	0.2 mg

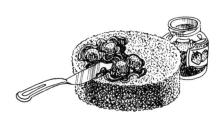

CAKES

Jack-O-Lantern Cake (Halloween)

Skill Level: Advanced   Serves 20

INGREDIENTS
nonstick vegetable cooking spray
1½ teaspoons cinnamon, divided
2   cups all-purpose flour
1½ cups whole wheat flour
1½ cups sugar
2   teaspoons baking soda
½   teaspoon salt
1   teaspoon nutmeg
2   cups cooked or canned pumpkin
1   cup safflower oil
2   eggs plus 3 egg whites, lightly beaten
⅔   cup hot water
½   cup chopped pecans

Icing
8   ounces light cream cheese
2   tablespoons brown sugar
1   tablespoon low-fat (2%) milk
½   teaspoon cinnamon
green food coloring
yellow food coloring

EQUIPMENT
10-inch nonstick bundt pan
measuring spoons
large mixing bowl
dry measuring cups
sifter
liquid measuring cup
electric mixer
rubber spatula
hot pads
cake tester
cooling rack
2 serving plates
serrated knife
small mixing bowl
small bowl
2 spoons
pastry bag with a small open star tip

1. Preheat oven to 350°F. Coat a 10-inch nonstick bundt pan with nonstick vegetable cooking spray and sprinkle with ½ teaspoon cinnamon.

2. Into a large mixing bowl, sift together all-purpose flour, whole wheat flour, sugar, baking soda, salt, 1 teaspoon cinnamon, and nutmeg.

CAKES

3. Add pumpkin, oil, eggs and egg whites, and hot water to dry ingredients. Blend with an electric mixer, starting on low speed and increasing to medium, about 2 to 3 minutes. Stir in pecans with a rubber spatula.
4. Pour mixture into prepared bundt pan. Bake for 1 hour, or until a tester inserted in center of cake comes out clean.
5. Using hot pads, place cake on a cooling rack and cool for 5 minutes in the pan. Invert cake onto the rack to cool completely.
6. Invert cake again onto a plate. Using a serrated knife, slice ½ inch off the bottom of the cake.
7. Invert cake right side up on second serving plate. Fill center hole of cake with pieces cut from the bottom slice.

Icing and Decoration:

1. In a small mixing bowl, combine cream cheese, brown sugar, milk, and cinnamon. Cream together with an electric mixer until smooth.
2. Place a rounded ¼ cup icing in a small bowl. Add a few drops of green food coloring to the icing and stir to distribute color evenly.
3. Spoon green icing on top of cake's center. Using your fingers, shape green icing into a stem for the pumpkin.
4. Add a few drops of yellow food coloring to the remaining icing and stir together. Put icing in a pastry bag fitted with a small open star tip. Pipe a Halloween face on the Jack-O-Lantern Cake.

NUTRITIONAL INFORMATION	
Calories per serving 297	**Fiber.** .... 0.6 g
Carbohydrate .... 34 g	**Vitamin A.** .... 1725 IU
Protein .... 5 g	Vitamin C .... 1 mg
Total fat. .... 16 g	Calcium. .... 26 mg
Saturated fat .... *3 g*	*Sodium.* .... *196 mg*
Cholesterol .... *36 mg*	Iron . . . . 0.9 mg

CAKES

Parve-Honey Cake

Skill Level: Intermediate   Serves 18

INGREDIENTS
- nonstick vegetable cooking spray
- 2½ cups all-purpose flour
- 1 tablespoon baking powder
- ½ teaspoon baking soda
- 1 teaspoon cinnamon
- ¼ teaspoon salt
- ¾ cup sugar
- ½ cup safflower oil
- 4 egg substitutes
- 1 cup honey
- 1 cup fresh orange juice

EQUIPMENT
- 10-inch nonstick bundt pan or two 9×5-inch loaf pans
- 2 mixing bowls
- sifter
- dry measuring cups
- measuring spoons
- electric mixer
- liquid measuring cup
- rubber spatula
- cutting board
- serrated knife
- juicer
- hot pads
- cake tester
- cooling rack

1. Preheat oven to 325°F. Coat a 10-inch nonstick bundt pan or two 9×5-inch loaf pans with nonstick vegetable cooking spray.
2. Sift together flour, baking powder, baking soda, cinnamon, and salt into a mixing bowl. Set aside.
3. In a second mixing bowl, cream together sugar and oil with an electric mixer on high speed for about 1 minute.
4. Add egg substitutes, and mix on high speed 2 to 3 minutes until frothy.
5. Add honey, and mix well about 1 minute on high speed.
6. Add about ⅓ of the flour mixture and ⅓ cup of orange juice to batter at a time, mixing well after each addition. Scrape batter from sides with rubber spatula.

7. Pour batter into prepared bundt pan or loaf pans. Bake for 50 minutes, or until tester inserted in center of cake comes out clean.
8. Invert pan(s) on rack to let cake cool.

NOTE: Jewish people who observe the Kosher dietary laws do not eat meat and dairy foods at the same meal. *Parve* designates a recipe or food that may be served with either meat or dairy foods.

NUTRITIONAL INFORMATION

Calories per serving 216	Fiber................ 0 g
Carbohydrate .... 37 g	Vitamin A.......... 236 IU
Protein .... 3 g	Vitamin C .... 5 mg
Total fat .... 7 g	Calcium............ 10 mg
Saturated fat .... *0.6 g*	*Sodium*............ *120 mg*
Cholesterol.......... *0 mg*	Iron .... 0.8 mg

COOKIES

Apple Jack Cookies

Skill Level: Intermediate   Yield: 36   1 serving = 1 cookie

INGREDIENTS
nonstick vegetable cooking spray
2   cups all-purpose flour
1   teaspoon baking powder
¼   teaspoon baking soda
¾   teaspoon cinnamon
½   cup margarine
½   cup sugar
1   egg
½   cup unsweetened applesauce
1   teaspoon vanilla
⅓   cup chopped pecans

EQUIPMENT
2 baking sheets
2 mixing bowls
sifter
dry measuring cups
measuring spoons
electric mixer
rubber spatula
2 spoons
hot pads
cooling racks
metal spatula

1. Preheat oven to 400°F. Coat 2 baking sheets with nonstick vegetable cooking spray.
2. Sift together flour, baking powder, baking soda, and cinnamon in a mixing bowl. Set aside.
3. In a second mixing bowl, cream margarine and sugar together until fluffy by using an electric mixer on high speed for 1 minute.
4. Add egg, applesauce, and vanilla, then beat with the electric mixer on high speed for 1 minute, until the mixture is creamy. Push batter from sides with a rubber spatula.
5. Add dry ingredients. Beat with electric mixer on high speed until well blended, about 1 to 1½ minutes. Add pecans, then beat about 20 seconds to combine.
6. Drop dough by teaspoonfuls 1½ inches apart onto prepared baking sheet using 2 spoons, one to scoop the dough and one to push it from the spoon onto baking sheet.

7. Bake for 10 minutes or until lightly browned.

8. Transfer baking sheets to cooling racks, and cool for 10 minutes. Loosen cookies with a metal spatula while still warm. Remove when cool.

NUTRITIONAL INFORMATION

Calories per serving..... 67	Fiber............... 0 g
Carbohydrate .... 8 g	Vitamin A......... 114 IU
Protein .... 1 g	Vitamin C .... 0 mg
Total fat .... 3 g	Calcium............ 4 mg
Saturated fat........ 0.6 g	*Sodium .... 47 mg*
Cholesterol.......... 8 mg	Iron .... 0.1 mg

COOKIES

Easter Fudge Baskets

Skill Level: Intermediate   Yield: 36   1 serving = 1 basket

INGREDIENTS
Fudge Balls (see page 259)
1 cup multicolored yogurt-covered raisins

EQUIPMENT
3 12-cup miniature muffin tins
miniature muffin paper liners
spoon

1. Follow Fudge Ball recipe (page 259) through Step 4.
2. Place paper liners in muffin tins.
3. Spoon mixture into muffin cups, then use a spoon or your thumb to make an indentation in center to form a cup. Store in the refrigerator.
4. At serving time, place cups with liners on a serving tray. Fill fudge baskets with yogurt-covered raisins.

NUTRITIONAL INFORMATION

Calories per serving	81	Fiber	0.1 g
Carbohydrate	14 g	Vitamin A	85 IU
Protein	1 g	Vitamin C	0 mg
Total fat	3 g	Calcium	12 mg
Saturated fat	0.4 g	*Sodium*	33 mg
Cholesterol	0 mg	Iron	0.4 mg

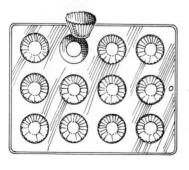

Fudge Balls

Skill Level: Intermediate Yield: 6 dozen 1 serving = 2 balls

INGREDIENTS
- 1 cup sugar
- ½ cup low-fat (2%) milk
- 6 tablespoons margarine
- ¼ cup unsweetened cocoa powder
- 1 teaspoon vanilla
- 3 cups rolled oats

EQUIPMENT
- dry measuring cups
- liquid measuring cup
- cutting board
- small, sharp knife
- heavy saucepan
- hot pads
- wooden spoon
- measuring spoons
- 2 spoons
- wax paper
- airtight container

1. Combine sugar, milk, margarine, and cocoa in a heavy saucepan. Bring mixture to a boil over medium heat, stirring frequently.
2. Continue to boil for 5 to 6 minutes, stirring frequently, until mixture thickens to a sauce consistency.
3. Remove cocoa mixture from the stove to a heatproof surface. Add vanilla and oats and stir to combine.
4. Drop mixture by teaspoons onto wax paper using 2 spoons, one to scoop batter, the other to push batter onto wax paper. Let dough cool and harden slightly, then roll into small balls using your hands. Store in the refrigerator in an airtight container.

NUTRITIONAL INFORMATION

Calories per serving..... 67	Fiber .... 0.4 g
Carbohydrate .... 10 g	Vitamin A .... 85 IU
Protein .... 1 g	Vitamin C .... 0 mg
Total fat .... 3 g	Calcium .... 10 mg
Saturated fat........ 0.4 g	*Sodium* .... 32 mg
Cholesterol......... 0 mg	Iron .... 0.3 mg

COOKIES

Ginger Faces

Skill Level: Intermediate   Yield: 4 dozen   1 serving = 1 cookie

INGREDIENTS
- ½ cup margarine
- ½ cup brown sugar
- ½ cup molasses
- ¼ cup water
- 2½ cups all-purpose flour
- ¾ teaspoon salt
- ¾ teaspoon baking soda
- 1 teaspoon ground ginger
- ½ teaspoon cinnamon
- ¼ teaspoon nutmeg
- ⅛ teaspoon allspice
- nonstick vegetable cooking spray
- ¼ cup raisins
- ¼ cup carob chips

EQUIPMENT
- large mixing bowl
- dry measuring cups
- liquid measuring cup
- electric mixer
- rubber spatula
- sifter
- measuring spoons
- plastic wrap or foil
- 2 baking sheets
- hot pads
- cooling racks
- metal spatula

1. In a large mixing bowl, cream margarine and brown sugar together with an electric mixer on high speed for 30 seconds.
2. Add molasses and water. Blend together for about 1 minute.
3. Sift flour, salt, baking soda, ginger, cinnamon, nutmeg, and allspice into batter. Beat with an electric mixer just until blended, about 1 minute, scraping batter from sides of bowl as needed with a rubber spatula.
4. Wrap the dough in plastic or foil and chill for several hours or overnight.
5. Preheat oven to 375°F. Coat 2 baking sheets with nonstick vegetable cooking spray.
6. Form dough into 1-inch balls and place them on prepared baking sheets, 2 inches apart. Press with palm to flatten.
7. Press raisins and carob chips into cookies to create eyes and mouths.

8. Bake for 8 to 12 minutes or until lightly browned on edges.

9. Place the baking sheets on cooling racks for 3 minutes, then remove cookies from baking sheets with a metal spatula and place them on cooling racks.

NUTRITIONAL INFORMATION

Calories per serving..... 59	Fiber............... 0 g
Carbohydrate .... 10 g	Vitamin A .... 80 IU
Protein .... 1 g	Vitamin C .... 0 mg
Total fat .... 2 g	Calcium........... 10 mg
Saturated fat........ *0.4 g*	*Sodium* .... *74 mg*
Cholesterol.......... *0 mg*	Iron............. 0.3 mg

COOKIES

Jack-O-Lantern Cookies (Halloween)

Skill Level: Advanced   Yield: 2½ dozen   1 serving = 1 cookie

INGREDIENTS
nonstick vegetable cooking spray
1 cup whole wheat flour
1½ cups all-purpose flour
1 tablespoon baking powder
½ teaspoon salt
1½ teaspoons pumpkin pie spice
¼ teaspoon ground ginger
1 cup margarine, room temperature
1 cup brown sugar
2 eggs
1 cup cooked or canned pumpkin
1 teaspoon vanilla
1 teaspoon fresh lemon juice
⅔ cup coarsely chopped walnuts, divided
Orange Frosting (see below)
60 candy corns
1 cup raisins

EQUIPMENT
2 baking sheets
dry measuring cups
measuring spoons
mixing bowl
sifter
large mixing bowl
electric mixer
cutting board
serrated knife
juicer
rubber spatula
2 spoons
hot pads
2 cooling racks
metal spatula
spreader or small spatula

1. Preheat oven to 375°F. Lightly coat 2 baking sheets with nonstick vegetable cooking spray.
2. Sift together whole wheat flour, all-purpose flour, baking powder, salt, pumpkin pie spice, and ginger into a mixing bowl. Set aside.
3. In a large mixing bowl, cream together margarine and brown sugar with an electric mixer on medium-high speed until blended, about 1 minute.
4. Beat eggs into margarine mixture, one at a time.
5. Add pumpkin, vanilla, and lemon juice, and beat until well combined. Push batter from sides with a rubber spatula.
6. Add flour mixture to batter and blend together until dough forms, about 1 minute. Stir ½ cup walnuts into dough with a rubber spatula.

COOKIES

7. Using 2 spoons, one to scoop dough and the other to push, drop cookie dough by tablespoons 2 inches apart on prepared baking sheets.
8. Bake for 12 to 14 minutes or until cookies are lightly browned. (Prepare frosting while cookies are baking.)
9. Place baking sheets on cooling racks. Loosen cookies with a metal spatula.
10. Spread cooled cookies with frosting and create faces using 2 candy corns for eyes, raisins for a mouth and nose, and a walnut piece for a stem.

Orange Frosting
Yield: about 3½ cups

INGREDIENTS	EQUIPMENT
½ cup margarine	mixing bowl
¼ cup fresh orange juice	cutting board
3 cups sifted powdered sugar	serrated knife
2 teaspoons vanilla	electric mixer
5 drops orange food coloring	dry measuring cups
	rubber spatula
	juicer
	measuring spoons

1. In a mixing bowl, beat margarine and orange juice with an electric mixer until smooth. Add powdered sugar a cup at a time, beating after each addition until mixture is smooth.
2. Add vanilla and orange food coloring. Beat together until light and fluffy, about 1 minute.

NUTRITIONAL INFORMATION

Calories per serving 240	Fiber . . . . 0.3 g
Carbohydrate . . . . 35 g	**Vitamin A** . . . . **918 IU**
Protein . . . . 2 g	Vitamin C . . . . 1 mg
Total fat. . . . . 11 g	Calcium. . . . . 22 mg
Saturated fat . . . . 2 g	*Sodium*. . . . . *194 mg*
Cholesterol. . . . . 18 mg	Iron . . . . 0.8 mg

Meringue Kisses

Skill Level: Intermediate   Yield: 24   1 serving = 1 meringue

INGREDIENTS
- 4 egg whites
- 1 cup sugar
- 2 tablespoons candy sprinkles

EQUIPMENT
- 2 baking sheets
- parchment paper
- mixing bowl
- electric mixer
- dry measuring cups
- rubber spatula
- large spoon
- pastry bag with ⅝-inch open star tip (optional)
- 2 spoons (optional)
- hot pads
- measuring spoons

1. Preheat oven to 200°F. Line 2 large baking sheets with parchment paper.
2. In a large, grease-free mixing bowl, beat the egg whites at medium speed with an electric mixer while gradually adding the sugar. When the egg whites form soft peaks, increase the mixer speed to medium-high. Beat another 5 to 6 minutes, until the meringue is thick, glossy, and forms firm peaks when the beaters are lifted. Scrape the sides of the bowl with a rubber spatula.
3. "Glue" the parchment paper to the baking sheet with a few pinches of meringue.
4. Spoon meringue into a pastry bag fitted with a ⅝-inch open star tip and pipe meringue onto parchment paper or drop meringues by teaspoonfuls using 2 spoons, one to scoop the meringue and the other to push it onto parchment paper. Sprinkle meringues with candy sprinkles.

5. Bake meringues for 2 hours—no peeking during baking! Turn oven off but do not open it. Let meringues cool in oven at least 1 hour or overnight. Carefully lift meringues from parchment.

NOTE: It is said that when Queen Elizabeth I tasted meringues for the first time, she kissed the napkin on which they had been served and named these charming delicacies "kisses."

NUTRITIONAL INFORMATION

Calories per serving	39	Fiber	0 g
Carbohydrate	10 g	Vitamin A	0 IU
Protein	1 g	Vitamin C	0 mg
Total fat	0 g	Calcium	1 mg
Saturated fat	*0 g*	*Sodium*	*8 mg*
Cholesterol	*0 mg*	Iron	0 mg

COOKIES

Oatmeal-Raisin Cookies

Skill Level: Intermediate   Yield: 2 dozen   1 serving = 1 cookie

INGREDIENTS
nonstick vegetable cooking spray
1½ cups rolled oats
½ cup whole wheat flour
½ teaspoon baking powder
¼ teaspoon salt
½ teaspoon cinnamon
⅓ cup margarine
½ cup brown sugar
1 egg
½ teaspoon vanilla
3 tablespoons low-fat (2%) milk
½ cup chopped walnuts
½ cup raisins

EQUIPMENT
2 baking sheets
2 large mixing bowls
dry measuring cups
measuring spoons
electric mixer
rubber spatula
2 spoons
hot pads
cooling racks
metal spatula

1. Preheat oven to 350°F. Coat 2 baking sheets with nonstick vegetable cooking spray.
2. In a large mixing bowl, stir together oats, flour, baking powder, salt, and cinnamon. Set aside.
3. Combine margarine and brown sugar in a second large mixing bowl and cream with an electric mixer at medium speed until fluffy, about 30 seconds to 1 minute. Scrape mixture from sides with a rubber spatula.
4. Add egg and vanilla to creamed mixture and beat at medium speed until combined, about 1 minute.
5. Add dry ingredients and milk to creamed mixture and beat well with electric mixer until dough forms, about 30 seconds.
6. With the spatula, stir in walnuts and raisins.
7. Drop dough onto prepared baking sheets by teaspoons using 2 spoons, one to scoop mixture and the second to push dough onto baking sheets. Cookies should be placed about 2 inches apart.

8. Bake cookies for 12 to 14 minutes or until browned. Transfer baking sheets to cooling racks. Loosen cookies with a metal spatula. Remove when cool.

NUTRITIONAL INFORMATION

Calories per serving 103	Fiber . . . . 0.2 g
Carbohydrate . . . . 13 g	Vitamin A. . . . . 132 IU
Protein . . . . 2 g	Vitamin C . . . . 0 mg
Total fat . . . . 5 g	Calcium. . . . . 21 mg
Saturated fat . . . . *0.8 g*	*Sodium* . . . . *80 mg*
Cholesterol . . . . *11 mg*	Iron . . . . 0.7 mg

COOKIES

1-2-3 Peanut Butter Cookies

Skill Level: Intermediate   Yield: 2 dozen   1 serving = 1 cookie

INGREDIENTS	EQUIPMENT
nonstick vegetable cooking spray	baking sheet
1 cup natural peanut butter (plain or crunchy)	mixing bowl
	dry measuring cups
½ cup brown sugar	measuring spoons
½ cup rolled oats	wooden spoon or electric mixer
1 egg	2 spoons
1 teaspoon vanilla	fork (optional)
	hot pads
	cooling rack
	metal spatula

1. Preheat oven to 350° F.
2. Coat a baking sheet with nonstick vegetable cooking spray.
3. In a mixing bowl, combine peanut butter, brown sugar, oats, egg, and vanilla with a wooden spoon or electric mixer.
4. Drop by teaspoonfuls onto prepared cookie sheet using 2 spoons, one to scoop the dough and one to push it onto the baking sheet. Flatten dough with a fork or your fingers.
5. Bake for 8 to 10 minutes or until golden brown. Transfer baking sheet to cooling racks. Loosen cookies with a metal spatula. Remove when cool.

NUTRITIONAL INFORMATION

Calories per serving	110	Fiber	0.3 g
Carbohydrate	10 g	Vitamin A	13 IU
Protein	4 g	Vitamin C	0 mg
Total fat	7 g	Calcium	15 mg
Saturated fat	*1.3 g*	Sodium	*83 mg*
Cholesterol	*14 mg*	Iron	0.6 mg

Painted Holiday Cookies

Skill Level: Intermediate   Yield: 32   1 serving = 1 cookie

INGREDIENTS
- 2½ cups all-purpose flour plus 2 tablespoons, divided
- 1 teaspoon baking powder
- ¼ teaspoon salt
- ½ cup margarine
- 1 cup sugar
- 1 teaspoon vanilla
- 1 egg
- 3 egg whites, divided
- 2 tablespoons toasted wheat germ
- 2 tablespoons nonfat powdered milk
- 1 tablespoon low-fat (2%) milk
- nonstick vegetable cooking spray
- food coloring

EQUIPMENT
- 2 mixing bowls
- sifter
- dry measuring cups
- measuring spoons
- electric mixer
- rubber spatula
- plastic wrap or foil
- rolling pin
- 2 baking sheets
- holiday cookie cutters
- fork
- small mixing bowl
- 3 small bowls
- 3 thin paintbrushes
- hot pads
- 2 cooling racks
- metal spatula

1. In a mixing bowl, sift together 2½ cups flour, baking powder, and salt. Set aside.
2. In a second mixing bowl, cream together margarine, sugar, and vanilla using an electric mixer on high speed for about 30 seconds. Add whole egg plus 1 egg white, and beat for about 30 seconds.
3. Add wheat germ, powdered milk, and low-fat milk to creamed mixture and beat until smooth, about 30 seconds.
4. Add dry ingredients to creamed mixture in 3 equal portions. Beat after each addition, scraping sides of bowl with a rubber spatula as needed.
5. Form dough into a ball. Wrap in plastic wrap or foil. Refrigerate dough for several hours, or place it in freezer until firm but not hard.

Continued on next page

6. When dough is firm, sprinkle work surface with remaining flour and place dough on it.
7. Preheat oven to 375°F. Coat 2 baking sheets with nonstick vegetable cooking spray.
8. Flatten dough with your hands, then use a rolling pin to roll it out until it is about ¼ inch thick. Roll from the center toward the edges, stopping just before rolling over edges.
9. Cut shapes from dough with holiday cookie cutters, then place them on a baking sheet.
10. Using a fork, stir 2 egg whites in a small mixing bowl until blended. Divide egg whites among 3 small bowls. Using paintbrushes, stir several drops of food coloring into each bowl.
11. Use the paint brushes to decorate the cookies with egg white paints.
12. Bake cookies for about 12 to 15 minutes or until lightly browned on bottom.
13. Transfer baking sheets to cooling racks. Loosen cookies with metal spatula and cool.

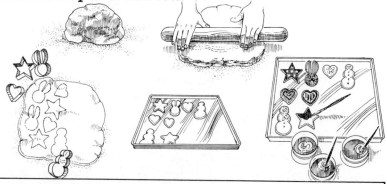

NUTRITIONAL INFORMATION

Calories per serving..... 87	Fiber................ 0 g
Carbohydrate .... 13 g	Vitamin A......... 133 IU
Protein .... 2 g	Vitamin C .... 0 mg
Total fat .... 3 g	Calcium............ 8 mg
Saturated fat........ 0.6 g	Sodium .... 72 mg
Cholesterol.......... 9 mg	Iron .... 0.1 mg

Peanut Puff Cookies

Skill Level: Intermediate   Yield: 30   1 serving = 1 cookie

INGREDIENTS
- 1¼ cups all-purpose flour
- ¼ teaspoon baking soda
- ¼ teaspoon salt
- 1 egg
- 1 teaspoon vanilla
- ¼ cup margarine
- ¼ cup natural peanut butter
- ⅓ cup brown sugar
- 1 tablespoon apple juice concentrate
- nonstick vegetable cooking spray
- 1 tablespoon granulated sugar

EQUIPMENT
- 2 baking sheets
- small mixing bowl
- mixing spoon
- dry measuring cups
- electric mixer
- measuring spoons
- rubber spatula
- shallow dish
- hot pads
- cooling racks
- metal spatula

1. Stir flour, soda, and salt together in a small mixing bowl. Set aside.
2. In a mixing bowl, combine egg and vanilla. Beat together using an electric mixer until frothy, about 20 seconds.
3. Add margarine, peanut butter, brown sugar, and apple juice concentrate to egg mixture.
4. Blend ingredients together on medium until well mixed, about 1 minute. Push batter from sides with a rubber spatula.
5. Add flour mixture to batter.
6. Blend together until dough forms, about 30 seconds to 1 minute. Chill dough for at least 2 hours.
7. Preheat oven to 325°F. Coat 2 baking sheets with nonstick vegetable cooking spray.
8. Roll dough into small balls. Place sugar in a shallow dish. Lightly roll each dough ball in sugar.
9. Place balls 1½ inches apart on prepared baking sheet.

Continued on next page

COOKIES

10. Flatten balls lightly with the palm of your hand.
11. Bake for 10 to 14 minutes or until cookies are lightly browned on the bottom.
12. Transfer baking sheets to cooling racks. Loosen cookies with a metal spatula.

NUTRITIONAL INFORMATION

Calories per serving..... 57
Carbohydrate .... 7 g
Protein .... 1 g
Total fat .... 3 g
Saturated fat........ *0.6 g*
Cholesterol.......... *9 mg*
Fiber .... 0.1 g
Vitamin A .... 71 IU
Vitamin C .... 0 mg
Calcium........... 4 mg
Sodium .... *58 mg*
Iron............. 0.1 mg

FROZEN DESSERTS

Citrus Icee

Skill Level: Intermediate   Serves 16
Conventional and Microwave Methods

INGREDIENTS
- ½ cup sugar
- 2 cups water
- 2 ripe bananas
- 10 strawberries, hulled
- 3 oranges
- 1 lemon

Conventional Method

EQUIPMENT
- dry measuring cups
- liquid measuring cup
- small saucepan
- hot pad
- wooden spoon
- mixing bowl
- fork
- cutting board
- serrated knife
- juicer
- 16 3-ounce disposable cups or popsicle molds
- 12-cup muffin tins (optional)
- 16 popsicle sticks

1. Combine sugar and water in saucepan and cook over medium heat for 3 minutes. Stir at end of cooking with a wooden spoon.
2. Remove saucepan from the stove and cool.
3. Peel bananas and put in a bowl with the strawberries. Mash together with a fork.
4. Roll the oranges and lemon on a cutting board to soften them. Cut the oranges and lemon in half with a serrated knife. Juice with a juicer. Add juice to the bowl with the bananas and strawberries. Stir together.
5. Pour the sugar water into the fruit mixture and stir well.
6. Pour fruit mixture into disposable cups or popsicle molds and freeze for about 30 minutes. (If using disposable cups, place cups in muffin tins to prevent spills.) When they begin to freeze, insert a popsicle stick in the center of each. Then freeze again for several hours until solid.
7. Remove popsicle from cup or popsicle mold, and enjoy.

Continued on next page

FROZEN DESSERTS

Microwave Method

EQUIPMENT
Same as above, with 8-cup microwave-safe bowl substituted for saucepan

1. Combine sugar and water in an 8-cup microwave-safe bowl. Microwave on high (100%) power for 3½ minutes. Stir to dissolve all sugar. Cool.
2. Continue with Step 3.

NUTRITIONAL INFORMATION

Calories per serving..... 51	Fiber .... 0.2 g
Carbohydrate .... 13 g	Vitamin A .... 66 IU
Protein .... 0 g	Vitamin C .... 20 mg
Total fat .... 0 g	Calcium............ 13 mg
Saturated fat .... *0 g*	*Sodium* .... *0 mg*
Cholesterol.......... *0 mg*	Iron.............. 0.1 mg

Frozen Pumpkin Pie

Skill Level: Beginner   Serves 8

INGREDIENTS
- 30 gingersnaps, divided
- 1 cup cooked or canned pumpkin
- ¼ cup sugar
- ¼ teaspoon salt
- ½ teaspoon cinnamon
- ¼ teaspoon ground ginger
- ¼ teaspoon nutmeg
- pinch of ground cloves
- ¼ teaspoon vanilla
- ½ cup chopped pecans
- 1 quart low-fat vanilla frozen yogurt, softened

EQUIPMENT
- plastic bag
- rolling pin
- 9-inch pie plate
- medium mixing bowl
- dry measuring cups
- measuring spoons
- rubber spatula
- mixing spoon
- plastic wrap

1. Crush 20 gingersnaps into coarse crumbs by placing them in a plastic bag and rolling over them with a rolling pin. Press the crumbs into the bottom of a 9-inch pie plate.
2. In a medium mixing bowl, combine pumpkin, sugar, salt, cinnamon, ginger, nutmeg, cloves, vanilla, and pecans by stirring with a mixing spoon.
3. Fold softened low-fat vanilla frozen yogurt into the pumpkin mixture with a rubber spatula.
4. Spoon yogurt mixture carefully into the pie plate, spreading it evenly to the edges.
5. Use the remaining 10 gingersnaps to decorate the pie by breaking them in half and placing them end to end between the pie plate and yogurt, with the straight edges down. The half circles will create a scalloped border.
6. Cover pie with plastic wrap and freeze.
7. Remove from the freezer a few minutes before serving to allow to soften.

Continued on next page

FROZEN DESSERTS

NUTRITIONAL INFORMATION

Calories per serving.... 302	**Fiber.............. 0.6 g**
Carbohydrate .... 50 g	**Vitamin A....... 2075 IU**
Protein .... 6 g	Vitamin C .... 2 mg
Total fat............ 10 g	Calcium .... 169 mg
Saturated fat........ 2.4 g	Sodium........... 232 mg
Cholesterol.......... 7 mg	Iron .... 1.0 mg

"Frozen Yogie" Sandwich

Skill Level: Beginner   Serves 1

INGREDIENTS
1 large graham cracker (2½ × 5 inches)
2 tablespoons low-fat raspberry frozen yogurt (softened)

EQUIPMENT
small spatula
measuring spoons
plastic wrap

1. Break graham cracker in half crosswise.
2. Carefully spread frozen yogurt onto a graham cracker half. Cover frozen yogurt with the other graham cracker half.
3. Tightly wrap the sandwich in plastic wrap. Freeze.

NOTE: You can substitute your favorite flavor of yogurt for raspberry. Make several sandwiches at a time to keep on hand for snacks or dessert.

NUTRITIONAL INFORMATION			
Calories per serving	83	Fiber	0.2 g
Carbohydrate	15 g	Vitamin A	22 IU
Protein	2 g	Vitamin C	0 mg
Total fat	2 g	Calcium	40 mg
Saturated fat	0.7 g	Sodium	115 mg
Cholesterol	2 mg	Iron	0.2 mg

FROZEN DESSERTS

 # Frozen Yogurt Pie

Skill Level: Beginner   Serves 8

INGREDIENTS
- 6 graham crackers (2½ × 5 inches each)
- ¼ cup chopped pecans
- ¼ cup light brown sugar
- ¼ cup margarine, melted
- 1 pint low-fat strawberry frozen yogurt, softened

EQUIPMENT
- plastic storage bag
- dry measuring cups
- meat pounder (optional)
- measuring spoons
- 8-inch pie plate
- rubber spatula

1. In a plastic storage bag, crush graham crackers and pecans with a fist or a meat pounder.
2. Add brown sugar and margarine to the graham cracker crumbs in the plastic bag and knead to combine well. Reserve 2 tablespoons of the graham cracker mixture to be used later as the topping.
3. Press graham cracker crumbs firmly into an 8-inch pie plate.
4. Spread softened frozen yogurt over the crust with a rubber spatula and sprinkle with reserved crumbs.
5. Freeze pie until ready to serve. Remove 5 minutes prior to serving to allow to soften slightly.

NOTE: Any flavor of frozen yogurt can be substituted for the strawberry yogurt.

NUTRITIONAL INFORMATION

Calories per serving 185	Fiber . . . . 0.3 g
Carbohydrate . . . . 21 g	Vitamin A . . . . 292 IU
Protein . . . . 3 g	Vitamin C . . . . 0 mg
Total fat . . . . 11 g	Calcium . . . . 53 mg
Saturated fat . . . . 2.4 g	*Sodium* . . . . 164 mg
Cholesterol . . . . 5 mg	Iron . . . . 0.3 mg

FROZEN DESSERTS

Orange Sherbet Freeze (Halloween)

Skill Level: Intermediate   Serves 6

INGREDIENTS
6   medium oranges
1   quart orange sherbet
18 candy corns

EQUIPMENT
serrated knife
cutting board
spoon
dish cloth
black felt-tip markers with permanent ink

1. Place an orange on its side. Use a serrated knife to cut a slice about ½ inch from the stem. Repeat the process for all the oranges.
2. Run a serrated knife around the inside edge of each orange to help loosen orange sections. Remove orange sections with a spoon.
3. Dry orange skins thoroughly with a dish cloth. Decorate oranges with black markers so that they look like jack-o-lanterns.
4. Spoon sherbet into hollowed oranges. Garnish the top of each orange with three candy corns.
5. Freeze oranges for 4 or more hours. Remove a few minutes before serving to allow to soften slightly.

NOTE: Save orange juice and sections for a cool snack.

NUTRITIONAL INFORMATION

Calories per serving.... 216	Fiber................ 0 g
Carbohydrate .... 48 g	Vitamin A......... 123 IU
Protein .... 1 g	Vitamin C.......... 3 mg
Total fat .... 2 g	Calcium........... 71 mg
Saturated fat........ 1.6 g	Sodium .... 62 mg
Cholesterol.......... 9 mg	Iron............. 0.4 mg

FROZEN DESSERTS

Phyllo Flowers With Frozen Vanilla Yogurt and Raspberry Sauce

Skill Level: Advanced   Serves 6

Phyllo Flowers

INGREDIENTS
nonstick vegetable cooking spray
3   sheets phyllo dough
2   tablespoons margarine, melted
3   cups low-fat frozen vanilla yogurt
Raspberry Sauce (recipe below)

EQUIPMENT
cutting board
plastic wrap or foil
small, sharp knife
6-cup muffin tin
measuring spoons
hot pads
cooling rack
dry measuring cups

1. Preheat oven to 375°F. Spray a 6-cup muffin tin with nonstick vegetable cooking spray.

2. Carefully unfold phyllo dough on a work surface. Remove one sheet of dough at a time, then stack 3 sheets together on a cutting board. Roll remaining dough into original log shape, and securely wrap in plastic wrap or foil. Store in the refrigerator.

3. Cut dough into nine 4-inch squares with a small, sharp knife.

4. Place a phyllo square into each cup, then dab each square with melted margarine. Place a second square over the first, staggering the corners so that an octagon is formed, and dab each square with margarine. Place 2 more squares over each octagon, once again staggering the corners and dabbing with margarine between layers. Press each stack of squares into the muffin cup, leaving the corners over the edge to form petals.

5. Bake for about 5 minutes, or until very lightly browned. Transfer muffin tin to cooling rack. Cool phyllo flowers in muffin tins before removing.

Raspberry Sauce

INGREDIENTS
- 2 10-ounce packages frozen raspberries in light syrup, thawed
- 2 tablespoons fresh orange juice

EQUIPMENT
- sieve
- 2 bowls
- food processor or blender
- rubber spatula
- spoon
- measuring spoons
- cutting board
- serrated knife
- juicer

1. Drain raspberries by placing them in a sieve over a bowl. Reserve the juice.
2. Puree raspberries in a food processor or blender until smooth. To remove the seeds, put the puree in a sieve over a bowl, and use a rubber spatula to force the puree through the sieve.
3. Stir orange juice into the raspberry puree. If raspberry sauce is too thick, add a small amount of the reserved raspberry juice until desired consistency. Chill.

Assembly of Flowers

Place phyllo flowers on dessert plates. Fill with frozen yogurt and top with raspberry sauce.

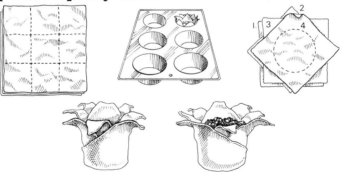

NUTRITIONAL INFORMATION

Calories per serving 234	**Fiber** .... **2 g**
Carbohydrate .... 41 g	Vitamin A .... 321 IU
Protein .... 4 g	Vitamin C .... 18 mg
Total fat .... 7 g	Calcium .... 106 mg
Saturated fat .... *3 g*	*Sodium* .... *122 mg*
Cholesterol .... *9 mg*	Iron .... 0.8 mg

Index

BEVERAGES
Apple-Lime Cooler (B), 41
Banana Smoothy (B), 42
Fruit Frappé (B), 43
Lemon-Apple-Ade (B), 44
Mighty Milk Shake (B), 45
Orange Juliette (B), 46
Orange Squeeze (B), 47
Strawberry Shake (B), 48
Thunderbird (B), 49

BREADS
Banana Bran Muffins (I), 50
Blueberry-Citrus Muffins (I), 51
Cinnamon Bears (I), 53
Cornmeal Pancakes (A), 54
Drop Biscuits (I), 56
Frenchy Toast (I), 57
Garlic Bread (I) (Micro.), 58
Good Morning Coffee Cake (I), 59
Parmesan Bread Sticks (I), 61
Powerhouse Oatmeal Muffins (I), 62
Tiny Tart Shells (I), 64
Valentine Scones (I), 65
Whole Wheat Crepes (A), 67

BREAKFAST
Apple Strudel (A), 231
Baked Apple Chunks (A), 233
Banana Bran Muffins (I), 50
Blueberry-Citrus Muffins (I), 51
Breakfast Sundae (B), 72
Cinnamon Bears (I), 53
Cornmeal Pancakes (A), 54
Creamy Oatmeal for One (I) (Micro.), 83
Frenchy Toast (I), 57
Good Morning Coffee Cake (I), 59
Homemade Turkey Sausage (I), 165
Powerhouse Oatmeal Muffins (I), 62
Orange Juliette (B), 46
Orange Spread (I), 90
Orange Squeeze (B), 47
Star Egg (I), 110

DESSERT
Cakes
"Full of Surprises" Chocolate Cake (I), 246
Gingerbread (I), 248
Happy Birthday Cake (White Cake) (A), 250
Jack-O-Lantern Cake (A), 252
Parve-Honey Cake (I), 254

Cookies
Apple Jack Cookies (I), 256
Easter Fudge Baskets (I), 258
Fudge Balls (I), 259
Ginger Faces (I), 260
Jack-O-Lantern Cookies (A), 262
Meringue Kisses (I), 264
Oatmeal-Raisin Cookies (I), 266
1-2-3 Peanut Butter Cookies (I), 268
Painted Holiday Cookies (I), 269
Peanut Puff Cookies (I), 271

Frozen Desserts
Citrus Icee (I) (Micro.), 273
Frozen Pumpkin Pie (B), 275
"Frozen Yogie" Sandwich (B), 277
Frozen Yogurt Pie (B), 278
Orange Sherbet Freeze (I), 279
Phyllo Flowers with Frozen Vanilla Yogurt and Raspberry Sauce, 280

ENTREES
Beef
Beef and Snow Peas (A), 122
Beef with Chinese Barbecue Sauce (A), 124
Father's Day Beef Kabobs (A), 126
Meatballs on Top of Spaghetti (A), 128
Meaty Macaroni and Cheese (A), 130
Mini Burgers (I), 132
Roast Beef and Turkey Roll-Ups (B), 169
Sloppy Muffin (I) (Micro.), 134
Soft Tacos (I), 136
Spaghetti Pie (A) 138

Chicken
"Always a Favorite" Chicken Salad (B), 149
Barbecued Chicken (A), 150
Chicken Drumsticks (I), 152
Chicken Enchiladas (A), 154
Chicken "Nuggets" with Dipping Sauce (I), 156
Chicken on a Skewer (A), 158
Hidden Lemon Chicken (I), 160
Pan-Fried Chicken with Lemon (A), 161
Rosemary Grilled Chicken (A), 162
Warm Chicken Salad Vinaigrette (I), 163

Fish
Baked Fish (A), 174
Fish Bites (I), 175
Our Favorite Fish Fillets (A), 176
Snapper Kabobs (I) (Micro.), 177

INDEX

Trout Parmesan (A), 178

Lamb
Easter Brunch Lamb Chops (A), 140
St. Patrick's Day Irish Stew (I), 141

Pork
Grilled Pork Loin with Lime Spread (A), 142
Honey-Mustard Pork Tenderloin (I), 144
Rob's Grilled Pork Chops (A), 145

Turkey
Homemade Turkey Sausage (I), 165
Mama Mia Pizza (A), 166
Roast Beef and Turkey Roll-Ups (B), 169
Roasted Turkey Breast (A), 170
Turkey and Rice Combo (A), 171
Turkey Salad (B), 173

Seafood
Breaded Shrimp (A), 179
Hickory Smoked Shrimp (A), 181
Shrimp Peel (A), 182

Veal
Grilled Veal Chops (A), 146
Veal Scallopini with Potatoes (A), 147

FRUITS
Ape over Apples and Grapes (B), 229
Apple Cartwheels (I), 230
Apple Strudel (A), 231
Baked Apple Chunks (A), 233
Breakfast Sundae (B), 72
Charoses (B), 235
Cranberry Orange Sauce (I) (Micro.), 236
Fresh Fruit Kabobs (B), 84
Fresh Fruit Salad (I), 238
Fun Fruits with a Dip (I), 85
Melon Melody (B), 240
Rosh Hashanah Apples and Honey (B), 97
Strawberry Souffle (I), 241
Summer Peach Crisp (A), 243
Sweet and Tart Pineapple (A), 245

HOLIDAY MEALS
Christmas Party
Breaded Shrimp (A), 179
Christmas Spinach Dip (I), 76
Christmas Vegetable Tree (I), 77
Painted Holiday Cookies (I), 269
Reindeer Sandwich (B), 109

Easter Brunch
Easter Brunch Lamb Chops (A), 140
Easter Fudge Baskets (I), 258
Gratinéed Rice (A), 214
Stir-Fried Snow Peas and Carrots (A), 200

Father's Day Dinner
Father's Day Beef Kabobs (A), 126
Fresh Fruit Salad (I), 238
Garlic Bread (I) (Micro.), 58
New Potatoes in Their Jackets (I), 195
Thunderbird, 49

Fourth of July Picnic
Fourth of July Strawberry Soup (B), 116
Lemon-Apple-Ade (B), 44
Pasta Primavera Salad (A), 209
Quick Corn-on-the-Cob (I) (Micro.), 199
Rosemary Grilled Chicken (A), 162
Summer Peach Crisp (A), 243

Halloween Treats
Cheesy Popcorn (I), 74
"Full of Surprises" Chocolate Cake (I), 246
Ghost Treats (B), 87
Jack-O-Lantern Cake (A), 252
Jack-O-Lantern Cookies (A), 262
Orange Sherbet Freeze (I), 279
Peanut Butter Points (I) (Micro.), 91

Valentine Tea Party
Strawberry Spread (B), 100
Valentine Scones (I), 65

Special Days
Charoses (B), 235
Happy Birthday Cake (A), 250
Mashed Sweet Potato with Thanksgiving Garnish (A), 191
Parve-Honey Cake (I), 254
Rosh Hashanah Apples and Honey (B), 97
St. Patrick's Day Irish Stew (I), 141

PASTA
Fettucine with Parmesan (A), 206
Noodle Kugel (A), 207
Olive Oyl's Pasta Salad (A), 208
Meatballs on Top of Spaghetti (A), 128
Meaty Macaroni and Cheese (A), 130
Pasta Primavera Salad (A), 209
Power-Packed Pasta (A), 211
Spaghetti Pie (A), 138

RICE
Basic Rice (I) (Micro.), 212
Fried Rice (A), 213
Gratinéed Rice (A), 214

INDEX

Rice Pilaf (I), 216
Risotto with Celery (I) (Micro.), 217
Turkey and Rice Combo (A), 171

SALAD
Caesar Salad (I), 218
Citrus and Spinach Salad (B), 220
Italian Romas (B), 221
Lettuce and Cucumber Salad with Creamy Garlic Dressing (B), 222
Olive Oyl's Pasta Salad (A), 208
Pasta Primavera Salad (A), 209

Salad Dressing
French Dressing (B), 223
"Good for Fruit" Salad Dressing (B), 224
Sweet and Sour Salad Dressing (B), 225
Tangy Buttermilk Dressing (B), 226
Thousand Island Dressing (B), 227
Seasoned Salad Dressing (I), 228

SANDWICHES
Berry-Good Turkey Sandwiches (B), 103
CLT's (Cheese, Lettuce, and Tomato Sandwiches) (B), 104
Ghost Treats (B), 87
Ham and Cheese "Hot Dogs" (B), 105
Lox and Mini Bagels (I), 106
Mini Burgers (I), 132
PB&S (Peanut Butter and Strawberries) (B), 107
Pocket Sandwich with Ham and Cheese (B), 108
Reindeer Sandwich (B), 109
Star Egg (I), 110
Sweet-Treat Sandwich (B), 111
Tuna Pocket (B), 112
Turkey Sandwich with Secret Sauce (B), 113

SNACKS
Apple Leather (I), 69
Bean Dip (A) (Micro.), 70
Breakfast Sundae (B), 72
Cheese Pimento Spread in Celery Boats (B), 73
Cheesy Popcorn (A), 74
Chip-Dipping Salsa (I), 75
Christmas Spinach Dip (I), 76
Christmas Vegetable Tree (I), 77
Cinnamon Bears (I), 53
"Circles and Squares" Snack Mix (I) (Micro.), 79
Corn Tortilla Chips (I), 81
Cream Cheese Spread with Whole Wheat Crackers (B), 82
Creamy Oatmeal for One (I) (Micro.), 83
Fresh Fruit Kabobs (B), 84
Fun Fruits with a Dip (I), 85
Ghost Treats (B), 87
Honey Bear Granola (I), 88
Oatmeal Cups (I), 89
Orange Spread (I), 90
Peanut Butter Points (I) (Micro.), 91
Pico De Gallo (I), 93
Pizza Snack (I), 94
Popcorn Ole (A), 95
Ranch Dip (B), 96
Rosh Hashanah Apples and Honey (B), 97
Snap, Crackle, Pop Cheese Wafers (I), 98
Strawberry Spread (B), 100
Tuna Snacker (B), 101
Yogurt Vegetable Dip (B), 102

SOUPS
Corny Chowder (A), 114
Fourth of July Strawberry Soup (B), 116
Homemade Chicken Stock (A), 117
Smooth or Chunky Vegetable Soup (A), 118
Won Ton Soup (A), 120

VEGETABLES
Cauliflower with Lemon "Butter" (A) (Micro.), 184
Cheese Sauce for Vegetables (I), 186
Corn Fritters (I), 187
Green Beans Parmesan (A), 188
Green Beans Sesame (A) (Micro.), 189
Mashed Sweet Potato with Thanksgiving Garnish (A), 191
Miniature Corn Medley (A), 193
Mr. McGregor's Baby Cabbage Patch (A), 194
New Potatoes in Their Jackets (I), 195
Oriental Broccoli (A), 196
Parmesan Potato Sticks (A), 197
Pinto Beans with a Hidden Ingredient (I), 198
Quick Corn-on-the-Cob (I) (Micro.), 199
Stir-Fried Snow Peas and Carrots (A), 200
Stop-Light Peppers (A), 202
Stuffed Potato Boats (I), 203
Tomato Sauce (A), 205